# Wanderings Of An Artist Among The Indians Of North America: From Canada To Vancouver's Island And Oregon, Through The Hudson's Bay Company's Territory And Back Again

## Paul Kane

# WANDERINGS OF AN ARTIST

## AMONG THE

# INDIANS OF NORTH AMERICA.

LONDON
PRINTED BY SPOTTISWOODE AND CO.
NEW-STREET SQUARE.

Paul Kane del                                    Vincent Brooks lith.

PORTRAIT OF A HALF-BREED CREE GIRL.

*William Wilson*
*Castle Meadows*
*1860 —*

# WANDERINGS OF AN ARTIST

AMONG THE

# INDIANS OF NORTH AMERICA

FROM CANADA

TO VANCOUVER'S ISLAND AND OREGON

THROUGH THE HUDSON'S BAY COMPANY'S TERRITORY

AND

BACK AGAIN.

## BY PAUL KANE.

LONDON

LONGMAN, BROWN, GREEN, LONGMANS, AND ROBERTS.

1859

TO

# GEORGE WILLIAM ALLAN, ESQ.

OF MOSS PARK, TORONTO, CANADA WEST

This Work

DESIGNED TO ILLUSTRATE THE MANNERS AND CUSTOMS OF THE

INDIAN TRIBES OF BRITISH AMERICA

Is Respectfully Dedicated

AS A TOKEN OF GRATITUDE FOR THE KIND AND GENEROUS INTEREST

HE HAS ALWAYS TAKEN IN THE AUTHOR'S LABOURS,

AS WELL AS A SINCERE EXPRESSION OF ADMIRATION OF THE

LIBERALITY WITH WHICH, AS A NATIVE CANADIAN,

HE IS EVER READY TO FOSTER CANADIAN TALENT AND ENTERPRISE.

TORONTO: *July* 9, 1858.

# PREFACE.

On my return to Canada from the continent of Europe, where I had passed nearly four years in studying my profession as a painter, I determined to devote whatever talents and proficiency I possessed to the painting of a series of pictures illustrative of the North American Indians and scenery. The subject was one in which I felt a deep interest in my boyhood. I had been accustomed to see hundreds of Indians about my native village, then Little York, muddy and dirty, just struggling into existence, now the City of Toronto, bursting forth in all its energy and commercial strength. But the face of the red man is now no longer seen. All traces of his footsteps are fast being obliterated from his once favourite haunts, and those who would see the aborigines of this country in their original state, or seek to study their native manners and customs, must travel far through the pathless forest to find them. To me

the wild woods were not altogether unknown, and
the Indians but recalled old friends with whom I
had associated in my childhood, and though at the
commencement of my travels I possessed neither
influence nor means for such an undertaking, yet
it was with a determined spirit and a light heart
that I had made the few preparations which were
in my power for my future proceedings.

The principal object in my undertaking was to
sketch pictures of the principal chiefs, and their
original costumes, to illustrate their manners and
customs, and to represent the scenery of an almost
unknown country. These paintings, however,
would necessarily require explanations and notes,
and I accordingly kept a diary of my journey, as
being the most easy and familiar form in which I
could put such information as I might collect.
The following pages are the notes of my daily
journey, with little alteration from the original
wording, as I jotted them down in pencil at the
time; and although without any claim to public
approbation as a literary production, still I trust
they will possess not only an interest for the
curious, but also an intrinsic value to the his-
torian, as they relate not only to that vast tract of
country bordering on the great chain of American

lakes, the Red River settlement, the valley of
Sascatchawan, and its boundless prairies, through
which it is proposed to lay the great railway con-
necting the Atlantic and Pacific Oceans, through
the British possessions; but also across the Rocky
Mountains down the Columbia River to Oregon,
Puget's Sound, and Vancouver's Island, where the
recent gold discoveries in the vicinity have drawn
thousands of hardy adventurers to those wild
scenes amongst which I strayed almost alone,
and scarcely meeting a white man or hearing the
sound of my own language.

The illustrations—executed from my sketches, or
finished paintings, for the purpose of illustrating the
present work — constitute only a few specimens of
the different classes of subjects which engaged my
pencil during a sojourn of near four years among the
Indians of the North-west. In that period I executed
numerous portraits of chiefs, warriors, and medicine-
men of the different tribes among whom I so-
journed, and also of their wives and daughters. The
Indian fishing and hunting scenes, games, dances,
and other characteristic customs, also occupied my
pencil; while I was not forgetful of the interest
which justly attaches to the scenery of a new and
unexplored country, and especially to such parts

of it as were either intimately associated with native legends and traditions, or otherwise specially connected with the native tribes—as their favourite fishing or hunting grounds, the locations of their villages, or the burying-places of the tribes. The whole of these sketches are now in my possession, and I have already been honoured by a commission to execute a series of paintings from them for the Legislature of the Province of Canada, which now have a place in the Library of the Provincial Parliament. A much more extensive series of oil paintings had been executed by me, from my sketches, for George W. Allan, Esq., of Moss Park, the liberal patron of Canadian art; and I would gladly indulge the hope that the present work will not prove the sole published fruits of my travels among the Indian tribes of North America, but that it will rather be a mere illustration of the novelty and interest which attach to those rarely explored regions, and enable me to publish a much more extensive series of illustrations of the characteristics, habits, and scenery of the country and its occupants.

PAUL KANE.

# CONTENTS.

---

### CHAPTER I.

### CHAP. II.

### CHAP. III.

a

## CHAP. XXII.

## CHAP. XXIII.

## CHAP. XXIV.

## CHAP. XXV.

## APPENDIX.

# LIST OF ENGRAVINGS.

# WANDERINGS OF AN ARTIST

&c.

## CHAPTER I.

Departure from Toronto. — An Indian Village. — The "Big Pike's" Likeness. — The Chiefs of Saugeen. — An Island Labyrinth. — The Encampment.—An Indian Kettle of Fish.—The Household Drudge. — Manetouawning. — Anecdote of the Chief Sigennok. — The Egyptian Sphynx on Indian Pipes. — A Serenade. — The Conjuror. — The Power of Love. — The Escape. — Heraldic Devices. — Departure for the Sault St. Marie.

I LEFT Toronto on the 17th of June 1845, with no companions but my portfolio and box of paints, my gun, and a stock of ammunition, taking the most direct route to Lake Simcoe. Thence I took the steamboat for Orillia ; and crossed over to Sturgeon Bay on Lake Huron, where I had to hire an Indian with a canoe, the packet having left for Penetanguishene a few hours before I reached

B

" Cold Water."    After paddling all night, we overtook her the next morning at Penetanguishene,
or the "Rolling Sand Bank," which is seated in
a deep bay, forming a secure harbour for vessels
of any amount of tonnage: it has been so named
by the Indians from a high bank of rolling sand
at the entrance of the bay.   There is a small
naval depôt here, and a steamer is employed in
making trips of inspection round the lake and its
shores.   A larger one has been for some years laid
up in ordinary, and is no doubt now unfit for
use.   Besides this depôt, there is a village inhabited
by a few whites and half-breeds.

We left Penetanguishene on the 20th, and arrived at Owen's Sound the same evening.   I here
met with three men bound for Saugeen, about
thirty-five or forty miles west of this place, where
a council.of chiefs was to meet for the purpose
of negotiating the sale of a tract of land to the
Provincial Government.   After engaging an Indian
to carry my pack and act as guide, I started in
company with them on foot.   Our journey was
a disagreeable one, through woods and swamps, the
rain all the time coming down in torrents.   We
had to encamp at night supperless, and without
shelter of any kind, in our wet clothes, as we had

omitted to bring blankets or provisions under the expectation of reaching Saugeen the same evening. We made an early start the next morning, and arrived there about noon, where we found a large assemblage of Indians holding a camp meeting, with its usual accompaniments of boisterous singing and praying, under the superintendence of six or seven Methodist preachers.

The Indian village of Saugeen, meaning "the Mouth of a River," contains about 200 inhabitants (Ojibbeways). It is the site of a former battle-ground between the Ojibbeways, as usually pronounced, or Chippawas, and the Mohawks. Of this, the mounds erected over the slain afford abundant evidence in the protrusion of the bones through the surface of the ground. The land hereabouts is excellent, but only a small part is cultivated, as the inhabitants subsist principally on fish, which are taken in great abundance at the entrance of the river. They also kill hundreds of deer by erecting a fence of brushwood many miles in extent, behind which the Indians conceal themselves ; and as the deer, in their annual migrations, are seeking an opening through this fence, they fall a prey to the unerring aim of the red man. I sketched the principal chief, named Maticwaub, or " the Bow."

The band of which he is the head chief forms a part of the great nation of the Ojibbeways, which still inhabits the shores of Lakes Huron, Michigan, and Superior. There is also another large band of them on the upper Mississippi, 90 or 100 miles above the falls of Saint Anthony; they speak the same language; their medicine dances, called Matayway, and their feasts are in every respect the same, identifying them as one and the same people, although scattered so widely apart. Another branch of them, called the Pilleurs, is found some 200 or 300 miles farther north. They derive their name from their thievish propensities, and richly deserve it, as I unfortunately experienced some few years afterwards on visiting their country.

I also took a sketch of a chief named Maskuhnoonjee, or the " Big Pike." This man was very proud of having his likeness taken, and put on his chief's medal presented by the Government to those they acknowledge as chiefs. I have never known a chief to barter away one of these marks of distinction, which they seldom wear on unimportant occasions. An interesting girl, the daughter of a chief from Lake St. Clair, gave me much trouble in prevailing on her to sit for her likeness, although her father insisted upon it; her repugnance proceeded from a superstitious belief that by so doing she would place herself in the power of the possessor of what is regarded by an Indian as a second self. Wāh-pūs, "the Rabbit," also permitted me to take his portrait. He resides at Owen's Sound, and was formerly as much renowned for his unconquerable fierceness and intemperance as he is now for his temperance and wisdom. This change in his character is attributable to the influence of the Methodist missionaries, whose church he has joined. He was the first Indian I had seen whose hair had been pulled out, all except the scalp-lock ; this custom is common amongst many tribes of Indians, though not universal amongst any.

I remained at Saugeen about ten days, residing in the family of an Indian who had been educated as a Wesleyan missionary. I then returned to Owen's Sound, accompanied by a young man named Dillon, who was extremely desirous of joining in my excursion. On arriving at the Sound I bought a canoe and a stock of provisions, and embarked with my new companion for Penetanguishene in our route for the Manitoulin Islands. On the fourth day we passed Christian Island, on which are still standing the ruins of a fort, said to have

been built by two Jesuit priests who took refuge
on the island with a large band of Hurons, after
they had been defeated by the Iroquoisin. They defended the fort until they were nearly all destroyed
by hunger and disease, when the missionaries led
the survivors to Quebec. The day after passing
this island we again reached Penetanguishene,
where we obtained a fresh supply of provisions,
after which we threaded a labyrinth of islands
of every size and form, amounting, as is said, to
upwards of 30,000 ; and both being strangers to
the navigation, we continually lost ourselves in
its picturesque mazes, enchanted with the beauty
of the ever-varying scenery, as we glided along in
our light canoe. We fished and hunted for fourteen days, almost unconscious of the lapse of
time so agreeably spent. We saw only two or
three Indians, the greater part of them having
preceded us to Manetouawning to receive their
presents.

Sketch No. 1 represents an Indian encampment
amongst the islands of Lake Huron ; the wig-
wams are made of birch-bark, stripped from the
trees in large pieces and sewed together with long
fibrous roots ; when the birch tree cannot be
conveniently had, they weave rushes into mats,

called Apuckway, for covering, which are stretched round in the same manner as the bark, upon eight or ten poles tied together at the top, and stuck in the ground at the required circle of the tent, a

No. 1.—Encampment amongst the Islands of Lake Huron.

hole being left at the top to permit the smoke to go out. The fire is made in the centre of the lodge, and the inmates sleep all round with their feet towards it. These lodges are much more comfortable than one would at first suppose from their loose appearance — that is, as far as warmth is considered. The filth, stench, and vermin make them almost intolerable to a white man; but Indians are invariably dirty, and it must be something very terrible indeed which will induce them to take half an hour's trouble in moving their lodge. As to removing the filth, that is never done. Their canoes are also made of birch-bark stretched over a very light frame of split cedar laths; the greatest attention being paid to symmetry and form. They travel a great deal and are often exposed to rough weather in these boats, which, being extremely light, are carried across "portages"* with ease. They make their mohcocks, or kettles, of birch-bark, in which they cook fish and game. This is done by putting red hot stones into the water, and it is astonishing how quickly an Indian woman will boil a fish in this way. The Indians round Lake Huron raise a good deal of corn, which is dried and then

---

* It would be as well to note here that the word "*Portage*" is applied to such places as require the canoes to be taken bodily out of the water and carried up the ascent by the men, and "*Discharge*" to such shallows or rapids as will not allow the canoes to pass without being considerably lightened or entirely emptied, and then pulled or dragged by cords over the difficulty.

pounded in a sort of mortar, made out of a hollow log, as represented in the sketch.

The Indians in this neighbourhood having a direct communication with the whites, use guns and other weapons of civilised manufacture, bows and arrows being seldom seen except with the children. As amongst all other tribes of North American Indians, the women do all the household work, carrying wood, putting up lodges, and cooking. I here noticed a custom amongst the women bearing a curious resemblance to the ancient usages of the Jews. At certain stated periods they are not allowed the slightest intercourse with the rest of the tribe, but are obliged to build a little hut for themselves a short distance from the camp, where they live entirely secluded until their return to health.

Previous to entering the bay of Manetouawning, we put ashore on one of the Spider Islands, to escape from a heavy shower, where we found a single lodge. A woman and her two children were there, but the men were off in the distance fishing, which is the principal occupation of the Indians hereabouts in summer, there being very little game, except occasionally a bear or deer, and, at particular seasons, ducks. The afternoon being clear, I had a fine view of the La Cloche Mountains, and spent the remainder of the evening in sketching.

Manetouawning is situated at the extremity of a bay six miles long, in the great Manetoulin Island, and is 200 miles distant from Penetanguishene by the route we took.

The word Manetouawning signifies " the Spirit Hole." The village consists of forty or fifty loghouses built by the Provincial Government for the Indians. There is a mission, with a church and pastor, an Indian agent, a doctor, and a blacksmith, all paid by the Government. I found nearly 2000 Indians here, waiting the arrival of the vessel that was freighted with their annual presents, comprising guns, ammunition, axes, kettles, and other implements useful to the Indian.

The principal chief here is Sigennok; he is an acute and intelligent Indian; he is appointed to distribute to his tribe their due share of the presents annually consigned to them. He receives a salary from the British Government as interpreter. This is paid him from policy, for although useless as an interpreter, from not speaking the English language, his natural eloquence is such that he possesses great influence over his tribe;

indeed, it is to the untiring volubility of his tongue that he owes his name, which signifies " The Blackbird." The following anecdote, illustrative of character, was related to me by Captain Anderson, now superintendent of Indian affairs:—Sigennok was, in his younger days, in the continual habit of drinking to excess, and when under the influence of his potations was a perfect maniac, and only to be controlled by main force; but as the attempt to place him under due restraint was attended with no small personal danger, on account of his Herculean strength, it was the custom of his attendants to increase the amount of stimulus, and ply him with it until he became insensible, rather than expose themselves to danger from his ungovernable violence. One day, when in this state of drunken stupor, Captain Anderson—who at that time filled the post of Indian agent, — saw him lying in front of his lodge in one of these fits of oblivion, and bound him hand and foot with strong cords, placing a sickly decrepit boy to watch over him, with instructions to hasten to him (Captain Anderson) the moment the sleeper should awake, and by no means to let him know who it was that had bound him. After some hours he revived, and angrily demanded of the boy, who had dared to treat him with such indignity. The little fellow, without replying to the inquiry, hobbled away to the captain: he at once hastened to his prisoner, who put the same interrogatory to him as he had before done to the boy, and furiously demanded his instant liberation. The captain replied that the boy had bound him by his own orders, and that he had lain for hours exposed to the derision of the whole camp. He took the opportunity also of commenting forcibly on the disgrace to which so great a warrior had thus subjected himself, merely to gratify a vile and disgusting propensity, which reduced him manifestly beneath the level of the brute beast, which never sacrificed its reason, or the power to protect itself from annoyance or insult from its fellows.

Sigennok, his pride humbled, and greatly mortified at the degraded position in which he had placed himself — in the power, as it were, of the most helpless of his tribe—formed the prompt resolution of at once and for ever abandoning his favourite habit, and promised Captain Anderson that if he would release him from his bonds, he would never again taste ardent spirits. The captain took him at his word, and unbound him. Twenty-three years had elapsed since the occurrence, during which Sigennok had never been known to violate the promise then made.

Sketch No. 2 represents Awbonwaishkum. This head possesses the characteristics of the Indian to

No. 2.— Portrait of Aw-bon-waish-kum.

a striking degree: the small piercing eyes, high cheek-bones, large mouth, protuberant and hanging lips, are strongly indicative of the race. This chief is a man of great ingenuity and judgment.

The sketch No. 3 is that of a pipe carved by Awbonwaishkum out of a dark-coloured stone, his only tools being an old knife and broken file. I leave it to antiquaries to explain how the bowl of this pipe happens to bear so striking a resemblance to the head of the Egyptian sphynx. I questioned Awbonwaishkum as · to whether he

No. 3.—Indian Pipe.

knew of any tradition connected with the design, but the only explanation he could offer was, that his forefathers had made similar pipes with the same shaped head for the bowl, and that he therefore supposed the model had always existed among the Indians.

Strolling one evening in the vicinity of the camp, I heard the sound of some musical instrument, and upon approaching the performer, who was lying under a tree, I found that he was playing on an instrument resembling a flageolet in construction, but much softer in tone. This instrument is principally used by lovers, who play for hours in the vicinity of their mistress's lodge. I have often listened with pleasure to this music, as its simple and plaintive notes stole through the stillness of the forest. The lover made no secret of his object, but conversed with me freely upon the subject of his love.

The Indians assemble annually at Manetouawning from all parts of the shores of Lakes Huron, Nipissing, and Superior, as well as from all the neighbouring islands. On the arrival of the presents, the Indians, male and female, accompanied by their children, immediately seated themselves in rows on the grass, each chief heading his own little band, and giving in their number and names to Sigennok, who here appears in his proper element, dividing the goods among them with great impartiality. He is really a very useful man. His voice is heard everywhere above the universal din of tongues, his native eloquence is unceasing, and seems to have the effect of allaying every envious and unpleasant feeling, and keeping all in good humour and proper order.

Among the numerous Indians assembled here, was one that particularly attracted my attention from his venerable and dignified appearance. In reply to my inquiry, as to who he was, I learned that he was called Shawwanossoway, or "One with his Face towards the West," and that he was a great medicine-man, skilled in the past, present and future. As I happened to lose, some days previously, some articles from my tent, I resolved, for the sake of an introduction, and the gratification of my curiosity, to apply to the seer. On laying my case before him, he told me that his power was of no avail wherever the pale faces were concerned, and, notwithstanding my offer of a very liberal remuneration, I could not prevail upon him to put his incantations into practice. He had been, I was told, a celebrated warrior in his youth, but that owing to a romantic incident, he had abandoned the tomahawk and scalping-knife for the peaceable profession of the medicine-man, or, in common parlance, the necromancer or conjuror, in which he has obtained great repute among his people.

There dwelt many years before, on the shores of one of the great lakes, a band of Ojibbeways. Among them was a family consisting of a father and mother, with a grown-up son and daughter, the latter named Awh-mid-way, or, " There is music in her footsteps : " she exceeded in beauty the rest of the tribe, and was eagerly sought in marriage by all the young warriors of her nation. It was not long before Muck-e-tick-enow, or, " Black Eagle," renowned for his prowess in battle and the chase, had, by his assiduities, won her undivided affections ; nor did she conceal from him this favourable state of her feelings, but, in accordance with the customs of her people, she had unhesitatingly extinguished the blazing bark which he had sent floating down the stream that glided past her lodge, and thus acknowledged him as her accepted lover. Confident of possessing her heart, he directed all his endeavours to the propitiation of her parents, and eagerly sought how to compensate them for the loss they would undergo in relinquishing a daughter so dearly loved. For this purpose he departed on a long and distant hunt, and while straining every faculty of his mind and body in collecting trophies and presents wherewith to conciliate them, and show his entire devotion to the object of his adoration, their evil destiny brought Shawwanossoway, then a great war chief, in all the pride of manly strength and vigour, to their camp, on his return from a war excursion, in which he had greatly distinguished himself, and spread his fame far and wide, as the terror of his enemies and the boast of his friends.

Having heard of the transcendent charms of Awh-mid-way, he presented himself before her, girded with the scalps of his enemies, and loaded with other trophies of victory. No sooner did he behold her, than, overcome by her charms, he devoted himself to her service and endeavoured, by every art that the most passionate love could dictate, to win her regard. He recounted the numerous battles he had won, the enemies he had slain : he displayed the reeking scalps he had torn from the defeated enemy,—warriors who had been the terror of his nation : he named the many chiefs who had sued to him for peace, and at the same time plied every artifice to win the good-will of her parents, who, proud of what they considered their daughter's superb conquest, listened to him with delight, and urged her, by every persuasive argument, to accept so distinguished a chief as her husband, expatiating on the honour such an alliance would confer on their family. Constant, however, to her first love, she turned a deaf ear to all the protestations of his rival, whose tales of conquest and bloody trophies only excited her abhorrence.

But, nothing daunted, and determined to win her, either by fair means or by foul, Shawwanossoway persevered in his suit, trusting to time and accident to attain his object. The poor girl, now made truly wretched by his undeviating persecution, accompanied by the menaces of her parents, who were determined to conquer what they regarded as the rebellious obstinacy of their child, at length came to the resolution of appealing to the generosity and honour of her persecutor, and, in the hope of propitiating his forbearance, in an evil hour she confessed her long-cherished affection for Muck-e-tick-enow. He no sooner discovered the cause of her rejection of his suit, than rage and jealousy took full possession of his heart, and plans of vengeance rapidly succeeded each other, until he decided on the assassination of his rival. Having learned from his unsuspecting charmer the route her lover had taken, he tracked him, and came up with his camp, and, concealing himself from observation, crawled towards the fire, where his victim sat alone preparing his evening repast, and shot him from behind a tree. Hiding the body among some brushwood, he took posses-

sion of the game of his murdered rival as a means
of accounting for his own absence, and hastened
back to the village, where he renewed his suit more
ardently than before, to the utter disappointment
and distress of Awh-mid-way who still rejected all
his overtures with indignation, until, urged by the
positive commands and threats of her parents, she
at last, hoping by some artifice still to put off the
evil day, consented to name a time when she would
receive him as her husband, trusting that her
lover would in the meantime return and rescue
her from the impending sacrifice, and concealing,
as well as she could, her increasing aversion to her
persecutor.

The dreaded day at last, however, arrived, but
no lover of course returned.   Little did she think
that his mangled remains had fallen a prey to the
ravenous beasts of the forest — for still hope fondly
directed her gaze in the direction she had seen him
take at his departure, when all was sunshine and
prospective happiness.  With aching eyes and a
bursting heart she saw the evening approach that
was to bind her irrevocably to one she abhorred.

The bridal canoe which, according to the Indian
custom, had been prepared with all the necessary
stores to convey the betrothed pair on a month's

excursion together, which is, in fact, the only marriage ceremony, was already lying upon the beach. Night had come—the nuptial feast was prepared—the last she was to partake of in her father's lodge—when lo! the bride was missing, and consternation usurped the place of gaiety in the bridal throng. Eagerly did they seek her with torches and shouts through the neighbouring forests, but no answering sound met their ears, although the search was continued with untiring eagerness till daylight. Then, for the first time, it was discovered that the bridal canoe was gone, and, concluding that the bride had availed herself of it to aid her escape, Shawwanossoway, accompanied by her brother, started in pursuit on foot, following the direction of the shore.

After proceeding for several hours, they caught sight of the canoe and its fair occupant in the distance. Increasing their speed, they reached a point which the canoe must necessarily pass round. Here the lover swam out, hoping to intercept it. In vain did he endeavour, by every means he could devise, to induce her to stop and take him on board. Defeated by her resolute refusal and the vigour and skill with which she plied her paddle, he was obliged to relinquish the pursuit and return to the shore. He had scarcely landed, when a violent storm, accompanied with thunder, lightning, and heavy rain, compelled the pair to encamp for the night. Notwithstanding the tempest, she continued her efforts until the shades of night hid her from their view. The clouds dispersed with the dawning day, and they continued their pursuit until they at length espied the canoe lying on the shore. Thinking they had at last attained their object, they quickened their steps; but, on coming up to it, they encountered a troop of wolves, and their horror may well be conceived on discovering the remains of the being they loved almost wholly devoured, and only to be recognised by her torn and scattered garments. With aching hearts, they carefully gathered her cherished remains, and, placing them in the canoe, returned to the camp, where she was wept and mourned over for many weeks by her disconsolate relatives and friends, and buried with all the ceremonies of her tribe.

It was evident that the heavy storm had driven the canoe ashore, and it is probable that her materials for kindling a fire having become soaked with water, she had been debarred the only means of protecting herself from these ravenous animals.

Shawwanossoway was so much grieved at the misery which his ungovernable passions had brought upon the object of his warmest love, that he formed the resolution of abandoning his warlike pursuits; and, throwing up the tomahawk to the Great Spirit, that it might be employed only as an instrument of justice, he took in its stead the rattle of the medicine-man; nor did he ever after act inconsistently with his altered character.

Six miles from Manetouawning is another village called Wequimecong, comprising fifty or sixty houses, and a Catholic mission with a church. I made a sketch of the principal chief, named Asabonish, " the Racoon," and his daughter. He belongs to the tribe of Ahtawwah Indians. This tribe is now scarcely distinct from the Ojibbeways, with whom they have numerously intermarried, and speak the same language. The Indians of this village subsist chiefly on salmon and white fish, which they take in such quantities as to be able to barter away a surplus beyond their own wants for other necessaries. The inhabitants also make abundance of maple sugar, which they sell to the traders; nor are they so very deficient in agricultural skill and industry, having, under the able and kind guidance of the missionary, cultivated many patches of wheat, corn, and potatoes, as well as erected a neat little church.

While I was at Manetouawning, the successor of Mr. Anderson, Captain Ironsides, arrived there; and as he was a half-breed and chief of the Wyandots, I have introduced him among my Indian sketches. His name signifies, " Walk in the water :" he is a descendant of Tecumseh, and uses the same *to-tem*, a turtle, each Indian family having a sort of heraldic device, which they use as a signature on important occasions.  Sometimes a family passing through the woods will cut a chip out of a tree, and mark their to-tem on the fresh surface, so that the next may know who passed ; or should a chief wish to send to a post for any articles, he draws the articles on a piece of birch-bark, and puts his to-tem, a fox, a dog, a bear, or whatever it may be, at the bottom; these are perfectly well understood, and answer every purpose of a written order.

I remained at the Manetoulin Island a fortnight, parting with Mr. Dillon, who returned in the schooner that brought the presents.  I left for the Sault St. Marie on board the steamer " Experiment," a Government vessel; Captain Harper, who commanded, kindly taking my canoe on board, and giving me a passage.  At the Sault St. Marie I made the acquaintance of Mr. Ballantyne, the gentleman in charge of the Hudson Bay Company's Post, who was exceedingly kind. He strongly advised me against attempting to penetrate into the interior, except under the auspices of the Company, representing it as almost impossible and certainly very dangerous; but urged me to apply to Sir George Simpson, the Governor of the Company at Lachine, who, he thought, when aware of the object I had in view, would send me forward with the spring brigade of canoes next year. Hoping that, by following this advice, I should be able to travel further, and see more of the wilder tribes, I determined upon confining my travels for the present to a mere summer campaign.

## CHAP. II.

Mackenaw, the "Turtle Island."—Famished Dogs. — The Chief He-Devil.—Green Bay, a Commercial Port.—Consolation in Sorrow.—An Indian Council.—Gambling Habits.—Illicit Traffic in Spirits. — Anecdote of Revenge. — A young Assassin.—Day of Reckoning.—Scenes of Drunkenness.

As it is my intention to speak of the Sault St. Marie in my next trip, I will pass over any mention of it here. After remaining a few days, I embarked on board a steamer for Mackenaw, a distance of ninety miles. There I found a large band of Indians to the number of 2600, who had come from all quarters to receive their pay of $25,000 for land ceded to the United States; these Indians were also Ojibbeways and Ottawas. On arriving among them, I at once pitched my tent in their midst, and commenced to sketch their most remarkable personages. I soon had to remove my tent, from the circumstance that their famishing dogs, which they keep for the purpose of hunting and drawing their sleds in winter, con-

trived to carry off all my provisions, and seemed
likely to serve me in the same way. This will
appear by no means improbable, when I state
that, while I was one evening finishing a sketch,
sitting on the ground alone in my tent, with my
candle stuck in the earth at my side, one of
these audacious brutes unceremoniously dashed
in through the entrance, seized the burning candle
in his jaws and bolted off with it, leaving me in
total darkness.

The next day, as I approached my tent, I saw
a dog running away from it, and thinking it
probably the same rascal that had stolen my
candle, I thought to inflict summary justice upon
the marauder, and fired the contents of my pistol
into his carcase. Beyond my expectations, which
had only been to wound, I saw that I had killed
him, and was immediately assailed with a demand,
from the owner of the dog and his wife, for payment for the loss of his services, which I agreed
to liquidate on their paying me for the losses I
had sustained in hams and other provisions which
their dog had stolen from me. Hereupon they
balanced accounts, and considered that we were
about even, giving me an invitation to join them
at supper, and partake with them of the slaugh-

tered animal, in which operation I afterwards saw them happily engaged.

The Indian name of the island is Mitchi-macinum, or, "the Big Turtle," to which animal it bears a strong resemblance in form when seen from a certain point.

It is situated in the straits between Lakes Huron and Michigan; it contains some picturesque spots, one in particular, a natural bridge, which all strangers visit. There is a garrison on the island, consisting of a company of soldiers. The inhabitants support themselves chiefly by fishing, the straits here yielding an immense supply of large salmon and white fish. Many traders assemble at Mackenaw, at the periods of payment, bringing with them large quantities of spirituous liquors, which they sell clandestinely to these poor creatures, it being prohibited by Government; and many an Indian who travels thither from a long distance returns to his wigwam poorer than he left it, his sole satisfaction being that he and his family have enjoyed a glorious bout of intoxication.

I took the likeness of a chief named Mani-tow-wah-bay, or, "He-Devil." He anxiously inquired what I wanted the likenesses for. In order to induce him to sit, I told him that they were going

home to his great mother, the Queen.  He said
that he had often heard of her, and was very desirous of seeing her, and that had he the time and
means, he would pay her a visit.  It pleased him
much that his second self would have an opportunity of seeing her.  He told me, with much pride
that he had been a successful warrior, and had
taken nine scalps in his warfare.  He was very fond
of liquor, and, when under its influence, was one
of the most violent and unmanageable among them.

Having remained at Mackenaw for three weeks,
I left for Green Bay, which is well situated for a
commercial port, and must eventually become a place
of importance, from the rich farming country in its
vicinity; but owing to over speculation in every way
in the years 1836 and 1837, it has been paralysed,
and houses might now be obtained for the keeping
them in repair.  Here I amused myself with shooting snipe, which are met with in abundance.  In
about a week I left in company with three gentlemen going to Fox River to see the Manōmanee
Indians, who were now assembling to receive their
payment for lands sold to the United States Government in the vicinity of Lake Winebago.  We
embarked in my little canoe, and proceeded up
stream, arriving on the second night about 11

o'clock at an Indian log-house on the shore of
Lake Winebago, or, "Muddy Lake." Two Indian
girls, sisters, reside here alone. I remained with
them the next day, and took their likenesses ; the
elder was named Iwa-toke, or, "the Serpent," the
younger was called Ke-wah-ten, "the North Wind."
We then proceeded up the lake to Fox River,
entering which we found an Indian trading-house,
round about which a number of idlers were pledg-
ing everything they possessed for liquor, under
the influence of which dozens were lying about in
a state of beastly intoxication.

An Indian called Wah-bannim, or, "the White
Dog," sat to me for his likeness. He was in
mourning for his wife, who had died some three
months before; the mourning suit consisting of a
coat of black paint with which he had smeared his
face. He apologised for not appearing in full
mourning costume to have his likeness taken, la-
menting that a part of the paint had worn off ; he
was eagerly seeking to obtain whisky to console
him for his loss. We gladly quitted this disgusting scene of dissipation, and continued our
course up the monotonous stream. After paddling
for two days, we reached the Monōmanee camp.

The evening previous to our arrival, we saw

some Indians spearing salmon ; by night, this has
always a very picturesque appearance, the strong
red glare of the blazing pine knots and roots in the
iron frame, or light-jack, at the bow of the canoe

No. 4. — Spearing by torch-light on Fox River.

throwing the naked figures of the Indians into
wild relief upon the dark water and sombre woods.
Great numbers of fish are killed in this manner.
As the light is intense, and being above the head
of the spearsman, it enables him to see the fish
distinctly at a great depth, and at the same time

it apparently either dazzles or attracts the fish. In my boyish days I have seen as many as a hundred light-jacks gliding about the Bay of Toronto, and have often joined in the sport. This, I suppose, gave me additional interest in the scene; and although very tired with my long day's paddling, I sat down by the fire, and while my companion was cooking some fish in a moh-cock, Indian fashion (for we had lost our kettle), I made the sketch No. 4.

Here we found about 3000 Indians assembled, anxiously awaiting the arrival of the agent with their money; there was also a large number of traders collected, all busily occupied in the erection of booths for the display of their finery. In about a week the bank of the river wore the aspect of a little town; the booths, placed in rows, presented a scene of bustle and animation: the finery was, of course, all displayed to the best advantage on the outsides of the booths. On the arrival of the Indian agent a council was immediately. called in a place erected for the occasion, in which thirty chiefs assembled. I attended in compliance with an invitation I had received from the head chief, Oscosh, or, "the Bravest of the Brave."

He opened the council by lighting a pipe, and

handing it to all present, each person taking a whiff or two, and passing it to the next. The mingling clouds of smoke raised by each are supposed to ascend to the Great Spirit, in token of the harmony that pervades the assembly, and to attest the purity of their intentions. After this ceremony the main business of the council began : it almost exclusively consisted of complaints to be forwarded to the Government. After several of the minor chiefs had delivered their sentiments, Oscosh himself rose, and spoke for about an hour, and a finer flow of native eloquence — seasoned with good sense — I never heard, than proceeded from the lips of this untutored savage. Although a small man, his appearance, while speaking, possessed dignity ; his attitude was graceful, and free from uncouth gesticulation. He complained of numerous acts of injustice which he supposed their great father, the President, could not possibly know, and which he desired might be represented to him, through the agent, accompanied with a pipe-stem of peace richly ornamented.

One of the grievances he specified was, that their money passed through too many hands before it reached them, and that a great part of it was thus lost to them. He wound up his long harangue by descanting upon the narrow limits in which they were pent up, which did not allow them sufficient hunting grounds without encroaching upon the rights of other tribes. He said that, like the deer chased by the dogs, they would have to take to the water.

When Oscosh aspired to the dignity of head chief, his election was opposed in the council by another chief, who insisted on contesting the post of honour with him. Oscosh replied, that as there could be only one head chief, he was quite willing on the instant to settle the dispute with their knives by the destruction of one or the other. This proposal was declined, and his claim has never since been disputed. This tribe is remarkably partial to gaudy decorations, and ornament themselves with great quantities of beads, silver ornaments, and feathers. This passion for display is confined chiefly to the men.

They are much addicted to gambling, and I have seen them commence playing, covered with highly-prized decorations, which have gradually changed hands, as the game proceeded, until its close has left the original possessor without a blanket to cover him. The principal despoilers of the Manōmanees are the Pottowattomies, some of

whom make it their business to visit the Manōmanee camp on a regular black-leg expedition at
the time the latter receive their Government pay,
in order to fleece them of whatever they can,
and they generally return home laden with booty.
Liquor, whenever they can obtain it, is their chief
bane, and lays them more open to the fraudulent
schemes of their despoilers.

I made a sketch of Coe-coosh, "the Hog,"
one of these Pottowattomie black-legs, whom I saw
intently engaged in gambling. The introduction
of spirits among the Indians is, as before mentioned, prohibited under severe penalties by the
laws of the United States, and with the greatest
propriety, as an Indian, when under its influence, is
one of the most dangerous animals in existence,
and there being so few whites to control them at
the period of payment, we should have been in no
small danger of losing our lives had it been readily
attainable.

I was myself, on this occasion, called up in the
dead of the night by the United States' marshal,
who had been commissioned to prevent its introduction among them ; he required my assistance, in
common with all the other whites on the spot, in
order to make a search throughout the camp to

detect the person who was selling liquor, as some of
the Indians were already drunk.   Having a suspicion that a half-breed was engaged in the illicit
traffic, we all proceeded to his tent.   Although we
plainly smelt the liquor in his tin pots, not a single
keg was to be found in spite of the most vigilant
search, carried even to the extent of digging up
the earth in his tent.   When I was leaving the
neighbourhood, I got him to confess that he had
sunk several kegs, with buoys attached to them, in
the middle of the river.   By keeping watch by
turns through the night, it fortunately passed over
without mischief.

Among other Indians whose likeness I took, is
that of Kitchie-ogi-maw, or, "the Great Chief," a
Manōmanee, who was celebrated among his tribe
for many acts of daring, one of which was narrated to me by his half brother : it occurred eight
or ten years previously.

His maternal uncle, who was then at Mackenaw,
chanced to be present in a grocery store, where
ardent spirits were sold, when two soldiers entered,
one of whom treated him with so much indignity,
that, seizing him in his powerful grasp, and being
the stronger and more active man, he threw the
soldier down with great violence on the ground

upon his back, and planting his knee upon his breast, assured him that he would do him no further injury, if he would behave himself properly. This assurance, given in his own language, was, unfortunately, not understood by either of the soldiers; the second of whom, seeing his comrade in the power of a savage, and his life, as he thought, in peril, instantly drew his side-arms and stabbed the ill-fated Indian to the heart. No punishment of any importance followed the commission of this crime; the offender was merely sent away from Mackenaw to escape the vengeance of the relatives of the murdered man.

A year or two subsequently to this unhappy occurrence, as two white men, a Mr. Clayman and a Mr. Burnett, were coming down the Fox River in a canoe, they chanced to pass the lodge of Kitchie-ogi-maw's father, the brother-in-law of the deceased Indian, who, with his family, was camped on the banks of the river. They were noticed by the squaw, the dead man's sister, who called to her husband that now had arrived the opportunity of revenging her brother's death, and that it was his duty, as a man, not to let so good a chance escape him; but her husband, unwilling to risk so hazardous an encounter without other aid than that of his son,

Kitchie-ogi-maw, then a stripling of only fourteen years, hesitated to comply with her request. On which, in order to show her contempt of what she considered his pusillanimity, she hastily divested herself of the breech cloth usually worn by Indian women, and, throwing it insultingly in his face, told him to wear it, for that he was no man. The husband, stung by the opprobrious imputation, caught up his gun, and commanded his son to follow him. The boy declined having any concern in killing the white men, but consented to accompany him for his protection.

The two Americans had now landed and were preparing their camp for the night; one of them was upon his knees engaged in kindling a fire, the other approaching at a distance with an armful of wood; the father raised his gun, but dropped it again to his side in evident agitation; the boy thereupon turned to him, saying, " Father, you tremble too much; give me the gun, and let me do it," and, taking the weapon from his father's hands, he approached the kneeling man from behind, and shot him dead; the other one, hearing the report and catching sight of the Indians, threw down the wood he had collected and ran for his life; the boy seeing a double-barrelled gun lying on the ground near the man he had killed, seized it and followed the fugitive, telling his father to assist in the pursuit, as if this man escaped.they might be punished through his evidence for killing the other.

The father was unable to keep up with the boy, who gained on the white man, and, when within twenty or thirty yards of him, took aim and endeavoured to fire; but being unused to the double trigger, and not having cocked both locks, he pulled the wrong one: determined to make sure of his next aim, he cocked both and pulled the two triggers together; part of the charge entered the victim's shoulder, but the recoil of the two barrels going off at once, knocked the boy backwards on the ground. He was, however, only stunned for the moment, and soon recovered his feet; drawing his scalping knife, the young assassin continued his pursuit of the now almost exhausted man, who, in endeavouring to leap over a log lying on the ground, stumbled and fell.

The bloody young wretch now made sure of his victim, and before the latter could recover his feet, had come up within a few yards of him. The white man seeing that the youngster was alone, and the father not within sight, faced his pursuer, armed

likewise with a knife, and resolved to grapple with
him. But the boy dexterously kept out of his
reach, dodging him round the fallen log, until his
father should come up when they could unitedly
overpower him. The wounded fugitive having now
recovered breath, and noticing the father in the
distance, took to flight once more, dogged by his
indefatigable tormentor, and continued his speed
till the morning dawned, when he fell in with
some friendly Indians, who protected him and
dressed his wounds, none of which were mortal:
they supplied all his wants, until he was strong
enough to return to his home. Kitchie-ogi-maw
now deemed it the safest plan to keep away from
any of the White Settlements, and he continues
still to observe the same precaution.

I found some Indians of the Winebago tribe at
the camp on a visit. The word Winebago signifies " dirty water ; " and they are so called from
living on the margin of a lake of that name. They
are easily distinguished from other tribes, as they
have the custom of pulling out their eyebrows.

I took the likeness of their chief, Mauza-pau-Kan,
or the " Brave Soldier." I remained here for three
weeks, and received much kindness and attention
from the Manōmanees. Hearing that I was taking

sketches of the most noted Indians in the camp, a fellow named Muck-a-ta paid me a visit. He was one of the most ill favoured of any that had been the subjects of my pencil, and by all accounts his physiognomy did not belie his character.

The Indians had no sooner received their money than a scene ensued that baffles description. Large quantities of liquor immediately found their way into the camp from some unknown quarter, and the sad effect was almost instantaneous. There was scarcely a man, woman, or child, old enough to lift the vessel to its mouth, that was not wallowing in beastly drunkenness; and we gladly availed ourselves of the arrival of a small steamer that plies on Lake Winebago and the Fox River to make our escape from the disgusting and dangerous scene of singing and dancing and fighting going on around us. We disembarked at a place called " Fond du Lac," where we hired a waggon, and crossed over to the Sheboygan on Lake Michigan, and embarked on board another steamer for Buffalo, which I left again on the 30th of November and arrived the day following at Toronto.

## CHAP. III.

In the ensuing March I repaired to Lachine to seek an interview with Sir George Simpson. Having exhibited to him the sketches which I had made, and explained the nature of the objects which I had in view, Sir George entered cordially into my plans; and, in order to facilitate them, ordered a passage in the spring brigade of canoes.

Accordingly, on the 9th of May, 1846, I left Toronto in company with Governor Simpson for the Sault St. Marie, in order to embark in the brigade of canoes which had left Lachine some time previously, taking the route of the Ottawa and Lake Huron.

On my arrival at Mackenaw in the evening, I

was informed by the master of the steamboat that he would not leave until 9 o'clock next morning. Trusting to this assurance, I went on shore for the night; but on coming down to the wharf on the following day, I found that the vessel with Sir George Simpson had departed about twenty minutes previously. This was indeed a damper of no ordinary magnitude, as, should I fail in seeing Sir George before he left the Sault, I should not be able to accompany the canoes. I was aware, likewise, that the governor would not remain longer than a few hours; but how to overtake him was the difficulty, as no boat would leave for four days.

Determined, however, not to be disappointed in my proposed expedition, I used every exertion to procure a mode of conveyance. Walking along the beach, I saw a small skiff lying, and having found the owner, inquired if I could hire it, and whether there was any chance of procuring a crew. The man strongly advised me not to attempt such a perilous voyage, as it was blowing hard, and that it was not in mortal power to reach the Sault by daylight next morning. Resolved, however, to make the attempt, I at length succeeded in chartering the skiff and engaging a crew, consisting of three boys, the eldest being under nineteen years of age. It must be added that they were all well acquainted with boating. The striplings held out no hopes of being able to accomplish the undertaking within the given time, and were only induced to make the attempt by the offer of a high reward. Thus, in a tiny skiff, with a blanket for a sail, and a single loaf of bread along with a little tea and sugar for stores, we launched out in the lake to make a traverse of forty-five miles.

The wind being favourable, the boat shot ahead with tremendous rapidity, but the danger was imminent and continuous from the moment we left the shore until we reached the mouth of the river of St. Marie, which we did at sunset.

Here we remained about twenty minutes, and discussed our tea and bread with appetites sharpened to intensity. But now commenced another difficulty, the navigation of forty-five miles of a river with which we were totally unacquainted, in a dark night against the current and through a channel dotted with numerous islands. All this was to be accomplished by daylight, or the toil and anxiety would be of no avail.

We however set forth unflinchingly; and after a night of the most violent exertion, after running into all sorts of wrong places and backing out again, after giving up half a dozen times in despair, and as often renewing the struggle, our exertions were crowned with success. When morning dawned, there lay the eagerly looked-for steamer not two miles from us.

On getting up in the morning, Sir George Simpson was astonished at seeing me; and his amazement was not lessened when he learned the mode of my conveyance. The voyage on no former occasion had been performed in so short a time under corresponding circumstances, and to this day the undertaking is still talked of as a rather notable adventure in Mackenaw and the Sault.

The Sault St. Marie is situated at the lower extremity of Lake Superior, where it debouches into the river St. Marie, in its course to Lake Huron: having in this part of the river a considerable fall, for about a mile and a half in length, it soon becomes a foaming torrent, down which, however, canoes, steered by practised guides, ordinarily descend safely, although with terrific violence. Sometimes, indeed, the venture is fatal to the bark and its occupants. A short time before our arrival on the present occasion, a canoe, in running down the rapid, had struck upon a sunken rock that made a hole through her bottom. She instantly filled, but, owing to the extreme buoyancy of the birch-bark these canoes are made of, the men, by balancing themselves adroitly in her, and squatting up to their necks in the water, thereby lessening their weight materially, were enabled to steer her with safety down the foaming billows, and run her on the shore in an eddy at the foot of the rapids.

I took a sketch of the rapids above alluded to, from the American side. There is a small town called the Sault St. Marie, on the American side, containing 700 or 800 inhabitants, with a well-built garrison, prettily situated on the river's bank. On the Canadian side, about half a mile direct across, the Hudson's Bay Company have a trading establishment, and the Custom House officer, Mr. Wilson, a tolerably handsome house. With these two exceptions, the British side presents to the traveller a collection of poor miserable hovels, occupied solely by half-breeds and Indians. In strolling among these hovels, I made a sketch of a good-looking half-breed girl, whose sudden appear-

ance, emerging from such a wretched neighbourhood, took me by surprise.

As the brigade of canoes had passed up two
days before my arrival at the Sault, and Sir
George's canoes were too heavily laden, he was
unable to give me a passage. My only alternative
was to wait until the "White Fish," a small
schooner belonging to the Company, and lying
at the upper end of the portage, was unloaded,
and trust to the chance of her intercepting the
canoes at Fort William. This was very doubtful,
depending, as it entirely did, upon the wind; but
I had no alternative. Sir George had embarked
on the 14th in his canoe, leaving me to follow in
the way above named. It took four days to
unload the schooner, so that she was not ready
to leave before the 20th of May. We had a fair
wind at starting, which continued until the night
of the 23rd, when it came to blow a gale off
" Thunder Point." The night being very dark, we
were apprehensive of driving on the rocks at the
base of this formidable mountain — Thunder Point,
as it is called, being in fact, a perpendicular rock
of twelve or fifteen hundred feet high. Seeing it,
as I then did, for the first time, by the glare of the
almost incessant flashes of lightning, it presented

one of the grandest and most terrific spectacles I had ever witnessed. As our crew consisted of only two men, I was under the necessity of assisting to work the vessel, so that all hope of a comfortable sleep in my warm hammock had to be abandoned, and I was obliged to remain the whole night on deck.

At daybreak we succeeded in rounding this dangerous point, and soon passed El Royal, which island is supposed to contain valuable mineral wealth, and cast anchor near the mouth of the Kaministaqueah River, which we ascended about two miles to Fort William, in a small boat. This fort, during the existence of the North-west Company, was one of considerable importance as a depôt for all the trade carried on in furs, &c. This importance it has lost, in consequence of the goods which formerly passed by the route of Lake Superior, now passing by Hudson's Bay since the two rival companies have merged into one; but as it possesses the best land in the vicinity of Lake Superior, it might still be made a place of much consideration in an agricultural point of view.

On delivering my letter of introduction to Mr. Mackenzie, the gentleman in charge of the fort, I learned, to my great disappointment, that the brigade had passed up the river the day before. I was compelled, in this dilemma, to trespass on the kindness of this gentleman for the supply of a light canoe and three men, in order to overtake them if possible before they reached the mountain portage, forty miles in advance. In the course of half an hour, thanks to Mr. Mackenzie's kindness, we were straining at the paddles, and, ten hours afterwards, had the satisfaction of coming up with the brigade about thirty-five miles from our starting point.

I found a gentleman named Lane in charge of the brigade, which consisted of three canoes with eight men in each. We all camped immediately, and at 3 o'clock next morning were again *en route* in our canoes. These are constructed of the bark of the birch tree, and are about twenty-eight feet long and four to five feet beam, strong, and capable of carrying, besides their crew of eight men, twenty-five pieces; but at the same time so light as to be easily carried on the shoulders of two men. All goods taken into the interior, and all peltries brought out, are made into packs of 90 lbs. each, for the purpose of easy handling at the frequent *portages* and *discharges;* these packs are called pieces.

After pulling our canoes up a rapid current, we arrived about 8 o'clock at the mountain portage, whose falls surpass even those of Niagara in picturesque beauty; for, although far inferior in volume of water, their height is nearly equal, and the scenery surrounding them infinitely more wild and romantic. Whilst the men were engaged in making the portage, I took advantage of the delay to make a sketch.

I have since been informed that the large flat rock which divided the torrent in the centre has fallen in. The interruption thus caused by the falls is about two miles of very steep ascent, up which the men have to carry the canoes and baggage, the former on their shoulders, the latter on their backs, by means of what is technically named a portage-strap, both ends of which are attached to the load of two pieces, while the middle of the strap goes round the forehead, which thus supports the principal part of the burden. The men who usually work this brigade of canoes are hired at Lachine, and are called by the uncouth name of *Mangeurs du Lard,* or pork-eaters, among the old hands in the interior, to whom they are unequal in encountering the difficulties incident to a voyage from Lachine to the mouth of the Columbia, whither some of them are sent, and become almost skeletons by the time they reach their destination, through the unavoidable privations and hardships they have to undergo.

Launching our canoes again, we proceeded for about a mile, and made another portage called "The Lost Men's Portage," owing to three men having lost themselves in the woods in crossing it. I very nearly met with the same fate myself; for, having gone up to the rapids to take a sketch, I endeavoured, when I had finished, to find my way back, and spent two hours in an unsuccessful attempt to gain the path. I then fortunately thought of discharging my fowling-piece as a signal, and had the pleasure of immediately hearing an answering shot, which guided my steps to the party who were anxiously awaiting my return to embark.

Proceeding a few miles up the stream, we reached the "Pin Portage," so called from the rocks over which we had to carry the canoes being so sharp as actually to cut the feet of the men, who usually go barefooted or only wearing light mocassins. We made, in all, six portages in one day, viz., "Ecarté,"

" Rose Décharge," and " De l'Isle," and the three
before named, travelling a distance of forty-three
miles : the current was so impetuous, even where we
could avail ourselves of our canoes, that the men
found the greatest difficulty in forcing up against it
with poles.

On the 26th of May we journeyed twenty-six
miles, making the following portages and discharges,
viz. :—" Recousi Portage," " Couteau Portage,"
" Belanger Décharge," " Mauvais Décharge,"
" Tremble Décharge," " Penet Décharge," " Maître
Portage," " Little Dog Portage," " Dog Portage,"
and the " Big Dog Portage;" the latter affords a
splendid view from its summit of the Kaministaqueah river, meandering in the distance, as far as the
eye can reach, through one of the loveliest valleys in
nature.   This view I wished much to have sketched,
but time is of so much importance in the movements of these brigades, that I did not consider
myself justified in waiting.

The " Big Dog Portage" derives its name from
an Indian tradition that a big dog once slept on
the summit, and left the impression of his form
on the highest point of land, which remains to
this present time.   The length of this portage
is two miles ;  we camped at the upper end ;

and while here I made a sketch of the fall, during one of the heaviest showers of rain I ever experienced.

One of our *Mangeurs du Lard* presenting himself at the camp fire in a handsome rabbit-skin blanket, was asked by Mr. Lane where he had obtained it. He replied that he had found it among the bushes. Mr. Lane, knowing that it is customary among the Indians to place offerings of all descriptions upon the graves of their deceased relatives, first rendering them unserviceable to any evil disposed persons in this world, under the idea that the Great Spirit will repair them on the arrival of the deceased in the next, and that they hold in the greatest abhorrence, and never fail to punish, any one who sacrilegiously disturbs them, ordered him immediately to return to the place whence he took it, and replace it exactly as he had found it, unless he wished to have us all murdered. When the man understood what he had done, he replaced the blanket immediately.

On the 27th, Sir George Simpson passed us with his two canoes, accompanied by his secretary Mr. Hopkins. Sir George only stopped a few minutes to congratulate me on my having overcome the difficulties of my starting: he seemed to think that

the perseverance and determination I had shown
augured well for my future success, and as his
canoes were much lighter and better manned than
ours, he passed on rapidly in advance.   As there
were no more currents to overcome, the men this
day threw away their poles as useless, and started
on a race with their paddles for about fifteen miles
through "Dog Lake" and entered "Dog River."
We now had to make a long portage of three
miles over a high mountain into a small lake.
At the upper end of this portage we again overtook Sir George, and were invited to dine with
him at the next, some four or five miles further
on, but we unluckily could not again come up
with him.

On inquiring the cause of some loud shouting
that I heard in the woods, I was told that some of
our men had surrounded a bear which had given
them battle, but that, unarmed as they were, they
had deemed discretion the better part of valour,
and sounded a retreat.  We camped on the banks of
a small river.  We had hitherto stemmed against
the stream of waters that emptied itself into the
Atlantic ; but we had now reached streams that
flowed at a much more rapid rate, and coursed
on to Hudson's Bay.   At the close of this day we

had accomplished a distance of thirty-three miles, having made the following portages, viz.: —
" Barrière Portage," " Joudain Portage," and
" Prairie Portage."

## CHAP. IV.

Four Miles of Swamp. — Lake of a Thousand Isles. — Virtue of a
Silver Bullet. — A wild Tale. — Living One upon Another. —
The Great Medicine-Man. — A Timid " Little Rat." — A Cater-
pillar Plague.—Butter in the Wilderness. — A Leap into the Grave.
—Going down the Winnipeg. — A novel Viameter.

*May* 28*th.*—TO-DAY we passed over one of the
largest and most difficult portages in the whole
route, it is called the " Savan Portage;" it passes
through about four miles of swamp. It formerly
had logs laid lengthwise, for the convenience of
the men carrying the loads; but they are now for
the most part decayed, so that the poor fellows
had sometimes to wade up to the middle in mud
and water. In all, we made to-day about thirty
miles, including the following portages, viz.:—
" Milieu Portage" and " Savan Portage," from
whence we went twenty miles down the Savan
River, and camped near its mouth, where it
empties into " Mille Lacs."

On the 29th, we passed through the Lake of the
Thousand Islands, thirty-six miles long, a name it

well deserves.  The scenery surrounding us was truly beautiful; the innumerable rocky islands varying from several miles in length to the smallest proportions, all covered with trees, chiefly pine. This lake is filled with innumerable ducks, which the Indians entice in the following curious manner:—A young dog is trained by dragging a piece of meat attached to a string up and down the edge of the shore several times, and putting the dog on the scent, who follows it rapidly, wagging his tail. After the dog has followed it for some time, he is given the meat; this is done repeatedly until the dog will do so whenever he is ordered, and his motions attract the ducks swimming in the distance to within reach of the Indian, who lies concealed on the banks.  The flock of ducks is so crowded and numerous, that I have known an Indian kill forty ducks by firing at them whilst in the water, and rapidly loading and firing again whilst the same flock was circling above his head.  Our first portage after leaving this lovely lake was " Portage de Pente."  We camped at the end of the next portage, called " Little Discharge," having made a distance altogether of fifty-six miles.

*May* 30*th*.—We made an early start, reaching the "French Portage" by breakfast-time.  Here we lightened the canoes of the principal part of the baggage, and carried it across the portage, a distance of three miles, in order that we might be able to send the canoes round by the river, which had now become very shallow, to meet us at the further end of the portage. We camped this evening at a small lake called Sturgeon Lake, having come a distance of forty-eight miles, passing " French Portage," and " Portage de Morts."

*May* 31*st.*—We passed down the " Rivière Maligne" until we came to what are termed the First, Second, and Third portages, and, making the portage " De l'Isle" and " Du Lac," camped near " Lac la Croix Traverse," accomplishing a distance of only twenty-seven miles.

*June* 1*st.*—We passed down the river " Macau," where there are some beautiful rapids and falls. Here we fell in with the first Indians we had met since leaving the Lake of the Thousand Islands; they are called " Saulteaux," being a branch of the Ojibbeways, whose language they speak with very slight variation. We purchased from an Indian man and woman some dried sturgeon. The female wore a rabbit-skin dress: they were, as I afterwards learned, considered to be cannibals, the Indian term for which is *Weendigo*, or " One who eats Human Flesh." There is a superstitious belief among Indians that the Weendigo cannot be killed by anything short of a silver bullet. I was informed, on good authority, that a case had occurred here in which a father and daughter had killed and eaten six of their own family from absolute want. The story went on to state, that they then camped at some distance off in the vicinity of an old Indian woman, who happened to be alone in her lodge, her relations having gone out hunting. Seeing the father and daughter arrive unaccompanied by any other members of the family, all of whom she knew, she began to suspect that some foul play had taken place, and to feel apprehensive for her own safety. By way of precaution, she resolved to make the entrance to her lodge very slippery, and as it was winter, and the frost severe, she poured water repeatedly over the ground as fast as it froze, until it was covered with a mass of smooth ice; and instead of going to bed, she remained sitting up in her lodge, watching with an axe in her hand. When near midnight, she heard steps advancing cautiously over the crackling snow, and looking through the crevices of the lodge, caught sight of the girl in the attitude of listening, as if to ascertain whether the inmate was asleep; this the old woman feigned by snoring aloud. The welcome sound no sooner reached the ears of the wretched girl, than she rushed forward, but, slipping on the ice, fell down at the entrance of the lodge, whereupon the intended victim sprang upon the murderess and buried the axe in her brains: and not doubting but the villanous father was near at hand, she fled with all her speed to a distance, to escape his vengeance. In the meantime, the Weendigo father, who was impatiently watching for the expected signal to his horrid repast, crept up to the lodge, and called to his daughter; hearing no reply, he went on, and, in place of the dead body of the old woman, he saw his own daughter, and hunger overcoming every other feeling, he saved his own life by devouring her remains.

The *Weendigoes* are looked upon with superstitious dread and horror by all Indians, and any one known to have eaten human flesh is shunned by the rest; as it is supposed that, having once tasted it, they would do so again had they an opportunity. They are obliged, therefore, to make their lodges at some distance from the rest of the tribe, and the children are particularly kept out of their way; however, they are not molested or injured in any way, but seem rather to be pitied for the misery they must have endured before they could be brought to this state. I do not think that any Indian, at least none that I have ever seen, would eat his fellow-creature, except under the influence of starvation; nor do I think that there is any tribe of Indians on the North American continent to whom the word " cannibal" can be properly applied.

We traversed to-day a distance of forty-one miles, passing four portages before entering Lake Meican, which is nine miles long, to " Portage Neuf," entering the " Lac la Pluie," where we camped; its name did not seem inappropriate, for we were detained here two days by the incessant torrents of rain that poured down. It took us until the evening of the 4th to reach Fort Francis, at the lower end of the lake, a distance of fifty miles, where I found a letter from Sir George Simpson, enclosing a circular.

There is a beautiful fall of water here within sight of the fort, at the commencement of the river which runs from Lac la Pluie to the Lake of the Woods. Vast quantities of white fish and sturgeon are taken at the foot of the rapids, with which our mess-table at the fort was abundantly supplied; indeed, the chief food here consists of fish and wild rice, with a little grain grown in the vicinity of the fort, this being the first land I had seen fit for agricultural purposes since I had left Fort William. We continued at the fort until the morning of the 5th. There was a large camp of Salteaux Indians in the immediate vicinity: a considerable party of them came to the establishment in the morning to see the "great medicine-*man" who made Indians, Mr. Lane having given them to understand that my object in travelling through the country was to paint their likenesses.

I applied to the head chief, Waw-gas-kontz, "the Little Rat," to take his likeness, but was refused, on the grounds that he feared something bad would result to him; but after Iacaway, "the Loud Speaker," had sat for his, Waw-gas-kontz seemed ashamed of his cowardice, and became very anxious to have it done, following me down to the canoe. I had not time, however, to do so; but I could not get rid of him until I promised to take his likeness on my return.

*June 5th.*—We left the fort at 10 this morning; the rain continued all day, and obliged us to camp

* The Indians attach a mysterious meaning to the word "medicine," applying it to almost everything they cannot clearly understand.

at 4 in the afternoon, the distance we went being about thirty miles.

*June 6th.*—It was a remarkable fact that the trees on each side of the river, and part of the Lake of the Woods, for full 150 miles of our route, were literally stripped of foliage by myriads of green caterpillars, which had left nothing but the bare branches; and I was informed that the scourge extended to more than twice the distance I have named, the whole country wearing the dreary aspect of winter at the commencement of summer.

As it was impossible to take our breakfast on land, unless we made up our minds to eat them, dropping incessantly as they did from the trees among our food, and the ground everywhere covered with them *en masse*, we were compelled to take it in our canoes. We met some Indians, from whom we purchased seven fine sturgeons, each weighing perhaps forty or fifty pounds. We paid for the whole one cotton shirt. We next entered the Lake of the Woods, and camped on a beautiful rocky island, having made fifty-three miles in one day.

*June 7th.*—We passed through the above lake, sixty-eight miles long. When passing a small island about the middle of it, the steersman of my canoe

put ashore on this island, and running to a clump
of bushes returned with a small keg of butter,
which he told us he had left hidden, or, as they call
it, *en cache*, the year before: it proved an acquisi-
tion to our larder, although its age had not improved its flavour.  We next made the " Rat Portage," at the foot of which is the fort, a small establishment where they were so badly supplied with
provisions as to be able to afford us only two white
fish.  We consequently thought it advisable to leave
the place, although late in the evening, and camped
a few miles lower down the Winnipeg River; having
travelled to-day a distance of seventy-two miles.

*June 8th.*—We continued our course down the
river Winnipeg, which is broken by numerous
beautiful rapids and falls, being indeed one of the
most picturesque rivers we had passed in the whole
route.  Our bowsman caught a pike, which in appearance had two tails, one at each end; but we
found on examination that the tail and part of the
body of another fish or sucker, nearly as large as
himself, which he had tried to swallow, was protruding from his mouth, evidencing the extreme
voracity of this species.  We passed to-day a
Catholic missionary station called " Wabassemmung " (or White Dog), which, on my return, two

years and a half afterwards, I found deserted, from the circumstance that the Indians of this quarter did not prove very willing converts. We camped for the night a few miles below this station, and still found the caterpillars before alluded to extremely annoying, covering as they did completely our blankets and clothing. We had passed the following places, viz.: "the Dalles," "Grand Décharge," "Terre jaune Portage," "the Charrette Portage," "Terre blanche Portage," "Cave Portage," and Wabassemmung, a distance of seventy-one miles.

*June 9th.*—We passed the "Chute de Jaques," so called from a man thus named, who, being dared by one of his companions to run his canoe over a fall of fifteen or twenty feet, an exploit never attempted before or since, unhesitatingly essayed the bold feat, and pushing off his frail bark, jumped into it, and on rounding a small island darted down the main sheet, his companions meanwhile anxiously watching for his safety from the shore. As might have been expected, he was dashed to pieces and no more seen. We camped this evening, after completing a distance of sixty miles, and making the following portages, viz.: "Portage de l'Isle," "Chute de Jaques," "Point des Bois" (the

F

Indian name of this fall is Ka-mash-aw-aw-sing, or, "the Two Carrying-Places"); "Rochers Boules," "the Slave Falls," which is the highest of all the falls of the Winnipeg River; I never heard the reason of its bearing this name. At "Barrière Portage" we found the black flies and mosquitoes so annoying all night, as to deprive us entirely of sleep.

*June* 10*th.* — We ran three or four beautiful rapids to-day in our canoes, the men showing great expertness in their management, although so much risk attends it that several canoes have been lost in the attempt. We made about sixty miles to-day down the Winnipeg, passing the following places, viz.: the "Grand Rapid," six portages, all within sight of each other, and about five miles in length inclusively : they are known collectively by the name of "The Six Portages" — the first and second portage of the "Bonnet," "the Grand Bonnet," "Petits Rochers," and "Terre Blanche." We encamped about a couple of miles below the rapids at 5 o'clock — earlier than usual, as our canoes had received some little injury and required repairs. It is usual to start every morning between 3 and 4 o'clock and proceed till 8 for breakfast, then continue steadily on until an hour before dark, just so as to give the men time to prepare for the night. The only rest allowed being at intervals of about an hour, when all hands stop two or three minutes to fill their pipes. It is quite a common way of expressing the distance of one place to another to say that it is so many pipes; and this, amongst those who have travelled in the interior gives a very good idea of the distance. The evening was very beautiful, and soon after we had pitched our tents and lighted our fires, we were visited by some Saulteaux Indians. As I had plenty of time, I sketched the encampment. Our visitors, the clear stream reflecting the brilliant sky so peculiar to North America, the granite rocks backed by the rich foliage of the woods with Indians and voyageurs moving about, made a most pleasing subject.

## CHAP. V.

Fort Alexander.—Mr. Lane.—A Western Career.—Value of Bark to
the Indian.—The Medicine Lodge.—A Double Shot.—Fort Garry.
— The nearest Market Town. — Red River Settlement. — White
Horse Plain.—Hunting the Buffalo.

*June* 11*th*. — WE made an early start with a fine
breeze, filling our sail, and arrived at Fort Alexander to breakfast, a distance of seventeen or
eighteen miles including the three portages: " First
Eau Qui Merit," " Second Eau Qui Merit," " Third
Eau Qui Merit." Fort Alexander is situated on
Winnipeg River, about three miles above where
it disembogues into Lake Winnipeg, and has some
good farming land in its vicinity. I here took my
farewell of Mr. Lane with great regret, and left
the brigade of canoes, which proceeded with him to
Norway House, on his route to Mackenzie River.
Mr. Lane had entered the Hudson's Bay Company's
service when very young, and having served for
twenty-six years, he became dissatisfied with the

slowness of his promotion, and determined to resign and return to Ireland, his native land. However, on his return home, he found himself lost in civilised life, and quite unable to occupy himself with any business pursuits there; and when I met him, he was again in the employment of the Company, at a lower salary than he had before received, and was going to Mackenzie River, one of the most remote and bleak posts in the whole region, accompanied by his wife, a half-breed. The last that I heard of him was that he had arrived at his post almost starved to death, after travelling about 700 miles on snow shoes through the depth of winter.

Hearing that a camp of Indians lay within a few miles, I requested a Mr. Setler, in charge of the establishment, to procure me a guide to them. I found it indispensably necessary to wear a veil all the way, as a protection from the mosquitoes, which I had never before seen so numerous. I found a very large camp of Saulteaux Indians assembled. They have a medicine lodge erected in the centre of their encampment, to which I at once directed my steps. It was rather an oblong structure, composed of poles bent in the form of an arch, and both ends forced into the ground, so as to form, when completed, a long arched chamber, protected from the weather by a covering of birch bark. This bark is one of the most valuable materials that nature supplies to the Red-man, as by its friendly aid he is enabled to brave the inclemency of the weather on land, and float lightly and safely over the vast inland seas that so abound in his wild domain; and when any transient impediments present themselves to his using it on water, so light is its weight, that he easily carries it on his shoulder. Such also is its compactness and closeness of texture, that he forms his culinary and other utensils of it, and, as it is quite impervious to water, he is able, by the aid of heated stones, to boil his fish in them. It also serves for a material or papyrus on which to transmit his hieroglyphic correspondence.

On my first entrance into the medicine lodge — (the reader is already apprised of the mysterious meaning the Indian attaches to the term "medicine") — I found four men, who appeared to be chiefs, sitting upon mats spread upon the ground gesticulating with great violence, and keeping time to the beating of a drum. Something, apparently of a sacred nature was covered up in the centre of the group, which I was not allowed to see.

They almost instantly ceased their "pow-wow," or music, and seemed rather displeased at my intrusion, although they approached, and inquiringly felt the legs of my fustian pantaloons, pronouncing me a chief on account of their fineness.

On looking around me, which I now ventured to do, I saw that the interior of their lodge or sanctuary was hung round with mats constructed with rushes, to which were attached various offerings consisting principally of bits of red and blue cloth, calico, &c., strings of beads, scalps of enemies, and sundry other articles beyond my comprehension. Finding they did not proceed with their "pow-wow," I began to think I was intruding, and retired. But no sooner had I emerged from the lodge, than I was surrounded by crowds of women and children, whom nothing would satisfy short of examining me from head to foot, following me in swarms through the camp, not apparently with any hostile intentions, but for the mere gratification of their curiosity. I passed a grave surmounted with a scalp hung on a pole, torn, doubtless, from an enemy by the warrior buried beneath. I now returned to the fort, first engaging six of the Indians to proceed with me to Red River. We left at four o'clock in the afternoon in a small boat, accompanied by Mr. Setler, and camped on the shore of Lake Winnipeg.

*June 12th.* — I wrote this part of my journal by the light of a blazing fire in the above encampment, surrounded by my six painted warriors sleeping in the front of the tent, their hideous faces gleaming in the fire-light: a head wind all day had prevented our making any great progress.

*June 13th.* — We entered the mouth of the Red River about ten this morning. The banks of this river, which here enters the lake, are for five or six miles low and marshy. After proceeding up stream for about twenty miles, we arrived at the Stone Fort, belonging to the Company, where I found Sir George Simpson and several of the gentlemen of the Company, who assemble here annually for the purpose of holding a council for the transaction of business. I remained here until the 15th, and left for the Upper Fort, about twenty miles higher up. We rode on horseback, accompanied by Mr. Peter Jacobs, Wesleyan Indian missionary, and arrived there in about four hours, after a pleasant ride of eighteen or twenty miles through a considerable part of Red River Settlement. Here there are a judge and a court house. A Saulteaux Indian was hung here last year for shooting a Sioux Indian and another of his own tribe at one shot, the ball having passed through the Sioux and entered the Saulteaux's body: his intention was to kill the Sioux only, with whom his tribe then was, and had been from time immemorial, at war, so that the killing of the Saulteaux was accidental. The country here is not very beautiful; a dead level plain with very little timber, the landscape wearing more the appearance of the cultivated farms of the old country with scarcely a stick or stump upon it.

This settlement is the chief provision depôt of the Hudson's Bay Company, and it is also here that large quantities of pimmi-kon are procured from the half-breeds, a race who, keeping themselves distinct from both Indians and whites, form a tribe of themselves; and, although they have adopted some of the customs and manners of the French voyageurs, are much more attached to the wild and savage manners of the Red-man. Fort Garry, one of the most important establishments of the Company, is erected on the forks of the Red River and the Assiniboine, in long. 97° W., and in lat. 50° 6' 20" N., as will be seen in sketch No. 5. On the opposite side of the river is situated the Roman Catholic church, and two or three miles

further down there is a Protestant church. The
settlement is formed along the banks of the river
for about fifty miles, and extends back from the
water, according to the original grant from the In-

No. 5. — View at Red River Settlement.

dians, as far as a person can distinguish a man from
a horse on a clear day.

Lord Selkirk first attempted to form a settlement here in 1811, but it was speedily abandoned.
A few years afterwards several Scotch families,
including some from the Orkney Islands, emi-

grated under the auspices of the Hudson's Bay Company, and now number about 3000, who live as farmers, in great plenty so far as mere food and clothing are concerned. As for the luxuries of life, they are almost unattainable, as they have no market nearer than St. Paul's, on the Mississippi River, a distance of nearly 700 miles over a trackless prairie. The half-breeds are more numerous than the whites, and now amount to 6000. These are the descendants of the white men in the Hudson's Bay Company's employment and the native Indian women. They all speak the Cree language and the Lower Canadian patois; they are governed by a chief named Grant, much after the manner of the Indian tribes. He has presided over them now for a long period, and was implicated in the disturbances which occurred between the Hudson Bay and North-West Companies. He was brought to Canada charged with the murder of Governor Semple, but no sufficient evidence could be produced against him.

The half-breeds are a very hardy race of men, capable of enduring the greatest hardships and fatigues: but their Indian propensities predominate, and consequently they make poor farmers, neglecting their land for the more exciting pleasures of the chase. Their buffalo hunts are conducted by the whole tribe, and take place twice a year, about the middle of June and October, at which periods notice is sent round to all the families to meet at a certain day on the White Horse Plain, about twenty miles from Fort Garry. Here the tribe is divided into three bands, each taking a separate route for the purpose of falling in with the herds of buffaloes. These bands are each accompanied by about 500 carts, drawn by either an ox or a horse. Their cart is a curious-looking vehicle, made by themselves with their own axes, and fastened together with wooden pins and leather strings, nails not being procurable. The tire of the wheel is made of buffalo hide, and put on wet; when it becomes dry, it shrinks, and is so tight that it never falls off, and lasts as long as the cart holds together.

# CHAP. VI.

Plain of Roses.—A Desert Filter.—Making Pimmi-kon.—Canine Camp-followers.—Dry Dance Mountain.—Vigils of the Braves.— Death at the Feast.—Successful Ambush.—The Scalp Dance.—A Hunter's Appetite. — The Grand Chase. — Marking the Game. — Head over Heels.—Sketching under Difficulties.—A Troublesome Tenant.

I ARRIVED at Fort Garry about three days after the half-breeds had departed; but as I was very anxious to witness buffalo hunting, I procured a guide, a cart for my tent, &c., and a saddle horse for myself, and started after one of the bands. We travelled that day about thirty miles, and encamped in the evening on a beautiful plain covered with innumerable small roses. The next day was anything but pleasant, as our route lay through a marshy tract of country, in which we were obliged to strain through a piece of cloth all the water we drank, on account of the numerous insects, some of which were accounted highly dangerous, and are said to have the power of eating through the coats of the stomach, and causing death even to horses.

The next day I arrived at the Pambinaw River, and found the band cutting poles, which they are obliged to carry with them to dry the meat on, as, after leaving this, no more timbered land is met with until the three bands meet together again at the Turtle Mountain, where the meat they have taken and dried on the route is made into pimmi-kon. This process is as follows:—The thin slices of dried meat are pounded between two stones until the fibres separate; about 50lbs. of this are put into a bag of buffalo skin, with about 40lbs. of melted fat, and mixed together while hot, and sewed up, forming a hard and compact mass; hence its name in the Cree language, *pimmi* signifying meat, and *kon*, fat. Each cart brings home ten of these bags, and all that the half-breeds do not require for themselves is eagerly bought by the Company, for the purpose of sending to the more distant posts, where food is scarce. One pound of this is considered equal to four pounds of ordinary meat, and the pimmi-kon keeps for years perfectly good exposed to any weather.

I was received by the band with the greatest cordiality. They numbered about two hundred hunters, besides women and children. They live,

during these hunting excursions, in lodges formed
of dressed buffalo skins. They are always accompanied by an immense number of dogs, which follow
them from the settlements for the purpose of feeding on the offal and remains of the slain buffaloes.
These dogs are very like wolves, both in appearance
and disposition, and, no doubt, a cross breed between the wolf and dog. A great many of them
acknowledge no particular master, and are sometimes dangerous in times of scarcity. I have
myself known them to attack the horses and eat
them.

Our camp broke up on the following morning,
and proceeded on their route to the open plains.
The carts containing the women and children, and
each decorated with some flag, or other conspicuous
emblem, on a pole, so that the hunters might recognise their own from a distance, wound off in
one continuous line, extending for miles, accompanied by the hunters on horseback. During the
forenoon, whilst the line of mounted hunters and
carts were winding round the margin of a small
lake, I took the opportunity of making a sketch of
the singular cavalcade.

The following day we passed the Dry Dance
Mountain, where the Indians, before going on a

war party, have a custom of dancing and fasting
for three days and nights.   This practice is always
observed by young warriors going to battle for the
first time, to accustom them to the privations and
fatigues which they must expect to undergo, and
to prove their strength and endurance.   Should
any sink under the fatigue and fasting of this
ceremony, they are invariably sent back to the
camp where the women and children remain.

After leaving this mountain, we proceeded on
our route without meeting any buffalo, although we
saw plenty of indications of their having been in the
neighbourhood a short time previously.   On the
evening of the second day we were visited by twelve
Sioux chiefs, with whom the half-breeds had been
at war for several years.   They came for the purpose
of negotiating a permanent peace, but, whilst
smoking the pipe of peace in the council lodge,
the dead body of a half-breed, who had gone to a
short distance from the camp, was brought in newly
scalped, and his death was at once attributed to
the Sioux.   The half-breeds, not being at war with
any other nation, a general feeling of rage at once
sprang up in the young men, and they would
have taken instant vengeance, for the supposed act
of treachery, upon the twelve chiefs in their power,

but for the interference of the old and more tem-
perate of the body, who, deprecating so flagrant a
breach of the laws of hospitality, escorted them
out of danger, but, at the same time, told them
that no peace could be concluded until satisfaction
was had for the murder of their friend.

Exposed, as the half-breeds thus are, to all the
vicissitudes of wild Indian life, their camps, while
on the move, are always preceded by scouts, for the
purpose of reconnoitring either for enemies or buffaloes. If they see the latter, they give signal of
such being the case, by throwing up handfuls of
dust; and, if the former, by running their horses
to and fro.

Three days after the departure of the Sioux
chiefs, our scouts were observed by their companions
to make the signal of enemies being in sight. Immediately a hundred of the best mounted hastened
to the spot, and, concealing themselves behind the
shelter of the bank of a small stream, sent out two
as decoys, who exposed themselves to the view of
the Sioux. The latter, supposing them to be alone,
rushed upon them, whereupon the concealed half-
breeds sprang up, and poured in a volley amongst
them, which brought down eight. The others
escaped, although several must have been wounded,

as much blood was afterwards discovered on their track. Though differing in very few respects from the pure Indians, they do not adopt the practice of scalping; and, in this case, being satisfied with their revenge, they abandoned the dead bodies to the malice of a small party of Saulteaux who accompanied them.

The Saulteaux are a band of the great Ojibbeway nation, both words signifying "the Jumpers," and derive the name from their expertness in leaping their canoes over the numerous rapids which occur in the rivers of their vicinity.

I took a sketch of one of them, Peccothis, "the Man with a Lump on his Navel." He appeared delighted with it at first; but the others laughed so much at the likeness, and made so many jokes about it, that he became quite irritated, and insisted that I should destroy it, or, at least, not show it as long as I remained with the tribe.

The Saulteaux, although numerous, are not a warlike tribe, and the Sioux, who are noted for their daring and courage, have long waged a savage war on them, in consequence of which the Saulteaux do not venture to hunt in the plains except in company with the half-breeds. Immediately on their getting possession of the bodies, they commenced a scalp dance, during which they mutilated the bodies in a most horrible manner. One old woman, who had lost several relations by the Sioux, rendered herself particularly conspicuous by digging out their eyes and otherwise dismembering them.

The following afternoon, we arrived at the margin of a small lake, where we encamped rather earlier than usual, for the sake of the water. Next day I was gratified with the sight of a band of about forty buffalo cows in the distance, and our hunters in full chase; they were the first I had seen, but were too far off for me to join in the sport. They succeeded in killing twenty-five, which were distributed through the camp, and proved most welcome to all of us, as our provisions were getting rather short, and I was abundantly tired of pimmi-kon and dried meat. The fires being lighted with the wood we had brought with us in the carts, the whole party commenced feasting with a voracity which appeared perfectly astonishing to me, until I tried myself, and found by experience how much hunting on the plains stimulates the appetite.

The upper part of the hunch of the buffalo, weighing four or five pounds, is called by the

Indians the little hunch. This is of a harder and more compact nature than the rest, though very tender, and is usually put aside for keeping. The lower and larger part is streaked with fat and is very juicy and delicious. These, with the tongues, are considered the delicacies of the buffalo. After the party had gorged themselves with as much as they could devour, they passed the evening in roasting the marrow bones and regaling themselves with their contents.

For the next two or three days we fell in with only a single buffalo, or small herds of them; but as we proceeded they became more frequent. At last our scouts brought in word of an immense herd of buffalo bulls about two miles in advance of us. They are known in the distance from the cows, by their feeding singly, and being scattered wider over the plain, whereas the cows keep together for the protection of the calves, which are always kept in the centre of the herd. A half-breed, of the name of Hallett, who was exceedingly attentive to me, woke me in the morning, to accompany him in advance of the party, that I might have the opportunity of examining the buffalo whilst feeding, before the commencement of the hunt. Six hours' hard riding brought us within a quarter of a mile of the nearest of the herd. The main body stretched over the plains as far as the eye could reach. Fortunately the wind blew in our faces: had it blown towards the buffaloes, they would have scented us miles off. I wished to have attacked them at once, but my companion would not allow me until the rest of the party came up, as it was contrary to the law of the tribe. We, therefore, sheltered ourselves from the observation of the herd behind a mound, relieving our horses of their saddles to cool them. In about an hour the hunters came up to us, numbering about one hundred and thirty, and immediate preparations were made for the chase. Every man loaded his gun, looked to his priming, and examined the efficiency of his saddle-girths.

The elder men strongly cautioned the less experienced not to shoot each other; a caution by no means unnecessary, as such accidents frequently occur. Each hunter then filled his mouth with balls, which he drops into the gun without wadding; by this means loading much quicker and being enabled to do so whilst his horse is at full speed. It is true, that the gun is more liable to burst, but that they do not seem to mind. Nor does the gun carry so far, or so true; but that is of less consequence, as they always fire quite close to the animal.

Everything being adjusted, we all walked our horses towards the herd. By the time we had gone about two hundred yards, the herd perceived us, and started off in the opposite direction at the top of their speed. We now put our horses to the full gallop, and in twenty minutes were in their midst. There could not have been less than four or five thousand in our immediate vicinity, all bulls, not a single cow amongst them.

The scene now became one of intense excitement; the huge bulls thundering over the plain in headlong confusion, whilst the fearless hunters rode recklessly in their midst, keeping up an incessant fire at but a few yards' distance from their victims. Upon the fall of each buffalo, the successful hunter merely threw some article of his apparel—often carried by him solely for that purpose—to denote his own prey, and then rushed on to another. These marks are scarcely ever disputed, but should a doubt arise as to the ownership, the carcase is equally divided among the claimants.

The chase continued only about one hour, and extended over an area of from five to six square miles, where might be seen the dead and dying buffaloes, to the number of five hundred. In the meantime my horse, which had started at a good run, was suddenly confronted by a large bull that made his appearance from behind a knoll, within a few yards of him, and being thus taken by surprise, he sprung to one side, and getting his foot into one of the innumerable badger holes, with which the plains abound, he fell at once, and I was thrown over his head with such violence, that I was completely stunned, but soon recovered my recollection. Some of the men caught my horse, and I was speedily remounted, and soon saw reason to congratulate myself on my good fortune, for I found a man who had been thrown in a similar way, lying a short distance from me quite senseless, in which state he was carried back to the camp.

I again joined in the pursuit; and coming up with a large bull, I had the satisfaction of bringing him down at the first fire. Excited by my success, I threw down my cap and galloping on, soon put a bullet through another enormous animal. He did not, however, fall, but stopped and faced me, pawing the earth, bellowing and glaring savagely at me. The blood was streaming profusely from his mouth, and I thought he would soon drop. The position in which he stood was so fine that I could not resist the desire of making a sketch. I accordingly dismounted, and had just commenced, when he suddenly made a dash at me. I had hardly time to spring on my horse and get away from him, leaving my gun and everything else behind.

When he came up to where I had been standing, he turned over the articles I had dropped, pawing fiercely as he tossed them about, and then retreated towards the herd. I immediately recovered my gun, and having reloaded, again pursued him, and soon planted another shot in him; and this time he remained on his legs long enough for me to make a sketch. This done I returned with it to the camp, carrying the tongues of the animals I had killed, according to custom, as trophies of my success as a hunter.

I have often witnessed an Indian buffalo hunt since, but never one on so large a scale. In returning to the camp, I fell in with one of the hunters coolly driving a wounded buffalo before him. In answer to my inquiry why he did not shoot him, he said he would not do so until he got him close to the lodges, as it would

save the trouble of bringing a cart for the
meat. He had already driven him seven miles,
and afterwards killed him within two hundred yards
of the tents. That evening, while the hunters
were still absent, a buffalo, bewildered by the hunt,
got amongst the tents, and at last got into one,
after having terrified all the women and children,
who precipitately took to flight. When the men
returned they found him there still, and being unable to dislodge him, they shot him down from the
opening in the top.

## CHAP. VII.

Camping amongst the Slain. — Wholesale Slaughter. — A Sick
   Guide. — Parting from the Half-breeds. — A False Alarm. —
   Dismal Night's Lodging. — Dreadful Position. — Stinking River.—
   Death of the Guide. — Paternal Government. — The Fire-Water
   Curse.

OUR camp was now moved to the field of slaughter, for the greater convenience of collecting the
meat. However lightly I wished to think of my
fall, I found myself the next day suffering considerably from the effects of it, and the fatigue I
had undergone. The man whom I had brought
with me as a guide was also suffering much from
an attack of the measles. Next day our hunters
sighted and chased another large band of bulls
with good success. At night we were annoyed by
the incessant howling and fighting of innumerable
dogs and wolves that had followed us to the hunt,
seemingly as well aware of the feast that was preparing for them as we could be ourselves. The
plain now resembled one vast shambles : the

women, whose business it is, being all busily employed in cutting the flesh into slices, and hanging them in the sun on racks, made of poles tied together. In reference to the immense number of buffaloes killed, I may mention that it is calculated that the half-breeds alone destroy thirty thousand annually.

Having satisfied myself with buffalo hunting amongst the half-breeds, I was anxious to return to the settlement, in order to prosecute my journey. On proposing to set out I found my guide so unwell, that I feared he would not be able to travel. I tried to procure one of the hunters to take his place and return with me, but none of them would consent to travel alone over so large a tract of country, from fear of the Sioux, in whose territory we then were; and who they dreaded, from the late occurrence, would be watching to cut off any stragglers. Being unable to procure a fresh man, I was about to start alone, when my guide, who thought himself better, proposed to accompany me, on condition that he should ride in the cart, and not be expected to attend to the horses or cooking. This I readily agreed to, as his services as guide were of the utmost importance.

We started next morning for the settlement, a

distance which I supposed to be somewhat over two
hundred miles.    A party of twenty of the hunters
escorted us for eight or ten miles, to see that there
were no Sioux in the immediate vicinity.    We
then parted, after taking the customary smoke on
separating from friends.    I could not avoid a strong
feeling of regret at leaving them, having experienced many acts of kindness at their hands, hardly
to be expected from so wild and uncultivated a
people.    We found a great scarcity of water on
our return, most of the swamps that had supplied
us on our way out being now dried up by the heat
of the season.

We fell in with a great many stray dogs and
wolves, which appeared to be led on by the scent of
the dead carcases.    After hobbling the horses,
putting up my tent, and cooking the supper, I
then turned in for the night, not without some apprehensions of a hostile visit from the Sioux, as we
were still on their hunting grounds, and in the
territory of the United States, being still a few
miles south of the boundary line.    During the
night my guide, who was very ill and feverish,
cried out that the Sioux were upon us.    I started
up with my gun in my hand, for I slept with it by
my side, and rushing out in the dark, was near

shooting my own horse, which, by stumbling over one of the tent pins, had alarmed my companion.

We travelled on the next day with as great rapidity as the ill health of my guide would permit, and on the evening of the 30th of June, we encamped on the bank of the Pambinaw. I lost considerable time next morning in catching the horses, as they are able from habit to run a considerable distance, and pretty fast, in spite of their hobbles. In the afternoon we arrived at the Swampy Lake, about fourteen miles across. A little before sunset we reached about the middle of it, but my guide complained so much that I could not proceed further.

I succeeded in finding a small dry spot above water large enough for me to sit on, but not affording room for my legs, which had to remain in the water, there being no more room in the small cart than was necessary for the sick man. Having no means for cooking, I was compelled to eat my dried meat raw. I tried to compose myself to sleep, but found it impossible, from the myriads of mosquitoes which appeared determined to extract the last drop of blood from my body. After battling with them until 4 o'clock next morning, my eyes almost blinded by their stings, I went in search of the horses, which had strayed away to some distance into deeper water, tempted by some sort of flags growing there. I had to wade up to my middle in pursuit of them, and it was not until 9 o'clock that we were able to proceed.

After leaving this dismal swamp we were within a day's march of the settlement; and my guide, believing himself to be much better, insisted upon my leaving him to drive the cart, whilst I proceeded at a more rapid rate on horseback. This, however, I would not do until I had seen him safe across Stinking River, which the horses had almost to swim in crossing. Having got him over safely, I left him, and proceeded onwards in the direction of the fort. But I had not gone far before I encountered one of the numerous swampy lakes that abound in this region, and render travelling extremely difficult. I had no doubt got on a wrong track, for in endeavouring to cross, my horse quickly sank up to his neck in mud and water. Seeing that I could neither advance nor recede, I dismounted, and found myself in the same predicament, scarcely able to keep my head above the surface. I managed, however, to reach the dry land; and, with the lasso, or long line, which every voyageur in these parts invariably has attached to his horse's neck, succeeded in getting the animal out. I remounted, and endeavoured to cross in another direction, but with no better success. I now found myself surrounded on all sides, as far as I could see, with nothing but swamp. My horse refused to be ridden any further. I had therefore, to dismount, and drag him along as best I could, wading up to my very middle in mud and water abounding with reptiles.

That I had lost my way was now certain; and as it was raining hard, I could not see the sun, nor had I a compass. I, however, determined to fix upon one certain course, and keep that at all hazards, in hopes that I might reach the Assiniboine River, by following which I could not fail to reach the settlement. After travelling in uncertainty for ten or twelve miles, I had at length the satisfaction of reaching the river, and in two hours afterwards I arrived safe at Fort Garry. The next morning I learned that my guide had been brought in by two men who were looking for stray horses. The poor fellow had got rapidly worse after my leaving, and had only proceeded a short distance when he was compelled to

stop.    He only survived two days after his arrival.

Fort Garry is one of the best built forts in the
Hudson's Bay territory.    It has a stone wall, with
bastions mounted with cannon, inclosing large store-
houses and handsome residences for the gentlemen
of the establishment.    Its strength is such that it
has nothing to fear from the surrounding half-
breeds or Indians.    The gentleman in charge was
Mr. Christie, whose many acts of kindness and
attention I must ever remember with feelings of
grateful respect.

The office of Governor of the Red River Settlement is one of great responsibility and trouble, as
the happiness and comfort of the whole settlement
depend to a great extent upon the manner in
which he carries out his instructions.    The half-
breeds are much inclined to grumbling, and
although the Company treat them with great
liberality, they still ask almost for impossibilities;
indeed, as far as the Company is concerned, I cannot
conceive a more just and strict course than that
which they pursue in the conduct of the whole of
their immense traffic.    In times of scarcity they
help all around them, in sickness they furnish them
with medicines, and even try to act as mediators

between hostile bands of Indians.   No drunkenness or debauchery is seen around their posts, and so strict is their prohibition of liquor, that even their officers can only procure a small allowance, which is given as part of their annual outfit on voyages.

Without entering into the general question of the policy of giving a monopoly of the fur trade to one company, I cannot but record, as the firm conviction which I formed from a comparison between the Indians in the Hudson's Bay Company territories and those in the United States, that opening up the trade with the Indians to all who wish indiscriminately to engage in it, must lead to their annihilation.   For while it is the interest of such a body as the Hudson's Bay Company to improve the Indians and encourage them to industry, according to their own native habits in hunting and the chase, even with a view to their own profit, it is as obviously the interest of small companies and private adventurers to draw as much wealth as they possibly can from the country in the shortest possible time, although in doing so the very source from which the wealth springs should be destroyed.   The unfortunate craving for intoxicating liquor which characterises all the tribes of Indians, and the terrible effects thereby produced upon them, render it a deadly instrument in the hands of designing men.

It is well known that, although the laws of the United States strictly prohibit the sale of liquor to the Indians, it is impossible to enforce them, and whilst many traders are making rapid fortunes in their territories, the Indians are fast declining in character, numbers, and wealth, whilst those in contact with the Hudson's Bay Company maintain their numbers, retain native characteristics unimpaired, and in some degree share in the advantages which civilisation places within their reach.

# CHAP. VIII.

Catching the Boat. — Queer Fish. — Fatal Thunder-bolt. — Killing Portraits. —Raising the Wind. —An Island with Wings.—Norway House. — Playgreen Lake. — Bound to the Rock. — A Model Athlete. — Shooting a Buck Moose. — Luxury of a Clean Shirt. — Life for Life. — A Violent Puss. — Buffalo Pounds. — A Perfect Centaur.

HEARING that two small sloops belonging to the Company which ply between the Red River and Norway House would leave the Lower, or Stone Fort, immediately, I rode down on the 5th of July, in company with Mr. W. Simpson, a brother-in-law of Sir George's, and reached our destination in about three hours. This establishment is larger than the Upper Fort, and built with still greater strength, but not so neatly arranged in the interior. We rested about an hour, and then embarked in one of the sloops; two Catholic missionaries, Mr. Le Fleck and Mr. Taché, who were bound for Isle La Croix, occupying the other. We dropped down the river a few miles, and cast anchor in front of the residence of Mr. Smithers, the Episcopalian missionary, and his larder and

H 2

cellar being well supplied, we passed a most agreeable evening, notwithstanding the mosquitoes, which were very troublesome. Early next morning we went round his very extensive farm, which seemed to be in a high state of cultivation. He works it principally by Indians, who receive a share of the produce according to their labour.

After a hearty breakfast, we bid a reluctant farewell to our kind host, and drifted down the current, there not being enough wind to fill our sails. When night had set in, I distinctly heard the noise made by the Red River sun-fish, which I have only noticed in this river. The fish resemble our Canadian black bass, weighing from two to three pounds, and during the night they make a singular noise, resembling a person groaning; how they produced these sounds, I was unable to ascertain. We proceeded only a short distance to-day, the current running very slow. After casting anchor for the night, the mosquitoes became so troublesome on board, that Mr. Simpson and I took our blankets on shore and went to an Indian lodge within a short distance of the river, the smoke which pervades these places generally keeping them free from the nuisance. There were three or four families of women and children in the lodge, but the men were all absent hunting. They cleared a corner for us to sleep in, but one of the most awful thunder storms, accompanied by heavy rain, that I had ever witnessed, set in, and effectually prevented our repose. Such tempests are here of frequent occurrence; so vivid was the lightning, and so near the rattling and crashing of the thunder, that I fancied several times during the night that I heard our vessels dashed to pieces by it. The missionaries on board were much terrified, and spent, I believe, the whole night in prayer. A short time previously a lodge containing seven persons was struck by the electric fluid; four of them were immediately killed, the other three were much injured, but recovered. These accidents are of very frequent occurrence about Red River.

*July 7th.*—We embarked in the morning, and proceeded at a slow rate. On arriving at the mouth of the river we were obliged to cast anchor, as it still remained a dead calm.

*July 8th.*—This morning we had a strong head wind, putting a stop to our further progress for the present. Mr. Simpson and I took a small boat, and returned up the river to an Indian camp of Saulteaux which we had passed the day before.

The Indians crowded round the boat on our arrival, inquiring what we wanted. Our interpreter told them that I had come to take their likenesses. One of them, a huge ugly-looking fellow, entirely naked, stepped up telling me to take his, as he was just as the Great Spirit had made him. I declined, however, as I wanted to sketch one of the females, but she refused, as she could not dress herself suitably for such an occasion, being in mourning for some friends she had lost, and therefore only wearing her oldest and dirtiest clothes.

After some difficulty, I succeeded in getting a young girl to sit in the costume of this tribe, although her mother was very much afraid it might shorten her life. But on my assuring her that it was more likely to prolong it, she seemed quite satisfied. After finishing my sketch, which they all looked at with great astonishment, a medicine-man stepped up and told us that he would give us three days' fair wind for a pound of tobacco. As the demand was so enormous for so small a supply of wind, we declined the bargain, whereupon he hesitatingly reduced his price, offering a greater quantity of wind for a smaller amount of tobacco, till at length, having reduced his price to a small plug for six days, we closed the bargain, declining his invitation to stay and partake of a large roasted dog, which we had seen slaughtered on our arrival. We returned to our vessel to pass another uncomfortable night, tormented by the mosquitoes, which all our efforts at smoking failed to drive out of our hot little cabin.

*July 9th.*—Hauled up our anchor and left the mouth of the river with a fair wind, and proceeded up Lake Winnipeg.

*July 10th.*—To-day we were wind-bound under the lee of a low rocky island, and although the surf ran very high on the beach, we determined to explore it as a relief to the monotony of our voyage. The attempt furnished us with plenty of excitement, as the boat filled before we reached the shore. We, however, arrived safe, and walked across the island about half a mile. It was literally covered with gulls and pelicans, which were hatching, and all rose in one body on our approach in such a dense mass as to give the appearance of the island itself taking wings. The rocks were so covered with eggs and young birds, that it was difficult to tread without crushing them. Wearied with the discordant screeching of the birds over our heads, and the smell from their dung being very offensive, we soon returned to our vessels. Large quantities of eggs are collected on this island by the voyageurs and Indians, gull's eggs being considered a great delicacy at certain seasons. There did not appear to be any considerable collection of guano here, as probably the island is washed almost clean by the high water and heavy rains in the spring of the year.

*July* 11*th.* — We entered the Straits between Lake Winnipeg and Playgreen Lake. The lake derives its name from a green plain which the Indians frequent to play their great game of ball. We cast anchor here, and having a small net on board, we set it, and caught a great number of jack-fish or pike, which we found excellent eating.

*July* 12*th.*—Sailed on through Playgreen Lake, a distance of twenty-five miles, the channel lying between numerous small rocky islands, some of them so near that we could easily have sprung on shore from the vessel; from Playgreen Lake we entered Jack-fish River, and the current soon carried us to Norway House, a distance of nine miles, where we arrived in the afternoon. Mr. Ross, the gentleman in charge, received us with great kindness and hospitality. Notwithstanding the barrenness of the soil and the severity of the cold in this region, which prevents all hope of deriving any advantage from agricultural pursuits, a Wesleyan Methodist mission is established within a few miles of the fort. It is under the superintendence of the Reverend Mr. Mason, and consists of about thirty small log houses, with a church and dwelling-house for the minister. It is supported by the Company with the hope of improving the Indians; but, to judge from appearances, with but small success, as they are decidedly the dirtiest Indians I have met with, and the less that is said about their morality the better.

The Indians belong to the Mas-ka-gau tribe, or "Swamp Indians," so called from their inhabiting the low swampy land which extends the whole way from Norway House to Hudson's Bay. This race is rather diminutive in comparison with those who inhabit the plains, probably from their suffering often for want of food; and instances of their being compelled by hunger to eat one another are not uncommon. Their language somewhat resembles the Cree, but is not so agreeable in sound. I made a sketch of one of them, called the I-ac-a-way, "the Man who is gone on a Hunt without raising his Camp."

I remained at Norway House until the 14th of August, waiting for the brigade of boats which had gone down in the Spring to York Factory, in Hudson's Bay, with the furs, and was now expected back on their return with the outfit of goods for the interior trade. Our time passed very monotonously until the 13th, when Mr. Rowand, chief factor, arrived with six boats: one of the boats under the charge of a clerk, Mr. Lane, was entirely devoted to the carriage of the furs paid annually by the Hudson's Bay Company to the Russian Government, for the privilege of trading in their territory. These consisted of seventy pieces or packs, each containing seventy-five otter skins of the very best description. They are principally collected on the Mackenzie River, from whence they are carried to York Factory, where they are culled and packed with the greatest care; they have then to be carried up the Saskatchawan, across the Rocky Mountains, down the Columbia River, to Vancouver's Island, and then shipped to Sitka. I mention these furs particularly here, as they were the source of much trouble to us in our future progress.

On the morning of the 14th we left Norway House, in the boats, for Playgreen Lake. These boats are about twenty-eight feet long, and strongly built, so as to be able to stand a heavy press of sail and rough weather, which they often encounter in the lakes: they carry about eighty or ninety packs of 90 lbs. each, and have a crew of seven men, a steersman and six rowers. Mr. Lane was accompanied by his wife, a half-breed, who travelled with us all the way to Fort Vancouver, on the Columbia. We had scarcely got into Playgreen Lake when a heavy gale separated the boats and drove ours on to a rock in the lake. Here we were compelled to remain two nights and a day, without a stick to make a fire, and exposed to the incessant rain, as it was not possible to raise our tents. In the distance we could perceive our more fortunate companions, who had succeeded in gaining the mainland, comfortably under canvas, with blazing fires; but so terrific was the gale that we dared not venture to leave the shelter of the rock.

On the 16th, the wind having somewhat abated, we were enabled to join the rest of the party, when the blazing fires and comfortably cooked food soon restored our spirits. Being sufficiently recruited, and the wind being fair, we again embarked, although the lake was still very rough.

This lake is about 300 miles long, but so shallow, that in high winds the mud at the bottom is stirred up, from which it derives the name of Winnipeg, or Muddy Lake. On the present occasion the waves rose so high that some of the men became sick, and we were obliged to put into a lee shore, not being able to find a landing-place. On nearing the shore some of the men jumped into the water and held the boats off, whilst the others unloaded them and carried the goods on their heads through the dashing surf. When the boats were emptied, they were then enabled to drag them up on the beach. Here we were compelled to remain until the 18th, occupying ourselves in shooting ducks and gulls, which we found in great abundance, and which proved capital eating.

The waves having abated on the morning of the 18th, we made an early start, and arrived in the afternoon at the mouth of the Saskatchawan River. The navigation is here interrupted by what is called the Grand Rapid, which is about three miles long, one mile of which runs with great rapidity, and presents a continual foamy appearance, down which boats are able to descend, but in going up are obliged to make a portage.

I was told a story of one of the steersmen of our brigade, named Paulet Paul, who in steering his boat down by an oar passed through a ring in the stern of the boat, fell overboard, from the oar, on which he was leaning with his whole force, suddenly breaking. His great bodily strength enabled him to gain a footing, and to stand against the rapid until the boat following came past, into which he sprang, and urging the men to pull, he eventually succeeded in jumping into his own boat and guiding her safely down, thereby saving the valuable cargo which might have otherwise been lost. He was a half-breed, and certainly one of the finest formed men I ever saw, and when naked, no painter could desire a finer model. We encamped on the shore, and were obliged to remain here till the third day, for the purpose of getting the goods across, as it required the crews of all the boats to haul each over in succession. There are usually Indians to be met at this portage, who assist the men for a small consideration, but on this occasion they were un• fortunately absent.

*August* 21*st.*—Embarked in the afternoon, and on the 22nd passed through Cedar Lake, and again entered the Saskatchawan River; the land in the neighbourhood of which is very flat and marshy, innumerable small lakes being scattered over the whole region. We met with nothing worth recording till the 25th, when we arrived at the " Pau," a Church of England missionary station, occupied by the Rev. Mr. Hunter. He resides in a neat house most brilliantly decorated inside with blue and red paint, much to the admiration of his flock, which consists of only a small band of the same tribe of Indians as are met with about Norway House. Mr. Hunter and his amiable lady invited us to their table, where we found some bread made from wheat of their own raising, ground in a hand-mill, and they spared no exertions to make us as comfortable as possible.

Mr. Hunter accompanied me to a medicine-man's lodge, a short distance from his own residence. Seeing a very handsomely worked otter-skin bag, apparently well filled, hanging up in the lodge, I inquired as to its purpose, when the Indian informed me it was his medicine-bag, but would not let me examine its contents until he had seen some of my sketches, and was informed that I was a great medicine-man myself, upon which he opened it for my inspection. The contents consisted of bits of bones, shells, minerals, red earth, and other heterogeneous accumulations, perfectly incomprehensible to my uninitiated capacity.

*Aug. 26th.* — We left the hospitable mansion of Mr. Hunter with many kind wishes for our safety and success, and continued our journey along the low and swampy banks of the river. On the

28th, we passed the mouth of the Cumberland River. Here the men had to harness themselves to the boats with their portage straps and drag the boats up the river for several days. We passed a large quantity of the bones of buffaloes which had been drowned in the preceding winter in attempting to cross the ice. The wolves had picked them all clean.

On the 29th I fired both barrels loaded with ball at a large buck moose, which was swimming across the river. He, however, arrived at the other side and trotted up the bank. Thinking I had missed him, I went on, but on my return the following year, two Indians, who had been attracted by the shots, told me that he had dropped 200 yards from the river.

*Aug. 30th.* — We this day fell in with a small band of Crees, from whom we procured some buffalo meat, tongues, and beaver tails; the last is considered a great delicacy. It is a fat, gristly substance, but to me by no means palatable; the rest of our party, however, seemed to enjoy it much. The tongues were decidedly delicious; they are cured by drying them in the smoke of the lodges.

The river as we ascended presented a more

inviting appearance, the banks becoming bolder and covered principally with pine and poplar, the latter trees springing up wherever the former are burned off. The men suffered severely from the heat, which was very oppressive.

*September 6th.* — We were within about eighteen or twenty miles of Carlton, when about dark in the evening we heard a tremendous splashing in the water, but so far off that we could not see the cause. Mr. Rowand at once conjectured it to be a large party of Blackfeet swimming their horses across the river, which they do by driving the horse into the water till he loses his footing, when the rider slips off and seizes the tail of the animal, and is thus towed to the opposite shore. We were somewhat alarmed, and immediately loaded our guns, the Blackfeet being the most hostile tribe on the continent; but on coming up to the spot, we found it was the horsekeeper of Fort Carlton, who was swimming his horses across to an island in the middle of the river to save them from the wolves, which had killed several of them, owing to the scarcity of buffaloes. As we had but a short distance to travel next day we encamped for the night.

*Sept. 7th.* — When we arrived within a couple

of miles of Carlton, we halted for the purpose of arranging our toilets previous to presenting ourselves at the establishment. This consisted chiefly of a thorough washing; some, indeed, put on clean shirts, but few, however, could boast of such a luxury. This compliment to the inhabitants was by no means unnecessary, as we were in a most ragged and dirty condition.

The country in the vicinity of Carlton, which is situated between the wooded country and the other plains, varies much from that through which we had been travelling. Instead of dense masses of unbroken forest, it presents more the appearance of a park; the gently undulating plains being dotted here and there with clumps of small trees. The banks of the river rise to the height of 150 or 200 feet in smooth rolling hills covered with verdure. The fort, which is situated about a quarter of a mile back from the river, is enclosed with wooden pickets, and is fortified with blunderbusses on swivels mounted in the bastion. This fort is in greater danger from the Blackfeet than any of the Company's establishments, being feebly manned and not capable of offering much resistance to an attack. Their horses have frequently been driven off without the inmates of the fort daring to leave it for their rescue. The buffaloes are here abundant, as is evident from the immense accumulation of their bones which strew the plains in every direction.

The whole of the boats not having yet arrived, we remained here for several days. On the second evening after our arrival we were rather alarmed by the rapid approach of fire, which had originated far off to the west on the prairies. Fortunately, when within about half a mile of the fort, the wind changed, and it turned to the south. We, however, remained up nearly all night for fear of accidents. There were some Cree Indians about the fort, which is one of the trading ports of that nation who extend along the Saskatchawan to the Rocky Mountains, and is one of the largest tribes of Indians in the Hudson's Bay Company's dominions. This tribe has been from time immemorial at war with the Blackfeet, whom they at one time conquered and held in subjection: even now the Crees call the Blackfeet slaves, although they have gained their independence, and are a fierce and warlike tribe. These wars are kept up with unremitting perseverance from year to year; and were they as destructive in proportion to the numbers engaged as the wars of civilised nations, the continent would soon be depopulated of the whole Indian race; but, luckily, Indians are satisfied with small victories, and a few scalps and horses taken from the enemy are quite sufficient to entitle the warriors to return to their friends in triumph and glory.

I made a sketch of Us-koos-koosish, "Young Grass," a Cree brave. He was very proud of showing his many wounds, and expressed himself rather dissatisfied with my picture, as I had not delineated all the scars, no matter what was their locality. He had a younger brother killed by one of his own tribe in a quarrel; this he considered incumbent on him to revenge, and tracked the offender for upwards of six months before he found an opportunity of killing him, which he however effected at last.

This custom of taking life for life is universal amongst all Indians; and the first death often leads to many, until the feud is stayed either by the intervention of powerful friends, or by one party paying the other a satisfaction in horses or other Indian valuables. An Indian, however, in taking revenge for the death of a relative does not in all cases seek the actual offender; as should the party be one of his own tribe any relative will do, however distant. Should he be a white man, the Indian would most probably kill the first white man he could find.

Mr. Rundell, a missionary, whose station was at Edmonton, was at Carlton awaiting our arrival, for the purpose of returning in company with us. He had with him a favourite cat which he had brought with him in the canoes from Edmonton, being afraid to leave her behind him, as there was some danger of her being eaten during his absence. This cat was the object of a good deal of amusement among the party, of great curiosity amongst the Indians, and of a good deal of anxiety and trouble to its kind master.

Mr. Rowand, myself, and Mr. Rundell, having determined to proceed to Edmonton on horseback, as being the shortest and most agreeable route, we procured horses and a guide and, on the morning of the 12th September, we arose early for our start. The Indians had collected in numbers round the fort to see us off, and shake hands with us, a practice which they seem to have taken a particular fancy for. No sooner had we mounted our rather skittish animals than the Indians crowded around, and Mr. Rundell, who was rather a favourite amongst them, came in for a large share of their attentions, which seemed to be rather annoying to his horse. His cat he had tied to the pummel of his saddle by a string, about four feet long, round her neck, and had her safely, as he thought, concealed in the breast of his capote. She, however, did not relish the plunging of the horse, and made a spring out, utterly astonishing the Indians, who could not conceive where she had come from. The string brought her up against the horse's legs, which she immediately attacked. The horse now became furious, kicking violently, and at last threw Mr. Rundell over his head, but fortunately without much injury. All present were convulsed with laughter, to which the Indians added screeching and yelling as an accompaniment, rendering the whole scene indescribably ludicrous. Puss's life was saved by the string breaking; but we left her behind for the men to bring in the boats, evidently to the regret of her master, notwithstanding the hearty laugh which we had had at his expense.

We were accompanied by a party of hunters proceeding to a buffalo pound about six miles off. These pounds can only be made in the vicinity of forests, as they are composed of logs piled up roughly, five feet high, and enclose about two acres. At one side an entrance is left, about ten feet wide, and from each side of this, to the distance of half a mile, a row of posts or short stumps, called dead men, are planted, at the distance of twenty feet each, gradually widening out into the plain from the entrance. When we arrived at the pound we found a party there anxiously awaiting the arrival of the buffaloes, which their companions were driving in. This is accomplished as follows :—A man, mounted on a fleet horse, usually rides forward till he sees a band of buffaloes. This may be sixteen or eighteen miles distant from the ground, but of course the nearer to it the better. The hunter immediately strikes a light with a flint and steel, and places the lighted spunk in a handful of dried grass, the smoke arising from which the buffaloes soon smell and start away from it at the top of their speed. The man now rides up alongside of the herd, which, from some unaccountable propensity, invariably endeavour to cross in front of his horse. I have had them follow me for miles in order to do so. The hunter thus possesses an unfailing means, wherever the pound may be situated, of conducting them to it by the dexterous management of his horse. Indians are stationed at intervals behind the posts, or dead men, provided with buffalo robes, who, when the herd are once in the avenue, rise up and shake the robes, yelling and urging them on until they get into the enclosure, the spot usually selected for which is one with a tree in the centre. On this they hang offerings to propitiate the Great Spirit to direct the herd towards it. A man is also placed in the tree with a medicine pipe-stem in his hand, which he waves continually, chaunting a sort of prayer to the Great Spirit, the burden of which is that the buffaloes may be numerous and fat.

As soon as all the herd are within the pound, the entrance is immediately closed with logs, the buffaloes running round and round one after another, and very rarely attempting to break out, which would not be difficult, from the insufficiency of the structure. Should one succeed in doing so the whole herd immediately follow. When once in the enclosure the Indians soon despatch them with their arrows and spears.

Whilst the buffaloes were being driven in, the scene was certainly exciting and picturesque; but the slaughter in the enclosure was more painful than pleasing. This had been the third herd that had been driven into this pound within the last ten or twelve days, and the putrefying carcases tainted the air all round. The Indians in this manner destroy innumerable buffaloes, apparently for the mere pleasure of the thing. I have myself seen a pound so filled up with their dead carcases that I could scarcely imagine how the enclosure could have contained them while living. It is not unusual to drive in so many that their aggregate bulk forces down the barriers. There are thousands of them annually killed in this manner ; but not one in twenty is used in any way by the Indians, so that thousands are left to rot where they fall. I heard of a pound, too far out of my direct road to visit, formed entirely of the bones of dead buffaloes that had been killed in a former pound on the same spot, piled up in a circle similarly to the logs above described. This improvidence, in not saving the meat, often exposes them to great hardships during the seasons of the year in which the buffalo migrates to the south.

As is frequently the case on buffalo hunts, a large band of wolves hovered round us in expectation of a feast, and a young Indian, for the purpose of showing his dexterity, galloped off towards them mounted on a small Indian horse. He succeeded in separating one from the pack, and notwithstanding all the dodging of the wolf, managed to drive him quite close to us. As he approached he entirely abandoned his bridle, and to look at them, one would imagine, from the rapid turnings of the horse without the apparent direction of the rider, that he was as eager in the pursuit as his master. When he had succeeded in getting the wolf close to us, he transfixed him with an arrow at the first shot. We selected a comfortable place on the banks of the river, and, on the boats coming up, we formed our encampment for the night.

*Sept.* 13*th.*—In the morning we passed a small island on which we saw a herd of eighteen deer. Our hunter went round to the other side, the water being shallow enough to wade across, and, getting behind the bushes, fired twice at them before they could escape, and brought down two. The rest crossed over to our side of the river, and, as a noble buck was ascending the bank, we all fired at him. He escaped, notwithstanding, into the woods, and I hobbled my horse and pursued him on foot, tracking him readily by the blood which flowed from his wounds. I soon saw him lying down, apparently so exhausted that I forbore to fire again. This forbearance cost me the deer, for on my coming up, he made a sudden plunge into a thicket and escaped. I followed his track a long distance, but could not come up to him. On my return I found two wolves making a dead set at my poor horse, who was trembling with fear. One of them was in the act of springing at him. It was impossible for him to get away, as his fore feet were tied together. I instantly levelled my double-barrelled gun and killed both, one after the other.

## CHAP. IX.

Beautiful Valley.—Crossing the Water. — The curious Cabree.—A
shouting Aide-de-Camp.—Strange Memento Mori. — The Love of
Indian Mothers.—No Coat, no Fire. — The " Little Slave." — A
Voyageur's Trust.—Surrounded by Beef.—A spirited Cow.

On my coming back to the party, I found them
hanging up the two deer for the use of the crews
of the boats, having taken what they wanted for
themselves.  This they did by forming a triangle
with poles about twelve feet high in a conspicuous
place on the bank, so that the wolves could not
reach the meat, and fastening a red handkerchief
above it to keep off the crows.  Towards evening, as
we were approaching the place where we were to
cross the river, I saw some buffaloes idly grazing
in a valley, and as I wished to give a general idea
of the beauty of the scenery which lies all along
the banks of the Saskatchawan from this point to
Edmonton, I sat down to make a sketch, the rest of
the party promising to wait for me at the crossing

place. It was the commencement of Indian summer; the evening was very fine, and threw that peculiar soft, warm haziness over the landscape, which is supposed to proceed from the burning of the immense prairies. The sleepy buffaloes grazing upon the undulating hills, here and there relieved by clumps of small trees, the unbroken stillness, and the approaching evening, rendered it altogether a scene of most enchanting repose.

On coming up to Mr. Rowand, we prepared to cross for the purpose of avoiding a strong bend in the river. Our ammunition, and other things that required to be kept dry, were put into a sort of basket made of a few willow twigs, with a buffalo skin drawn by a running string over them, something in the form of large bowls. This basket was floated in the water, and dragged by a string held in the teeth. The horse was then driven in, and the traveller, holding on by his tail, was safely ferried to the other side with his baggage.

*Sept. 14th.*—Saw an immense number of cabrees, or prairie antelopes. These are the smallest of the deer tribe, amazingly fleet, and very shy, but, strange to say, possessed of great curiosity, apparently determined to look at everything they do not understand, so long as they do not scent it.

Our hunter set off into the valley, to show me the manner of shooting them, while I made a sketch. A small stream wound its way through this most beautiful and picturesque valley in a course unusually tortuous, and was fringed on each side by a border of small, dense, and intensely green and purple bushes, contrasting beautifully with the rich yellow grass of the gradually sloping banks, about 200 feet in height, and the golden hues of the few poplars which had just begun to assume the autumnal tints.

The hunter stole forward and hid himself behind a small bush, so as to have the wind blowing from them, and gently waved a piece of rag tied to his ramrod; as soon as the cabrees perceived this, they gradually came up to him, until within shot, when he knocked one over; this was of course all he could expect, as the rest were off in an instant.

In the evening we saw smoke in the distance, which we supposed to proceed from a camp of Indians; we waited, therefore, till the boats arrived, with a view to our mutual protection, should they prove to be a hostile tribe. The boats arrived after a short time, and we remained with them all night without molestation.

*Sept. 15th.*—About an hour after leaving our encampment, we crossed the river again in our boat, and found a large camp of Cree Indians. They came down to us in great numbers. Mr. Rowand, being acquainted with their chiefs, they were very friendly with us, and we bought a large quantity of dried meat from them. About a year and a half after this, on my return, I met the head chief, Kee-a-kee-ka-sa-coo-way, or the " Man who gives the War-whoop," and learned something of his history, which will be introduced in the latter part of my journal. When I was in his company for some time at Fort Pitt, in January 1848, the second chief, Muck-e-too, or " Powder," acted as a sort of aide-de-camp to the other, the head chief issuing his commands in a low tone, while the other mounted his horse and delivered them to the rest of the camp in a loud commanding manner. Muck-e-too is a great warrior and horse thief, the two most important qualifications for a chief, skill in stealing horses being regarded with as much respect as taking scalps. We had much difficulty in getting away from them, as they wished to have a long talk, but our time not permitting, we resumed our journey. They, however, adroitly detained a boat that had not yet come up, and the persons in charge had to give them some tobacco before they would allow them to proceed.

*Sept.* 16*th.*—We rode on till the middle of the day through a most delightful country, covered with luxuriant herbage, the plains being enamelled with flowers of various kinds, presenting more the aspect of a garden than of uncultivated land. While roasting some meat before the fire for our breakfast, and allowing our horses to feed, we espied a party of Indians on the opposite side of the river, who were evidently making signals to another party in our rear whom we did not see. Upon this, eight of their young men came down to reconnoitre, and finding we were friends, kindly conducted us to their camp. We bartered with them for some horses.

I made a sketch of one of their chiefs, Otisskun, or " The Horn," or rather I made a sketch of his back. I did this for the purpose of showing his war-cap, and also to delineate the bag which he carries at his back. These bags are constantly worn, and contain some of the bones or hair of their deceased relatives. These relics they regard with the greatest veneration, and make them their constant companions, whether riding, walking, or sleeping. They are generally worn for a period of three years.   Not only amongst this tribe, but also amongst others, the affection for their relatives is very remarkable, though of course sometimes exhibited in a strange manner, as appears to us.   As an instance of this, I may mention the universal custom of Indian mothers eagerly seeking another child, although it may be of an enemy, to replace one of her own, whom she may have lost, no matter how many other children she may have.   This child is always treated with as great, if not greater, kindness than the rest; but all the mother's care evidently arises from, and has reference to, the love which she bore to the departed.

I had an unexpected trouble to catch my horse, which had got loose, in consequence of the hungry Indian dogs having eaten the lasso of raw hide with which I had fastened him.

*Sept. 17th.* — We were aroused in the night by our hunter, who told us that the horses were stolen, and as he would not leave the fire unless we accompanied him, we all started in pursuit.   After a run of about a mile, we came up with the horses pursued by a band of wolves; the billets of wood attached to their lassoes having retarded their further escape; the wolves were loth to leave their expected prey, but after a shot or two they took to flight. The horses were evidently much terrified, as they showed by remaining close to the camp-fires all night afterwards.

In the course of our ride to-day we killed a cabree, which was fortunate, as Mr. and Mrs. Lane arrived at our camp fire in the evening in a state of severe exhaustion, having left the boats in the morning and walked the whole day without tasting food. The boats had reached the other side of the river, and, for want of a channel, had been unable to · cross over and take them in. It was unfortunately a very cold night, and very little wood could be procured; besides which, we were unprovided with either tents or blankets, having dispensed with these luxuries since we left Carlton, where we began our journey on horseback. The greatest sufferer probably from the cold of the night was a young clerk who had walked with them, and left his coat and waistcoat in the boat.

*Sept.* 19*th.* — The boats this morning found a channel and crossed over to take in the party, who had left them the morning before. We reached Fort Pitt in the evening. It is a neat and compact little fort, and is, like all the rest of the forts except those at Red River, constructed of wood.

K

The country here abounds in buffalo; grain and other produce might be raised plentifully here if cultivated. We remained till the 23rd, and I took a sketch of Chimaza, the "Little Slave," a Chippewayeen Indian. He was the only one of that tribe I ever saw, as they live far north of Fort Pitt, on the Athabasca Lake; his prowess and dexterity in hunting won him a degree of notoriety amongst the traders. He had, when I saw him, upwards of a hundred moose skins, besides furs to a considerable amount, which he had brought to the fort to trade with.

*Sept.* 23*rd.* — I left the fort on horseback, accompanied by Mr. Rowand, Mr. Rundell, an Indian boy, and a fresh hunter; on reaching the river we crossed in a boat, and swam our horses by the bridle. We left this establishment in true voyageur style, unburthened with food of any kind, and, although contemplating a journey of 200 miles, trusting solely to our guns, having not even a grain of salt. After leaving the boat, we saddled our horses, and had not proceeded more than ten miles, when we fell in with immense numbers of buffaloes.

During the whole of the three days that it took us to reach Edmonton House, we saw nothing else but these animals covering the plains as far as the eye could reach, and so numerous were they, that at times they impeded our progress, filling the air with dust almost to suffocation. We killed one whenever we required a supply of food, selecting the fattest of the cows, taking only the tongues and boss, or hump, for our present meal, and not burdening ourselves unnecessarily with more. Mr. Rowand fired and wounded a cow, which made immediately for a clump of bushes ; he followed it, when the animal turned upon him, and bore him and his horse to the ground, leaping over them, and escaping among the rest. Fortunately, he received no hurt beyond the mortification of being thrown down and run over by an animal which he felt assured he should see roasting at our evening camp fire.

## CHAP. X.

*Sept. 24th.*— WE passed through what is called
the Long Grass Prairie.   The bones of a whole
camp of Indians, who were carried off by that fatal
scourge of their race, the small-pox, were here
bleaching on the plains, having fallen from the
platforms and trees on which it is their custom to
suspend their dead, covered with skins, — which
latter, as well as the supports, time had destroyed.
An immense grisly bear was drinking out of a pond,
and our hunter went ahead of the party to try and
get a shot at him.   The bear quietly awaited his
attack, and the Indian, seeing him so cool, rather
hesitated to advance, not deeming it prudent or

safe to depend on the fleetness of his horse unless he had a good start of the bear. He fired, therefore, at too great a distance for his shot to tell. The bear rose up very composedly on his hind legs, and regarding the hunter for a moment, turned about and walked away. I then determined to try my luck. As I was very well mounted, I rode up to within forty or fifty yards of him, and as he turned to look at me, I discharged both barrels; one wounded him in the shoulder, and, with a savage growl, he turned and pursued me. I set off at full gallop towards Mr. Rowand, who waited till he came within shot, when he put another ball into him, — but still the bear advanced.

In the meantime, the Indian and I had both managed to reload, and, as the bear came forward, the Indian fired, and must have hit, as the bear again rose on his hind legs ; when, taking deliberate aim, I lodged a ball in his heart, and the huge monster fell to the ground. The Indian now skinned him and cut off his paws, which we found most delicious picking when roasted in the evening. The claws, which I preserved, measured four and a half inches. There is no animal on the whole continent that the Indians hold in so much dread as the grisly bear, and few will attack one of them when alone, unless with a very fleet horse under him.

We had much difficulty that evening in finding a place to encamp away from the immense number of buffaloes that surrounded us, and we found it necessary to fire off our guns during the night to keep them away. We passed through a spot covered with great quantities of shed antlers of the deer. We had ridden so fast as to knock up Mr. Rowand's horse, but, having driven several loose horses with us, to provide against such emergencies, we were not inconvenienced, leaving the poor brute a prey to the wolves, which were constantly hovering about us.

We encamped this evening on the borders of a very beautiful fresh water lake. We had passed in our route daily many *dried-up* lakes, principally small, the basins covered with an incrustation of sub-carbonate of soda. Many of these are bordered with a dense growth of plants resembling in structure the well-known marine production called samphire, but of a rich purple colour. So unbroken is the incrustation of soda, as to give the spots the appearance of being covered with snow.

*Sept. 26th.* — Mr. Rundell remained at the encampment this morning with the Indian boy, being completely knocked up by the hard riding of the preceding days. We were reluctant to leave him, but were under the necessity of going on as fast as possible, as I had still a long journey before me, and the season was drawing to a close. Mr. Rowand and myself, therefore, left the camp at half-past 3 A.M., and pursued our journey almost at a gallop the whole way, having stopped only once for about an hour, for breakfast and to breathe our horses.

About 5 o'clock in the afternoon, when about eight or ten miles from Fort Edmonton, we were met by a party of gentlemen from the fort, who were out shooting wild geese, in which they had been very successful, and on seeing the jaded condition of our horses, they were kind enough to exchange with us, so that we started off for the remaining distance at a round gallop.

On getting to the edge of the river, which it was necessary to cross to reach the fort, Mr. Rowand, having a fine large horse under him, plunged in. Though my horse was very small, I did not hesitate in following him. Mr. Rowand's horse carried him over in fine style, but mine, not being equal to the task, sank under me; still, however, I held firmly on to him, till, drifting into the rapid, he struck a sunken rock in striving to obtain a footing, on which he nearly brought me under him; but, on drifting a little further down, he fortunately found footing in a more shallow part, and was able to ford across, Mr. Rowand appearing greatly to enjoy the scene from his safe position on the shore. We were greeted by the occupants of the fort in their gayest attire, the day being Sunday.

Edmonton is a large establishment: as it has to furnish many other districts with provisions, a large supply is always kept on hand, consisting entirely of dried meat, tongues, and pimmi-kon. There are usually here a chief factor and a clerk, with forty or fifty men with their wives and children, amounting altogether to about 130, who all live within the pickets of the fort. Their employment consists chiefly in building boats for the trade, sawing timber, most of which they raft down the river from ninety miles higher up, cutting up the small poplar which abounds on the margin of the river for fire-wood, 800 cords of which are consumed every winter, to supply the numerous fires in the establishment. The employment of the women, who are all, with-

out a single exception, either squaws or half-
breeds, consists in making moccasins and clothing
for the men, and converting the dried meat into
pimmi-kon.

On the night of our arrival at Edmonton, the
wind increased to a perfect hurricane, and we had
reason to be thankful to Providence for our timely
escape from the awful scene we now witnessed
from our present place of safety, for, had we been
one day later, we might have been involved in its
fiery embrace. The scene on which our attention
was now riveted, was the conflagration of the
prairie through which we had passed but a few
hours before. The scene was terrific in the extreme ; the night being intensely dark gave increased effect to the brilliancy of the flames. We
were apprehensive at one time of its crossing the
river to the side on which the fort is situated, which
must in that case have been destroyed. Our fears,
too, for Mr. Rundell, whom we had left behind
with the boys, were only relieved three days afterwards, when he arrived in safety. It appeared
that he had noticed the fire at a long distance off,
and immediately started for the nearest bend in the
river, which with great exertions he reached in
time, and succeeded in crossing. The mode re-

sorted to by the Indians, when in the immediate vicinity of a prairie on fire, is to set fire to a long patch in front of them, which they follow up, and thus depriving the fire in the rear of fuel, escape all but the smoke, which, however, nearly suffocates them.

As we had to remain here until the arrival of the boat with Mr. Lane and the Russian packs of otters, I took a sketch of the fort, and having leisure, I went a good deal amongst the Indians, who are constantly about the fort for the purpose of trading; they were principally Crees and Assiniboines: Potika-poo-tis, the "Little Round Man," an Assiniboine chief, sat for me. He was well known about the fort, and was commonly called the Duke of Wellington, I suppose from his small person and his warlike feats. He was on one occasion set upon by a party of Blackfeet, and, while in the act of discharging his gun, received a wound, which he showed me, of rather a remarkable nature. The ball entered his wrist, passed through the arm, entered the neck, and came out near the upper part of the spine. He had received several wounds, but none that seemed seriously to endanger his life, as at the time I saw him he was in good health.

After relating various stories of his war and hunting exploits, he, to my great astonishment, told me that he had killed his own mother. It appears that, while travelling, she told him that she felt too old and feeble to sustain the hardships of life, and too lame to travel any further, and asked him to take pity on her, and end her misery, on which he unhesitatingly shot her on the spot. I asked him whereabouts he had directed his ball. His reply was, " Do you think I would shoot her in a bad place? I hit her there;" pointing his finger to the region of the heart. "She died instantly, and I cried at first; but after I had buried her, the impression wore off."

It must not be supposed that Indians look on the softer sex with feelings at all resembling those entertained towards them in civilised life; in fact, they regard them more in the light of slaves than as companionable beings. As might be expected, this is most evident in their treatment of aged women, whom they consider as scarcely fit to live.

Some of the Company's servants were going up the Saskatchawan river on the ice in the winter, with a sledge of dogs drawing a load, comprising, among other things, an eight-gallon keg of spirits; and in crossing over a piece of bad ice, the dogs

went through sledge and all, and were instantly
carried under by the force of the current. In
the following summer, some Indians, while bathing
near the shore, picked up the cask safe and sound;
and finding, on examination, that it was full of
rum, made up their minds to have a booze. One
of them, however, suggested the possibility that
the white men had put poison in it, to be revenged
on them for having fired on the inland brigade of
canoes while going up the river the year before.
This deterred them from drinking any until they
had tested its quality. For this purpose they
selected eight of the oldest women in the camp
to try the experiment on. The women fell into
the snare; and, becoming intoxicated, commenced
singing with great glee. But an old chief soon put
a stop to their potations, saying there could be no
poison in it, and that it was far too good to be
thrown away upon old women. The whole tribe
then set to, and were not long in draining the
cask.

One day, whilst wandering some distance to the
south of the fort, I saw two Assiniboine Indians
hunting buffaloes. One was armed with a spear,
formed of an ashpole about ten feet long, ornamented with tufts of hair, and having an iron

head, which is procured from the trading posts;
the other with a bow formed of ash, with the
sinews of a buffalo gummed to the back of it.
These they use with great dexterity and force;
I have known an instance of the arrows passing
through the body of the animal, and sticking in
the ground at the opposite side.

## CHAP. XI.

Leaving Fort Edmonton. — The Last of the Buffaloes. — Sir George's Highland Piper. — An Indian Delicacy. — Freak of an Evil Spirit. — Singular Cradle. — Jasper's House. — The Snow and the Cold. — First-steps in Snow Shoes. — Nearly Roasted Alive. — Going down Hill. — Wading an Icy Torrent. — Making up for lost Time. — Shooting the Dalle de Mort. — A Narrow Escape. — A Wet Voyage.

WE remained at Edmonton till the morning of the 6th, preparing for the arduous journey which now lay before us. On that morning we started at daybreak. Our party consisted of Mr. Lane and his wife, a young man named Charles, a clerk, who was going to a post on the west side of the Rocky Mountains, a person of the name of M'Gillveray, and sixteen men. We had with us sixty-five horses to carry our baggage and provisions. This seems a large supply of horses for so small a party; but it must be taken into consideration that Edmonton is the last post at which we could get a supply of provisions on this side of the mountains; so that we were necessarily obliged to carry a large quantity with us, owing to the difficulty which always arises in getting the men away from comfortable quarters to commence a long and difficult journey, coupled with the wild-

No. 6.—Group of Buffaloes.

ness of the horses on a first day's march. We only succeeded in reaching Sturgeon Creek, a distance of about sixteen miles, on the first day. Seeing a group of buffaloes reposing near a small lake, I took a sketch (No. 6). They were the last that I should see for some time; and it was easy for me to keep up with the party at the slow rate at which they proceeded.

*Oct. 7th.*—The prairies were now fast receding behind us, our course lying to the northward. The track became almost impassable, being wet and swampy; and the horses often stuck fast, and threw off their loads in their struggles to extricate themselves from the mire. We were lucky enough to vary our provisions by killing a great many geese of the kind called "wavy." Could we have procured a little salt, I should have found them more palatable.

*Oct. 8th.*—The tremendous hurricane above alluded to had torn up immense trees by the roots, and scattered them in piles one on another in all directions, detaining us sometimes for hours, while the men cut a path through them for the horses. Our progress through the thick woods, which we had now fairly entered, was necessarily very slow and fatiguing.

*Oct. 9th.*—The track still continued bad, and we saw no game; so that our time passed very monotonously, as we had to keep pace with the loaded horses. A Highlander of the name of Colin Frazer had joined our party. He was on

his way to a small post, of which he had the charge,
at the head of the Athabasca River, in the Rocky
Mountains, where he had resided for the last eleven
years.  He had been brought to the country by
Sir George Simpson, in the capacity of his piper,
at the time when he explored Frazer's River, and
made an extensive voyage through a country
hitherto little known, and among Indians who
had seen few or no white men.  He carried the
pipes with him, dressed in his Highland costume;
and when stopping at forts, or wherever he found
Indians, the bagpipes were put in requisition,
much to the astonishment of the natives, who
supposed him to be a relation of the Great Spirit,
having, of course, never beheld so extraordinary
a looking man, or such a musical instrument,
which astonished them as much as the sound produced.  One of the Indians asked him to intercede with the Great Spirit for him; but Frazer
remarked, the petitioner little thought how limited
his influence was in that quarter.

*Oct.* 10*th.* — I left the party this morning and
proceeded on, and at two o'clock in the afternoon,
after a smart ride, I arrived at Fort Assiniboine, on
the Athabasca River.  This establishment, although
honoured with the name of a fort, is a mere post

L

used for taking care of horses, a common man or horsekeeper being in charge of it. The rest of the party arrived late the same evening.

*Oct. 11th.* —We found two boats here, which our men immediately overhauled and set to work to repair and pitch. At 2 o'clock P.M. we embarked, and continued travelling slowly on, against a very strong current, for five days. The water was very low, which added greatly to our difficulties. We saw no game nor Indians to break the monotony of our labour, and the nights and mornings were becoming very cold.

*Oct. 15th.* —When we stopped to take breakfast, it was very cold and snowing. We held a council, and it was determined that, as the weather had set in so bad, five men and one boat, with the clerk Charles, should return back to Fort Assiniboine with the Russian packs of otter skins. We were now all obliged to crowd into one boat, the others having gone back; and were frequently obliged to disembark and lighten the boat, owing to the unusual lowness of the river. We had almost continually to drag the boat onwards with a line, the men waist deep in the water. One of them slipped off a log into deep water, and it was with no small difficulty we saved him from being drowned. We had not extricated him from the river five minutes before his clothes were stiff with ice. I asked him if he was not cold, and his reply was characteristic of the hardihood of the Iroquois, of which tribe our party principally consisted, " My clothes are cold, but I am not."

*Oct.* 16*th.* — The weather had now set in so cold that we began to doubt the possibility of crossing the mountains this season. The line by which the men dragged the boat broke twice to-day in the rapids, and our boat was nearly dashed to pieces among the rocks. Had this misfortune happened, we should have lost all our provisions, and had a great chance of perishing with hunger.

*Oct.* 17*th and* 18*th.* — Weather fine. This is the most monotonous river that ever I have met with in my travels. Nothing but point after point appearing, all thickly covered with pine, any extensive view being entirely out of the question. The course of the river, although tortuous, is rapid, but unbroken by falls, running at the rate of six or seven miles an hour on an average.

*Oct.* 19*th.* — We fell in with an Indian hunter and his family. He had two bark canoes; he sold one of them to Colin Frazer, in which he embarked with four men, for the purpose of lightening our boat, and proceeded on in advance of us. We traded with them for some beaver meat and moose noses; the latter is the most delicate eating I ever met with, and is valued amongst the Indians beyond all other food.

*Oct. 20th and 21st.* — The weather was fine, and we made good progress.

*Oct. 22nd.* — The men were in extraordinarily good spirits. I measured a tree lying on the ground, which had been cut down by the beaver; it was seven feet in circumference. We found three bears left *en cache* by Colin Frazer, an old one and two cubs. He told me afterwards that he had killed the two cubs at one shot, while one was climbing over the back of the other to ascend a bank. The cubs proved fine eating, and were much relished, as our fresh provisions had been long exhausted.

*Oct. 23rd.* — We passed a camp fire still burning that had been left by Frazer the night previously.

*Oct. 24th.* — We passed the Rapids de Mort. The men had great difficulty in getting the boat up; we, of course, had all to walk. All the ponds and still water were frozen hard enough to bear. The rapidity of the current, however, prevented ice forming in the river. A small bag of pimmi-kon made in the usual way, except that it contained

Sasketome berries, was stolen, and a search being made for its recovery, a part of it was found in one of the men's bags. The only temptation to the theft could have been that it was more palatable than his own. M'Gillveray, being one of the most powerful men of the party, was called upon to administer the punishment, which he did by repeatedly knocking the delinquent down. This severity of punishment was called for by the fact, that the most disastrous consequences might arise on a journey through these desolate regions, if the most rigid care were not taken of the provisions.

*Oct. 25th to 27th.*—There was no change in the general aspect of the country; the same monotonous scenery still surrounded us.

*Oct. 28th.*—We passed the mouth of the Old Man's River. The Indians say that an evil spirit once came down this river—which is so rapid that no canoe can ascend it—and that having reached its mouth, where it enters the Athabasca, he made five steps down, leaving a rapid at every step. These rapids are a mile apart. After which he returned and went up his own river, and has not since been heard of. The river now became so shallow, that we were obliged to make two discharges.

*Oct. 29th.* — The bank of the river being very high, I ascended it, and saw for the first time the sublime and apparently endless chain of the Rocky Mountains. The outline was scarcely perceptible in the distance through the intervening smoky atmosphere, which is caused by the almost invariable conflagration of the woods at this season of the year. M'Gillveray wounded a moose while out with his gun. The deer took to the water, and swam across to the opposite side. I took the boat and followed him, and brought him down at the first shot. He was a fine large buck. It being nearly night, we encamped on the spot, and supped heartily off him, carrying his remains with us next morning.

*Oct. 30th.* — We had a fine view of the mountains from the boat for the first time; the men greeted them with a hearty cheer.

*Oct. 31st.* — The atmosphere clear but very cold. I made a sketch of the river and the mountains in the distance.

*November 1st.* — We entered Jasper's Lake in the morning. This lake is about twelve miles long, and from three to four miles wide, but at this season of the year very shallow, on account of its sources in the mountains being frozen. We had

to land three men on the south shore for the
purpose of decreasing the draft of our boat; but
even then we proceeded with great difficulty.
Shortly after we had put them on shore, it began
to blow a perfect hurricane, which drove us to the
north side, and a snow storm coming on, we were
compelled to encamp. This was unfortunate, as it
was impossible to communicate with the men
whom we had left at the other side, and who were
without either provisions or blankets, and we knew
from the intense cold that they must be suffering
severely.

*Nov. 2nd.*—We were now close upon the mountains, and it is scarcely possible to conceive the
intense force with which the wind howled through
a gap formed by the perpendicular rock called
" Miëtte's Rock," 1500 feet high, on the one side,
and a lofty mountain on the other. The former derives its appellation from a French voyageur, who
climbed its summit and sat smoking his pipe with
his legs hanging over the fearful abyss. M'Gillveray and the guide went on to Colin Frazer's, distant
about fourteen or fifteen miles, to procure horses,
as we found that further progress in the boat was
impossible, both on account of the shallowness of
the water and the violence of the wind.

*Nov. 3rd.* — The hurricane still continued, accompanied by very heavy snow; indeed, from what I heard, I believe it is always blowing at this place. The forest is composed entirely of very high pine trees, small in circumference, and growing thickly together; these had a very curious appearance in the storm, as they waved in the wind like a field of grain. The immense long roots seemed to be especially provided them by nature to prevent their being blown over; and, as the soil is very light, and upon a rocky foundation, these roots formed a net work near the surface, which was in constant motion, and rocked us to sleep as we lay round our camp fires.

Meanwhile, our guide returned from Jasper's House with several horses. We found our boat blown out of the water, and lying fifteen feet distant from it on the shore although its weight was so great, that the strength of our remaining nine men could not return it to its element.

I selected a horse, and, taking the guide with me, started for the establishment in advance of the rest of the party. After a severe ride of four hours, and having forded the river four times, dangerously crowded with drift ice borne down by a rapid current, sometimes coming over the saddle, I arrived at Jasper's House cold, wet, and famished. But I was soon cheered by a blazing fire and five or six pounds of mountain sheep, which I certainly then thought far more delicious than any domestic animal of the same species. About 10 o'clock that evening, to our great joy, the three men whom we had left on the south shore, came in. Their sufferings had been very great, as they had been wandering through the woods for three days without food, endeavouring to find the house, which none of them had been at before. One of them had not even taken his coat with him, and it was only by lying huddled together at night that they escaped being frozen. Another suffered dreadfully from the swelled state of his legs, caused by the strings usually tied round their leggings being too tight, and which, owing to his benumbed condition, he did not perceive. We had some difficulty in cutting them off, as they were buried in the swollen flesh.

*Nov. 4th.*—Mr. Lane and party arrived safe in the evening with the loaded horses. Jasper's House consists of only three miserable log huts. The dwelling-house is composed of two rooms, of about fourteen or fifteen feet square each. One of them is used by all comers and goers: Indians, voyageurs, and traders, men, women, and children being huddled together indiscriminately; the other room being devoted to the exclusive occupation of Colin and his family, consisting of a Cree squaw, and nine interesting half-breed children.  One of the

No. 7. — Jasper's House — Rocky Mountains.

other huts is used for storing provision in, when they can get any, and the other I should have thought a dog-kennel had I seen many of the canine species about.  This post is only kept up for the purpose of supplying horses to parties crossing the

mountains. I made a sketch of the establishment (No. 7).

*Nov. 5th.*—We started with a cavalcade of thirteen loaded horses, but as we did not expect to be
able to get the horses across the mountains, I got
an Indian to make me a pair of snow shoes. The
Indians about here do not number above fifteen or
twenty; they are the Shoo-Schawp tribe, and their
chief, of whom I made a sketch, is called " Capote
Blanc" by the voyageurs—in their own language
it is Assannitchay, but means the same. His
proper location is a long distance to the north-east;
but he had been treacherously entrapped, whilst
travelling with thirty-seven of his people, by a
hostile tribe, which met him and invited him to
sit down and smoke the pipe of peace. They unsus-
pectingly laid down their arms, but before they
had time to smoke, their treacherous hosts seized
their arms and murdered them all except eleven,
who managed to escape, and fled to Jasper's House,
where they remained, never daring to return to
their own country through the hostile tribe.
Capote Blanc was a very simple, kind-hearted old
man, with whom I became very friendly.

We left this inhospitable spot about noon, and
crossed the river in a small canoe to where the

men were waiting for us, with the horses, which they had swam across the river in the morning. We rode on till 4 o'clock, and encamped in a small prairie, of which I made a sketch.

*Nov. 6th.*—We made but few miles of progress to-day, being obliged to encamp at La Row's Prairie in order to pasture our horses, our next stopping place being too distant to reach that evening.

*Nov. 7th.*—We made a *long day;* our route lay sometimes over almost inaccessible crags, and at others through gloomy and tangled forest; as we ascended, the snow increased in depth, and we began to feel the effects of the increasing cold and rarefaction of the atmosphere.

*Nov. 8th.*—We saw two mountain goats looking down on us from a lofty and precipitous ledge of rock, not exceeding, to all appearance, a few inches in width. One of the Indians who accompanied us from Jasper's House to take back the horses, started to attain a crag above them, as these animals cannot be approached near enough to shoot them from below, their gaze being always directed downwards. They chanced, however, to see him going up, and immediately escaped to an inaccessible height.

*Nov. 9th.*—Finding the snow so deep, and knowing, not only that we were late, but that our further progress must be slow, we became apprehensive that the party who should be waiting for us with boats and provisions from Fort Vancouver, at the other side of the mountains, would give up all hopes of meeting us and might leave. This would have entailed the most fearful hardships upon us, if it did not produce actual destruction, as we should have had to recross the mountains with scarcely any or no provisions. We, therefore, despatched the guide and M'Gillveray, to hasten on to Boat Encampment. We encamped at the " Grand Batteur," where we found some snow shoes, which had been hidden by the party that had come out in the spring.

*Nov. 10th.*—We had not proceeded far before the horses stuck fast in the snow, and we were obliged to encamp on the spot to give those men who were unprovided time to make snow shoes, without which they could not proceed. We remained here all day, and sent the horses back with everything we could dispense with, our provisions and blankets being quite as much as the men could carry; and some of the new hands, who had only come into the country that year, were now so knocked up by their long and fatiguing voyage from Montreal, which they had left in the spring, as to be quite useless.

*Nov.* 11*th.*—We sent two experienced men in advance to beat the track for the new beginners, and made our first essay on snow shoes. Some of our men succeeded but indifferently in the attempt, having never used them before; and the shoes, which we made the day before not being of the best description, materially impeded our progress. The shoes which the Indian had made for me at Jasper House were particularly good ones, and I found little difficulty in their use. Mrs. Lane had also taken the precaution to bring a pair with her, and as she had been accustomed to them from her childhood at Red River, where they are a great deal used, she proved one of our best pedestrians. We encamped early, making for the first time what is called a regular winter encampment. This is only made where the snow is so deep that it cannot be removed so as to reach the ground. The depth to which the snow attains can be calculated by the stumps of the trees cut off at its former level for previous camp fires; some of these were twelve or fifteen feet above us at the present time, and the snow was nine or ten

feet deep under us. Some of the old voyageurs
amused themselves by telling the new hands or
*Mangeurs du Lard*, that the Indians in those
parts were giants from thirty to forty feet high,
and that accounted for the trees being cut off at
such an unusual height.

It is necessary to walk repeatedly with snow
shoes over the place chosen for the encampment until it is sufficiently beaten down to bear
a man without sinking on its surface. Five
or six logs of green timber, from eighteen to
twenty feet long, are laid down close together, in
parallel lines, so as to form a platform. The fire
of dry wood is then kindled on it, and pine
branches are spread on each side, on which the
party, wrapped in their blankets, lie down with
their feet towards the fire. The parallel logs
rarely burn through in one night, but the dropping
coals and heat form a deep chasm immediately
under the fire, into which the logs are prevented
from falling by their length. Into this hole an
Iroquois, who had placed himself too near the fire,
rolled a depth of at least six or seven feet, the snow
having melted from under him while asleep. His
cries awoke me, and after a hearty laugh at his fiery
entombment, we succeeded in dragging him out.

*Nov. 12th.* — To-day we attained what is called the Height of Land. There is a small lake at this eminence called the Committee's Punch-bowl; this forms the head waters of one branch of the Columbia River on the west side of the mountains, and of the Athabasca on the east side. It is about three quarters of a mile in circumference, and is remarkable as giving rise to two such mighty rivers; the waters of the one emptying in the Pacific Ocean, and of the other into the Arctic Sea. We encamped on its margin, with difficulty protecting ourselves from the intense cold.

*Nov. 13th.*—The lake being frozen over to some depth, we walked across it, and shortly after commenced the descent of the grand côte, having been seven days continually ascending. The descent was so steep, that it took us only one day to get down to nearly the same level as that of Jasper's House. The descent was a work of great difficulty on snow shoes, particularly for those carrying loads ; their feet frequently slipped from under them, and the loads rolled down the hill. Some of the men, indeed, adopted the mode of rolling such loads as would not be injured down before them. On reaching the bottom, we found eight men waiting, whom M'Gillveray and the guide had sent on to assist us to Boat Encampment, and we all encamped together.

*Nov. 14th.* — I remained at the camp fire finishing one of my sketches, the men having made a very early start in order to reach Boat Encampment, where they would get a fresh supply of provisions, ours being nearly exhausted. As soon as I had finished my sketch I followed them, and soon arrived at a river about seventy yards across, and with a very rapid current.

Having followed their track in the snow to the edge of the river, and seeing the strength of the current, I began to look for other tracks, under the impression that they might possibly have discovered a way to get round it. But I was soon undeceived by seeing in the snow on the other side the path they had beaten down on the opposite bank ; nothing, therefore, remained but for me to take off my snow shoes, and make the traverse. The water was up to my middle, running very rapidly, and filled with drift ice, some pieces of which struck me, and nearly forced me down the stream. I found on coming out of the water my capote and leggings frozen stiff. My difficulties, however, were only beginning, as I was soon obliged to cross again four times, when,

M

my legs becoming completely benumbed, I dared not venture on the fifth, until I had restored the circulation by running up and down the beach. I had to cross twelve others in a similar manner, being seventeen in all, before I overtook the rest of the party at the encampment. The reason of these frequent crossings is, that the only pass across the mountains is the gorge formed by the Athabasca at one side, and the Columbia at the other; and the beds of these torrents can only be crossed in the spring before the thaws commence, or in the fall after the severe weather has set in. During the summer the melting of the mountain snow and ice renders them utterly impracticable.

*Nov.* 15*th.* — It will be easily imagined with what regret we left a warm fire and comfortable encampment, to plunge at once into one of the deepest crossings we had yet encountered, covered like the preceding with running ice. Here, as in many other of the crossings, our only means of withstanding the force of the current was for all to go abreast shoulder to shoulder, in a line parallel with it, each man being supported by all below him. Mrs. Lane, although it was necessary to carry her in the arms of two powerful men across the river, acquitted herself in other respects as well as any of us. One of the greatest annoyances accompanying the use of snow shoes, is that of having to take them off on entering a river, and replacing them over the wet and frozen moccasins on coming out of it.

Before stopping to breakfast this morning, we crossed the river twenty-five times, and twelve times more before camping ; having waded it thirty-seven times in all during the day.

The Columbia here makes long reaches, to and fro, through a valley, in some parts three miles wide, and backed with stupendous mountains, rearing their snowy tops above the clouds, and forming here and there immense glaciers, reflecting the rays of the sun with extreme brilliancy and prismatic beauty. The last part of the route lay through a slimy lake or swamp, frozen over, but not with sufficient solidity to bear us, so that we had to wade above our knees in a dense mass of snow, ice, and mud, there being no such thing as a dry spot to afford a moment's respite from the scarcely endurable severity of the cold, under which I thought I must have sank exhausted.

At length, however, we arrived at Boat Encampment, about 5 P.M., almost perishing with cold and hunger, having tasted nothing since what I have already termed breakfast, which consisted only of a small. supply of soup made of pemmi-kon, this being the mode of making the most of a small quantity of it. On our arrival we found a good fire blazing, and some soup made from pork and corn, brought from Fort Vancouver, boiling in the pot, which I attacked with so much avidity, that one of the men, fearing I might take too much in my present exhausted state, politely walked off with the bowl and its contents.

The men had been here waiting our arrival for thirty-nine days, and would have returned to Fort Vancouver the next day, had not the guide and M'Gillveray opportunely arrived in time to prevent them, as they thought we had either been cut off by the Indians, or that we had found it impossible to cross the mountains. In fact, they were clearing the snow out of the boats preparatory to starting. Had our messengers not arrived in time, it would most likely have proved fatal to us all, as we could not have re-crossed the mountains without provisions.

On leaving Boat Encampment, I did not take any sketches, although the scenery was exceedingly grand; the rapidity with which we now

travelled, and the necessity for doing so owing to
the lateness of the season, prevented me; and as I
was determined to return by the same route, I
knew that I should then have plenty of time and
opportunity.   I shall therefore give a mere outline
of my rapid journey to Fort Vancouver, a distance
of 1200 miles down the Columbia River, which we
accomplished in fifteen days, and which afterwards
took me four months to ascend.

*Nov. 16th.* — Our two boats were by this time
ready; they were formed canoe fashion, with round
bottoms of boards, clinker built.    On leaving
Boat Encampment the scene is exceedingly grand;
immense mountains receding further and further
in the distance on every side.    Few who read this
journal, surrounded by the comforts of civilised
life, will be able to imagine the heartfelt satisfaction with which we exchanged the wearisome snow-
shoe for the comfortable boats, and the painful
anxiety of half-satisfied appetites for a well-stocked
larder.    True it was, that the innumerable rapids
of the Columbia were filled with dangers of no
ordinary character, and that it required the constant exercise of all our energy and skill to escape
their perils, but we now had health and high
spirits to help us.    We no longer had to toil on in

clothes frozen stiff from wading across torrents, half-famished, and with the consciousness ever before us, that whatever were our hardships and fatigue, rest was sure destruction in the cold solitudes of those dreary mountains.

About three hours after our departure, we shot the celebrated " Dalle de Mort." It is about three miles long and is the most dangerous of all the rapids on the Columbia.

17th and 18th. — We passed through the two lakes, and were obliged to work night and day to avail ourselves of the calm weather, although the snow fell without ceasing.

19th. — We again entered the current of the river, where the men were enabled to rest for a few hours.

Nov. 20th. — About noon we ran through the Little Dalle, which, though short, is a series of dangerous whirlpools, which can only be passed with the greatest precaution, and arrived safe at Colville at 6 o'clock in the evening. Colville is beautifully situated about a mile above the falls of the Chaudière or Kettle Falls; it exceeds in height any other fall on the Columbia, and derives its name from the round holes that the water has hollowed out in the rocks, resembling caul-

drons of various sizes. Here we were most hospitably entertained by Mr. Lewis, who was in
charge. To avoid this fall we had to carry our
boats a distance of two miles over a hill two or
three hundred feet high. We remained here three
days, during which time the men did little else
but eat and sleep. The rapidity with which they
changed their appearance was astonishing. Some
of them became so much improved in looks, that
it was with difficulty we could recognise our
voyageurs.

*Nov. 23rd.* — We encamped in the evening a
few miles below the falls. During the night some
Indians, who had been prowling about, crept into
the boats and stole some wearing apparel, which
proved very annoying to us, as our wardrobes were
rather limited.

*Nov. 24th.* — We arrived at the Grand Rapid,
which the boats were obliged to run. I, however,
preferred getting out to walk, with the object of
making some sketches. I had proceeded nearly
three miles along the shore, and felt somewhat
astonished at not seeing the boats following, when
I observed something in the water, which I at first
took to be the head of an Indian swimming across.
I accordingly prepared my gun in case of an

M 4

attack, as the Indians about here are considered
some of the worst on the Columbia. On close
observation, however, I made out the object to be
the hood which I had noticed Mrs. Lane to wear
in the morning, and soon afterwards I perceived
the paddles and oars of one of the boats. I now
began to feel alarmed for the safety of some of the
party, and immediately returned to the rapid as
fast as possible. There I saw one of the boats,
in which Mr. and Mrs. Lane were, in a most dangerous situation, having struck in the midst of
the rapids upon a rock, which had stove in her
side. The conduct of the men evinced great
presence of mind. The instant she struck, they
had sprung on the gunwale next the rock, and by
their united weight kept her lying upon it. The
water foamed and raged around them with fearful
violence. Had she slipped off, they must all have
been dashed to pieces amongst the rocks and rapids
below; as it was, they managed to maintain their
position, until the crew of the other boat, which
had run the rapids safely, had unloaded and
dragged the empty boat up the rapids again. They
then succeeded in throwing a line to their hapless
companions. But there was still considerable
danger, lest in hauling the empty boat towards

them they might pull themselves off the rock; they at length, however, succeeded by cautious management in getting the boat alongside, and in embarking in safety. In a moment afterwards their own boat slipped from the rock, and was dashed to pieces. Everything that floated we picked up afterwards, but still we lost a great many useful and necessary articles. We had, in consequence of this mishap, to send back overland to Colville for another boat. This detained us until the morning of the 26th. We now continued our journey rapidly and safely, and arrived at Okanagan on the evening of the 28th November. Our provisons had run short, and we were compelled to shoot one of the horses of the establishment, which we roasted, and found very palatable. In our emergency the men partook of it so voraciously that some of them were unable to work the next day.

*Nov. 29th.* — We continued our course, and in four days arrived at Fort Walla-Walla. Here we remained till December 4th, when we entered that part of the country which is annually visited by an almost continuous rain for five months of the year, and during the remainder of our voyage to Fort Vancouver, which we reached on the 8th December, we were exposed in our open boats to an incessant shower.  Mr. Douglas and Mr. Ogden, the two chief factors in charge of the fort, came down to the landing, a distance of about half a mile, to welcome us on our arrival, all hopes of which they had given up, and conducted us up to the fort, where we were entertained with the most liberal hospitality.

# CHAP. XII.

Fort Vancouver.—The Flatheads.—Hereditary Names.—Casanov.—
Ravages of Fever.—The Evil Genius.—How to flatten the Head.
—The Sign of a Slave.—An impracticable Tongue.—"Clark, how
are you?"—Revolting Habits.—Chinook Costume.—Baskets Water-
tight.—How they cook the Camas.—Chinook Olives.—Chinook
Lodges.—Good-tempered Gamblers.

Fort Vancouver, the Indian name of which is
Katchutequa, or "the Plain," is the largest post
in the Hudson's Bay Company's dominions, and
has usually two chief factors, with eight or ten
clerks and 200 voyageurs, residing there. Our
society was also enlivened by the addition of
the officers of Her Majesty's ship of war the
"Modeste," which had been on this station for
two years, and lay in the river opposite the establishment. The buildings are enclosed by strong
pickets about sixteen feet high, with bastions for
cannon at the corners. The men, with their Indian wives, live in log huts near the margin of
the river, forming a little village — quite a Babel

of languages, as the inhabitants are a mixture of English, French, Iroquois, Sandwich Islanders, Crees and Chinooks.

The Columbia is here, ninety miles from its mouth, a mile and a quarter wide ; the surrounding country is well wooded and fertile, the oak and pine being of the finest description.  A large farm is cultivated about eight miles up the river, producing more grain than the fort consumes ; the surplus being sent to the Sandwich Islands and the Russian dominions.  They have immense herds of domestic horned cattle, which run wild in unknown numbers ; and sheep and horses are equally numerous.  When first introduced from California, Dr. M'Laughlin, the gentleman then in charge, would not allow any of the horned cattle to be killed for the use of the establishment until their numbers had reached 600, by which means they have multiplied beyond calculation.  During the five months' autumn and winter, it rains almost continuously, with very little frost or snow.  The river, however, was frozen over for a short time during the winter I spent there, but it was remarked as the coldest season ever experienced ; during the other seven months the weather is dry and sultry.

The Flat-Head Indians are met with on the banks of the Columbia River, from its mouth eastward to the Cascades, a distance of about 150 miles; they extend up the Walhamette River's mouth, about thirty or forty miles, and through the district between the Walhamette and Fort Astoria, now called Fort George. To the north they extend along the Cowlitz River, and the tract of land lying between that and Puget's Sound. About two-thirds of Vancouver's Island is also occupied by them, and they are found along the coasts of Puget's Sound and the Straits of Juan de Fuca. The Flatheads are divided into numerous tribes, each having its own peculiar locality, and differing more or less from the others in language, customs, and manners. Those in the immediate vicinity of the fort are principally Chinooks and Klickataats, and are governed by a chief called Casanov. This name has no translation, the Indians on the west side of the Rocky Mountains differing from those on the east in having hereditary names, to which no particular meaning appears to be attached, and the origin of which is in many instances forgotten.

Casanov is a man of advanced age, and resides principally at Fort Vancouver. I made a sketch

(No. 8) of him while staying at the fort. Previously to 1829 Casanov was considered a powerful chief, and could lead into the field 1000 men, but in that year the Hudson's Bay Company and emigrants from the United States introduced the

No. 8. — Portrait of Ca-sa-nov.

plough for the first time into Oregon; and the locality, hitherto considered one of the most healthy, was almost depopulated by the fever and ague.

His own immediate family, consisting of ten wives, four children, and eighteen slaves, were reduced in one year to one wife, one child, and two slaves. Casanov is a man of more than ordinary talent for an Indian, and he has maintained his great influence over his tribe chiefly by means of the superstitious dread in which they held him. For many years, in the early period of his life, he kept a hired assassin to remove any obnoxious individual against whom he entertained personal enmity. This bravo, whose occupation was no secret, went by the name of Casanov's scoocoom, or, "the Evil Genius." He finally fell in love with one of Casanov's wives, who eloped with him. Casanov vowed vengeance, but the pair for a long time eluded his search; until one day he met his wife in a canoe near the mouth of the Cowlitz River, and shot her on the spot, and at last procured also the assassination of the lover.

A few years before my arrival at Fort Vancouver, Mr. Douglass, who was then in charge, heard from his office the report of a gun inside the gates. This being a breach of discipline he hurried out to inquire the cause of so unusual a circumstance, and found one of Casanov's slaves standing over the body of an Indian whom he had just

killed, and in the act of reloading his gun with
apparent indifference, Casanov himself standing
by.  On Mr. Douglass arriving at the spot, he was
told by Casanov, with an apology, that the man
deserved death according to the laws of the tribe,
who as well as the white man inflicted punishment
proportionate to the nature of the offence.  In this
case the crime was one of the greatest an Indian
could be guilty of, namely, the robbing the sepulchre
canoes.  Mr. Douglass, after severely reprimand-
ing him, allowed him to depart with the dead body.

Sacred as the Indians hold their burial places,
Casanov himself, a short time after the latter
occurrence, had his only son buried in the cemetery
of the Fort.  He died of consumption—a disease
very common amongst all Indians—proceeding no
doubt from their constant exposure to the sudden
vicissitudes of the climate.  The coffin was made
sufficiently large to contain all the necessaries supposed to be required for his comfort and convenience in the world of spirits.  The chaplain of the
Fort read the usual service at the grave, and after
the conclusion of the ceremony, Casanov returned
to his lodge, and the same evening attempted, as
narrated below, the life of the bereaved mother,
who was the daughter of the great chief generally

known as King Comcomly, so beautifully alluded
to in Washington Irving's "Astoria." She was
formerly the wife of a Mr. McDougall, who bought
her from her father for, as it was supposed, the
enormous price of ten articles of each description,
guns, blankets, knives, hatchets, &c., then in Fort
Astoria. Comcomly, however, acted with unexpected liberality on the occasion by carpeting her
path from the canoe to the Fort with sea otter
skins, at that time numerous and valuable, but now
scarce, and presenting them as a dowry, in reality
far exceeding in value the articles at which she
had been estimated.   On Mr. McDougall's leaving
the Indian country she became the wife of Casanov.

It is the prevailing opinion of the chiefs that
they and their sons are too important to die in a
natural way, and whenever the event takes place,
they attribute it to the malevolent influence of
some other person, whom they fix upon, often in
the most unaccountable manner, frequently selecting those the most dear to themselves and the
deceased.   The person so selected is sacrificed
without hesitation.   On this occasion Casanov selected the afflicted mother, notwithstanding she had
during the sickness of her son been one of the most
assiduous and devoted of his attendants, and of his

N

several wives she was the one he most loved ; but it is the general belief of the Indians on the west side of the mountains, that the greater the privation · they inflict on themselves the greater would be the manifestation of their grief, and the more pleasing to the departed spirit. Casanov assigned to me an additional motive for his wish to kill his wife, namely, that as he knew she had been so useful to her son and so necessary to his happiness and comfort in this world, he wished to send her with him as his companion on his long journey. She, however, escaped into the woods, and next morning reached the Fort imploring protection ; she was accordingly secreted for several days until her own relations took her home to Chinook Point. In the meantime a woman was found murdered in the woods, and the act was universally attributed to Casanov or one of his emissaries.

I may here mention a painful occurrence which took place on Thompson's River, in New Caledonia, as illustrative of this peculiar superstition.

A chief dying, his widow considered a sacrifice as indispensable, but having selected a victim of rather too much importance, she was unable for some time to accomplish her object ; at length the nephew of the chief, no longer able to bear the continual taunts of cowardice which she unceasingly heaped upon him, seized his gun and started for the Company's Fort on the river, about twenty miles distant.    On arriving he was courteously received by Mr. Black, the gentleman in charge of the Fort, who expressed great regret at the death of his old friend the chief.    After presenting the Indian with something to eat and giving him some tobacco, Mr. Black turned to leave the room, and while opening the door was shot from behind by his treacherous guest and immediately expired.    The murderer succeeded in escaping from the Fort, but the tribe, who were warmly attached to Mr. Black, took his revenge upon themselves and hunted him down.    This was done more to evince their high esteem for Mr. Black than from any sense of impropriety in the customary sacrifice.

Amongst the Chinooks I have never heard any traditions as to their former origin, although such traditions are common amongst those on the east side of the Rocky Mountains.    They do not believe in any future state of punishment, although in this world they suppose themselves exposed to the malicious designs of the scoocoom or evil genius, to whom they attribute all their misfortunes and ill luck.    The Good Spirit is called the *Hias Soch-*

*a-li Ti-yah,* that is the Great High Chief from whom they obtain all that is good in this life, and to whose happy and peaceful hunting grounds they will all eventually go, to reside for ever in comfort and abundance.

The Chinooks and Cowlitz Indians carry the custom of flattening the head to a greater extent than any other of the Flathead tribes. The process is as follows:—The Indian mothers all carry their infants strapped to a piece of board covered with moss or loose fibres of cedar bark, and in order to flatten the head they place a pad on the infant's forehead, on the top of which is laid a piece of smooth bark, bound on by a leathern band passing through holes in the board on either side, and kept tightly pressed across the front of the head,—a sort of pillow of grass or cedar fibres being placed under the back of the neck to support it. This process commences with the birth of the infant, and is continued for a period of from eight to twelve months, by which time the head has lost its natural shape, and acquired that of a wedge: the front of the skull flat and higher at the crown, giving it a most unnatural appearance.

It might be supposed, from the extent to which this is carried, that the operation would be attended

with great suffering to the infant, but I have never
heard the infants crying or moaning, although I
have seen the eyes seemingly starting out of the
sockets from the great pressure. But on the contrary, when the lashings were removed, I have
noticed them cry until they were replaced. From
the apparent dulness of the children whilst under
the pressure, I should imagine that a state of torpor
or insensibility is induced, and that the return to
consciousness occasioned by its removal, must be
naturally followed by the sense of pain.

This unnatural operation does not, however, seem
to injure the health, the mortality amongst the Flat-
head children not being perceptibly greater than
amongst other Indian tribes; nor does it seem to
injure their intellect. On the contrary, the Flatheads are generally considered fully as intelligent
as the surrounding tribes, who allow their heads to
preserve their natural shape, and it is from amongst
the round heads that the Flatheads take their slaves,
looking with contempt even upon the white for
having round heads, the flat head being considered
as the distinguishing mark of freedom.

The Chinooks, like all other Indians, pluck out
the beard at its first appearance. Slavery is carried
on to a great extent among them, and considering

how much they have themselves been reduced, they still retain a large number of slaves. These are usually procured from the Chastay tribe, who live near the Umqua, a river south of the Columbia, emptying near the Pacific. They are sometimes seized by war parties, but children are often bought from their own people. They do not flatten the head, nor is the child of one of them (although by a Chinook father) allowed this privilege. Their slavery is of the most abject description. The Chinook men and women treat them with great severity, and exercise the power of life and death at pleasure. I took a sketch of a Chastay female slave, the lower part of whose face, from the corners of the mouth to the ears and downwards, was tattooed of a blueish colour. The men of this tribe do not tattoo, but paint their faces like other Indians.

I would willingly give a specimen of the barbarous language of this people, were it possible to represent by any combination of our alphabet the horrible, harsh, spluttering sounds which proceed from their throats, apparently unguided either by the tongue or lip. It is so difficult to acquire a mastery of their language that none have been able to attain it, except those who have been born

among them. They have, however, by their intercourse with the English and French traders, succeeded in amalgamating, after a fashion, some
words of each of these tongues with their own,
and forming a sort of patois, barbarous enough
certainly, but still sufficient to enable them to
communicate with the traders. This patois I was
enabled after some short time to acquire, and could
converse with most of the chiefs with tolerable
ease; their common salutation is Clak-hoh-ah-yah,
originating, as I believe, in their having heard in
the early days of the fur trade, a gentleman named
Clark frequently addressed by his friends, " Clark,
how are you ?" This salutation is now applied to
every white man, their own language affording no
appropriate expression. Their language is also
peculiar in containing no oaths, or any words con-
veying gratitude or thanks.

Their habits are extremely filthy, their persons
abounding with vermin, and one of their chief
amusements consists in picking these disgusting
insects from each other's heads and eating them.
On my asking an Indian one day why he ate them,
he replied that they bit him, and he gratified his
revenge by biting them in return. It might naturally be supposed that they are thus beset from

want of combs, or other means of displacing the in-
truders; but this is not the case, as they pride
themselves on carrying such companions about
them, and giving their friends the opportunity of
amusing themselves by hunting and eating them.

The costume of the men consists of a musk-rat
skin robe, the size of our ordinary blanket, thrown
over the shoulder, without any breech-cloth, moccasins, or leggings.  The dress which Casanov is represented as wearing, in the picture, being one
that was presented to him by a friend from Walla-
Walla.  Painting the face is not much practised
amongst them, except on extraordinary occasions,
such as the death of a relative, some solemn feast,
or going on a war party.  The female dress consists
of a girdle of cedar-bark round the waist, with a
dense mass of strings of the same material hanging
from it all round, and reaching almost to the knees.
This is their sole summer habiliment.  They, however, in very severe weather, add the musk-rat
blanket.  They also make another sort of blanket
from the skin of the wild goose, which is here taken
in great abundance.  The skin is stripped from the
bird with the feathers on and cut in strips, which
they twist so as to have the feathers outwards.
This makes a feathered cord, and is then netted

together so as to form a blanket, the feathers filling up the meshes, rendering it a light and very warm covering. In the summer these are entirely thrown aside, not being in any case worn from feelings of delicacy. The men go quite naked, though the women always wear the cedar petticoat.

The country which the Chinooks inhabit being almost destitute of furs, they have little to trade in with the whites. This, coupled with their laziness, probably induced by the ease with which they procure fish, which is their chief subsistence, prevents their obtaining ornaments of European manufacture, consequently anything of the kind is seldom seen amongst them.

The Chinooks evince very little taste, in comparison with some of the tribes on the eastern side of the Rocky Mountains, in ornamenting either their persons, or their warlike or domestic implements. The only utensils I saw at all creditable to their decorative skill were carved bowls and spoons of horn, and baskets made of roots and grass, woven so closely, as to serve all the purposes of a pail, in holding and carrying water. In these they even boil their fish. This is done by immersing the fish in one of the baskets filled with water, into which they throw red hot stones until the fish is cooked; and I have seen fish dressed as expeditiously by them in this way, as if done in a kettle over the fire by our own people. The only vegetables in use among them are the camas and wappatoo. The camas is a bulbous root, much resembling the onion in outward appearance, but is more like the potato when cooked, and is very good eating. The wappatoo is somewhat similar, but larger, and not so dry or delicate in its flavour. They are found in immense quantities in the plains in the vicinity of Fort Vancouver, and in the spring of the year present a most curious and beautiful appearance, the whole surface presenting an uninterrupted sheet of bright ultra-marine blue, from the innumerable blossoms of these plants. They are cooked by digging a hole in the ground, then putting down a layer of hot stones, covering them with dry grass, on which the roots are placed, they are then covered with a layer of grass, and on the top of this they place earth, with a small hole perforated through the earth and grass down to the vegetables. Into this water is poured, which, reaching the hot stones, forms sufficient steam to completely cook the roots in a short time, the hole being immediately stopped up on the introduction of the water. They often adopt the same ingenious process for cooking their fish and game.

There is another article of food made use of amongst them, which, from its disgusting nature, I should have been tempted to omit, were it not a peculiarly characteristic trait of the Chinook Indian, both from its extraordinary character and its use, being confined solely to this tribe. The whites have given it the name of Chinook olives, and it is prepared as follows:—About a bushel of acorns are placed in a hole dug for the purpose close to the entrance of the lodge or hut, covered over with a thin layer of grass, on the top of which is laid about half a foot of earth. Every member of the family henceforth regards this hole as the special place of deposit for his urine, which is on no occasion to be diverted from its legitimate receptacle. In this hole the acorns are allowed to remain four or five months before they are considered fit for use. However disgusting such an odoriferous preparation would be to people in civilised life, the product is regarded by them as the greatest of all delicacies.

During the season the Chinooks are engaged in gathering camas and fishing, they live in lodges constructed by means of a few poles covered with mats made of rushes, which can be easily moved from place to place, but in the villages they build permanent huts of split cedar boards. Having selected a dry place for the hut, a hole is dug about three feet deep, and about twenty feet square. Round the sides square cedar boards are sunk and fastened together with cords and twisted roots, rising about four feet above the outer level; two posts are sunk at the middle of each end with a crotch at the top, on which the ridge pole is laid, and boards are laid from thence to the top of the upright boards fastened in the same manner. Round the interior are erected sleeping places, one above another, something like the berths in a vessel, but larger. In the centre of this lodge the fire is made, and the smoke escapes through a hole left in the roof for that purpose.

The fire is obtained by means of a small flat piece of dry cedar, in which a small hollow is cut, with a channel for the ignited charcoal to run over; this piece the Indian sits on to hold it steady, while he rapidly twirls a round stick of the same wood between the palms of his hands, with the point pressed into the hollow of the flat piece. In a very short time sparks begin to fall through the channel upon finely frayed cedar bark placed underneath, which they soon ignite. There is a great deal of knack in doing this, but those who are used to it will light a fire in a very short time. The men usually carry these sticks about with them, as after they have been once used they produce the fire more quickly.

The only native warlike instruments I have seen amongst them were bows and arrows; these they use with great precision. Their canoes are hollowed out of the cedar by fire, and smoothed off with stone axes. Some of them are very large, as the cedar grows to an enormous size in this neighbourhood. They are made very light, and from their formation, are capable of withstanding very heavy seas.

The principal amusement of the Chinooks is gambling, which is carried to great excess amongst them. You never visit the camp but you hear the eternal gambling song of "*he hah ha*," accompanied by the beating of small sticks on some hollow substance. Their games are few. The one most generally played amongst them consists in holding in each hand a small stick, the thickness of a goose quill, and about an inch and a half in length, one plain, and the other distinguished by a little thread wound round it, the opposite party being required to guess in which hand the marked stick is to be found. A Chinook will play at this simple game for days and nights together, until he has gambled away everything he possesses, even to his wife. They play, however, with much equanimity, and I never knew any ill feeling evinced by the loser against his successful opponent. They will cheat if they can, and pride themselves on its success; if detected, no unpleasant consequence follows, the offending party being merely laughed at, and allowed to amend his game. They also take great delight in a game with a ball, which is played by them in the same manner as the Cree, Chippewa, and Sioux Indians. Two poles are erected about a mile apart, and the company is divided into two bands, armed with sticks, having a small ring or hoop at the end, with which the ball is picked up and thrown to a great distance; each party then strives to get the ball past their own goal. There are sometimes a hundred on a side, and the play is kept up with great noise and excitement. At this game they bet heavily, as it is generally played between tribes or villages. The Chinooks have tolerably good horses, and are fond of racing, at which they also bet considerably. They are expert jockeys, and ride fearlessly.

# CHAP. XIII.

Leaving Fort Vancouver.—Seven degrees below Zero.—The Magic
  Bullet.—A Match for the Indians.—A Jesuit Mission.—Har-
  monious Gamesters. — A Wild Calf Chase.—The Swallow-tailed
  Coat.—The Haunted Volcano.—The Cocked Hat.—Dead Men's
  Canoes. — Filching a Good Name. — The Prairie de Bute.

I CONTINUED at Fort Vancouver for about a month,
and left on the 10th of January 1847, with Mr.
Mackenlie, a chief trader, for Oregon City, where
the company has an establishment. After going
down the Columbia about five miles, we entered
the mouth of the Walhamette River, and ascended
it twenty-five miles to Oregon City, passing two
cities that are to be. One of them contained but
two houses, and the other was not much more advanced. Oregon City contains about ninety-four
houses, and two or three hundred inhabitants.
There are a Methodist and a Roman Catholic
church, two hotels, two grist mills, three saw mills,
four stores, two watchmakers, one gunsmith, one

lawyer, and doctors *ad libitum.* The city stands near the Falls of the Walhamette which is here about thirty-two feet high.

The water privileges are of the most powerful and convenient description. Dr. M'Laughlin, formerly a chief factor in the Hudson's Bay Company, first obtained a location of the place, and now owns the principal mills. A great drawback, however, to its prosperity, is, that vessels cannot ascend the river nearer to it than fifteen miles, on account of the rapids. At the head of the navigation a city is building, which must eventually rival, if not eclipse Oregon in commercial prosperity. The morning after our arrival the thermometer stood at 7° below zero. Such intense cold had not been felt by the oldest inhabitants of these regions. It had the effect of killing nearly all the cattle that had become acclimated, as they are never housed. The Columbia, too, was frozen over, an unprecedented circumstance, so that my travels were for a time interrupted. I was, however, very comfortably quartered at Mr. Mackenlie's residence, who amused me in the long winter evenings over a good fire by his interesting tales of Indian life, with which he was well conversant. I will relate a couple of his anecdotes.

While he was in charge of a fort in New Caledonia, which is situated south of the Columbia
River, he had a carat of tobacco, or three pounds,
stolen from him.   It was all that he had at that
time, and of course was a serious loss.   Supposing
it to have been taken by some of the Indians, who
were trading in large numbers about the establishment at that time, he requested the chief to call a
council of all the tribe, as he had something to say
to them.   On this they all assembled and squatted
down, leaving an open space in the centre, into
which he walked with his fowling piece; this he
loaded with two balls in the presence of the assembly, after which he related the circumstance of his
loss, and stated his belief that some one of the
Indians then present had taken it.   He then told
them that he wished that every one present would
place his mouth to the muzzle of the gun, and blow
into it, assuring them that it would injure no one
innocent of the theft; but, on the other hand, if the
guilty party should attempt to do so, it would inevitably kill him.   He himself set the example of
blowing into the piece, standing muzzle upwards on
the ground; the chief followed, as well as the
whole tribe, with the exception of one man, who sat
hanging down his head, and when called upon by

the chief to follow the example of the rest refused, saying, that he would not tempt the Great Spirit, for that he had taken the tobacco, and would return it, which he accordingly did.

Whilst Mr. Mackenlie was in charge of Walla-Walla he exhibited an instance of great presence of mind under very trying circumstances. His clerk had a quarrel and fight with the son of the chief, whom he beat. The Indian thereupon collected a large party of the tribe, and rushed with them into the yard of the fort, and attempted to seize the offender for the purpose of taking his life. Mr. Mackenlie kept them off for some time, but finding he could do so no longer, he ordered one of the men to bring him out a keg of powder, the head of which he knocked in, and taking a flint and steel from his pocket, he stood over it as if about to ignite it, telling the Indians that if they did not immediately depart he would show them how a white chief could die and destroy his enemies. The Indians took the alarm, and fled through the gates, which he immediately barred against them, secretly sending the clerk the next day to another post out of their reach.

After remaining at Mr. Mackenlie's house for about three weeks, I ascended the Walhamette

River, in company with Father Acolti, a Jesuit missionary, for about thirty miles. We then disembarked and proceeded on horseback about eight miles to the Roman Catholic mission, where there is a large establishment of religieuses for the purposes of education, as well as a good brick church, situated in a beautiful prairie, surrounded with woods. It has also a nunnery occupied by six Sisters of Charity, who employ themselves in teaching the children, both white and red, amounting to forty-two pupils.

Father Acolti's residence is three miles from here, the Jesuit mission being distinct from the Roman Catholic; at least they are under separate authorities. Besides this one under Father Acolti, there are three Jesuit missions near the Rocky Mountains, and one in New Caledonia. This part of the country contains the largest tract of good land that is to be met with in Oregon. I enjoyed the hospitality of Père Acolti's establishment for three or four days, when I again returned to the Walhamette; and previously to embarking in the canoe, I ascended a high mountain, and made a sketch of the windings of the river, with the Umqua Mountains, where it takes its rise, in the distance.

After visiting Mr. Mackenlie at Oregon City
for a few days, I once more started for Fort
Vancouver. About four miles below Oregon the
Klackamuss enters the Walhamette; and, seated
on the banks at its mouth, I saw a party of
Indians of the Klackamuss tribe, and I put
ashore for the purpose of taking a sketch of them.
They were busy gambling at one of their favourite
games. Two were seated together on skins, and
immediately opposite to them sat two others,
several trinkets and ornaments being placed between them, for which they played. The game
consists in one of them having his hands covered
with a small round mat resting on the ground.
He has four small sticks in his hands, which he
disposes under the mat in certain positions, requiring
the opposite party to guess how he has placed them.
If he guesses right, the mat is handed round to the
next, and a stick is stuck up as a counter in his
favour. If wrong, a stick is stuck up on the
opposite side as a mark against him. This, like
almost all the Indian games, was accompanied
with singing; but in this case the singing was
peculiarly sweet and wild, possessing a harmony
I never heard before or since amongst Indians.

This tribe was once very numerous; but owing

to their close vicinity to Oregon City, and the ease with which they can procure spirits, they have dwindled down to six or eight lodges.

We arrived late that evening at Fort Vancouver, having paddled on all day through heavy rain and cold. This, however, is thought little of in the Columbia during the rainy seasons, as no one troubles himself with making vain attempts to avoid wet at these periods. I remained here until the 25th of March; and although the weather was very wet, I found plenty of amusement with the officers of the "Modeste," who had built stables, and selected some very good horses. With these we ran races, and chased the wild calves; the object of which latter exercise consisted principally in showing the dexterity of the rider, in stooping from his saddle and throwing the calf head-over-heels by the tail.

These sports we occasionally varied by shooting and fishing, ducks and geese and seal being in great quantities in the neighbourhood of the fort. One day, a tall, large-boned Indian came on board the "Modeste" while I was sitting below with some of the officers. The Indian was dressed, as usual, in full costume, as they would call it in California (where, it is said, a shirt collar and spurs are con-

sidered the only clothing indispensably necessary);
that is to say, he had his paddle in his hand, and
walked about the deck with great gravity, examining
the cannon, and other things equally incomprehensible to him, much to the amusement of the idle
sailors. The purser, no doubt from a feeling of
delicacy, took the Indian below, and gave him an
old swallow-tailed coat of his, which was adorned
with numerous brass buttons. The Indian, highly
delighted, struggled into the garment with the
greatest difficulty, as it was infinitely too small
for him, the cuffs reaching but little below the
elbow, and the front not meeting within a foot.
Having, however, succeeded in getting into it,
he perambulated the deck with tenfold dignity,
and the whole ship's crew yelled with laughter.
The extraordinary noise brought us all on deck,
and, amongst others, the captain came up. Even
his dignity could not withstand the absurdity of
the figure, to which he immediately added, by
sending his steward down for an old cocked hat
of his, which was given to the Indian. When
this was mounted the figure was complete; and
seldom has the deck of one of Her Majesty's ships
been the scene of such uproarious and violent
laughter. I made several efforts to make a sketch

of the Indian before I could succeed; and though I at length did so, yet I fear that the picture would give but a faint idea of the cause of all our merriment.

*March 25th.*—I started from the Fort for Vancouver's Island in a small wooden canoe, with a couple of Indians, and encamped at the mouth of the Walhamette.

*March 26th.* — When we arrived at the mouth of the Kattlepoutal River, twenty-six miles from Fort Vancouver, I stopped to make a sketch of the volcano, Mount St. Helen's, distant, I suppose, about thirty or forty miles. This mountain has never been visited by either Whites or Indians; the latter assert that it is inhabited by a race of beings of a different species, who are cannibals, and whom they hold in great dread; they also say that there is a lake at its base with a very extraordinary kind of fish in it, with a head more resembling that of a bear than any other animal. These superstitions are taken from the statement of a man who, they say, went to the mountain with another, and escaped the fate of his companion, who was eaten by the " Skoocooms," or evil genii. I offered a considerable bribe to any Indian who would accompany me in its exploration, but could not find one hardy enough to venture. It is of very great height, and being eternally covered with snow, is seen at a great distance. There was not a cloud visible in the sky at the time I commenced my sketch, and not a breath of air was perceptible: suddenly a stream of white smoke shot up from the crater of the mountain, and hovered a short time over its summit; it then settled down like a cap. This shape it retained for about an hour and a-half, and then gradually disappeared.

About three years before this the mountain was in a violent state of irruption for three or four days, and threw up burning stones and lava to an immense height, which ran in burning torrents down its snow-clad sides. About ten miles lower down we encamped for the night near Coffin Rock, much against the inclination of my men, whose superstition would have led them to avoid such a place. This rock gets its name from its being the place in which the Indians deposit their dead. I took a sketch of the rock before the night set in.

There is another rock lower down, on which were deposited two or three hundred of their burial canoes; but Commodore Wilkes having made a fire near the spot, it communicated to the bodies, and nearly the whole of them were consumed.

The Indians showed much indignation at the violation of a place which was held so sacred by them, and would no doubt have sought revenge had they felt themselves strong enough to do so.

*March 27th.*—As usual, the rain came down in torrents. As we neared one of the points on the river, we perceived a naked Indian watching us; as we came up he ran away to his lodge, and, to my astonishment, reappeared in the cocked hat and purser's coat aforesaid. He received me with great friendship, having recognised me, before landing, as one of the party he had seen on board the "Modeste." He took me to his lodge and gave me some boiled salmon. He seemed to take great care of his uniform; but, unfortunately, the coat would not stretch, and it now burst wide open all the way up the back, which, I have no doubt, added considerably to his comfort. After leaving him we entered the Cowlitz River, and proceeded up about eight miles and encamped on its banks. We saw a family of emigrants winding their toilsome way in quest of a spot to make their home. Their condition appeared miserable in the extreme.

*March 28th.*—One of my Indians falling sick here, I procured another Indian and proceeded up the river at a very slow rate, owing to the rapidity

of the current. The pine trees here are the largest
I have ever seen. I measured one, which had
drifted down the stream, and which had apparently
a third of its length broken off. It was still 180
feet long, and 26 feet in circumference 5 feet from
its root.

*March 29th.*—We came to another Indian burial
ground, which seemed to be highly decorated. I
wished my Indians to put ashore, but they would
not do so. I was obliged, therefore, to put them
out of the canoe on the opposite side of the river,
and paddle the canoe over by myself. I have no
doubt that they would have opposed my doing so
had it not been for the name which I had already
acquired amongst the Indians, of being a great
medicine-man, on account of the likenesses which
I had taken. My power of pourtraying the features
of individuals was attributed entirely to supernatural
agency, and I found that, in looking at my
pictures, they always covered their eyes with
their hands and looked through the fingers ; this
being also the invariable custom when looking at a
dead person. On arriving at the place I found it
lavishly decorated with numerous articles, of supposed
utility and ornament, for the convenience of
the defunct in the journey to the world of spirits.

These articles consisted of blankets, tin cups, pots, pans, kettles, plates, baskets, horn bowls, and spoons, with shreds of cloth of various colours. One canoe, which was decorated more highly than the rest, I examined particularly. All the articles

No. 9. — Burial-place on the Cowlitz River.

appended to it were rendered useless for this world by either tearing, breaking, or boring holes in them, the Indians believing that they would be made whole again by the Great Spirit. On examining the interior of a canoe I found a great number of ioquas and other shells, together with beads and rings: even the mouth of the deceased was filled with these articles. The body itself was carefully enveloped in numerous folds of matting made of rushes. At the bottom of the canoe lay a bow and arrow, a paddle, a spear, and a kind of pick, made of horn, for digging the camas roots; the top of the canoe, immediately over the body, had a covering of bark, and holes were bored in the bottom to allow the water to run out. These canoes are always placed on wooden supports, suspended in the branches of trees, or placed upon isolated rocks in the river, to keep them beyond the reach of ravenous animals. Sketch No. 9 represents this burial place.

During my stay the Indians watched me closely from the opposite bank, and, on my return, they examined me as minutely as they well could with their eyes to see that I had not brought anything away with me. Had I been so imprudent as to have done so I should probably have answered for the sacrilege with my life, death being the certain penalty to the most trifling violation of the sanctity of a coffin canoe. I endeavoured to discover who was buried in the richly decorated canoe, but the only information I could get from them was that the

deceased was the daughter of a Chinook chief. The Indians here have a superstitious dread of mentioning the name of any person after death, nor will they tell you their own names, which can only be found out from a third party. One of the men asked me if my desire to know his name proceeded from a wish to steal it. It is not an uncommon thing for a chief, when he wishes to pay you a very high compliment, to give and call you by his own name, and adopt some other for himself.

*March 30th.*—We landed at the Cowlitz farm, which belongs to the Hudson's Bay Company. Large quantities of wheat are raised at this place. I had a fine view of Mount St. Helen's throwing up a long column of dark smoke into the clear blue sky. Here I remained until the 5th of April, and took the likeness of Kiscox, the chief of the Cowlitz Indians, a small tribe of about 200. They flatten their heads and speak a language very similar to the Chinooks. They were very friendly to me and I was a good deal amongst them. Sketch No. 10 is Caw-wacham, a woman of the tribe, with her child under the process of having its head flattened. It was with some difficulty that I persuaded her to sit, as she seemed apprehensive that it would be injurious to her. On the 5th of April I procured

horses to cross to Nasquala at Puget's Sound, and
rain poured down in torrents the whole day, making the swamps nearly impassable. We encamped
in the evening near a small village of Cowlitz
Indians, whom we found unusually kind and civil.

*April 6th.* — We passed over what is called the
Mud Mountain. The mud is so very deep in this
pass that we were compelled to dismount and drag
our horses through it by the bridle; the poor
beasts being up to their bellies in mud of the
tenacity of bird-lime. This evening we encamped in
the Prairie de Bute. This is remarkable for having
innumerable round elevations, touching each other
like so many hemispheres, of ten or twelve yards in
circumference, and four or five feet in height. I
dug one of them open, but found nothing in it but
loose stones, although I went four or five feet
down. The whole surface is thickly covered with
coarse grass. I travelled twenty-two miles through
this extraordinary looking prairie.

*April 7th.* — We found some difficulty in crossing the Nasqually River, as the rains had flooded
it, and we were obliged to adopt the usual plan
where canoes cannot be obtained, that is, swimming
at our horses' tails, and floating our things over in
skin baskets. A couple of hours brought us to

Nasqually, which was established by a company called the Puget's Sound Company, for grazing and farming. When I visited it, it had about 6000 sheep and 2000 horned cattle. Its site is beautiful, on the banks of the eastern end of Puget's Sound. The land is inferior to that in some other parts of the same district, the soil being gravelly; the grass, however, grows luxuriantly, and the mildness of the climate adapts it well for grazing purposes, as it is never necessary to house the animals. The wool, which is good, finds its way to the English market by the Company's ships, and the cattle are slaughtered and salted for the Sandwich Islands and the Russian dominions. The Indians about here are of very large stature; indeed, the largest that I have met with on the continent. The women are particularly large and stout. The tribe numbers between five or six hundred. They flatten their heads, but use a language different from the Chinooks. I made a sketch of Lach-oh-lett, their head chief, and his daughter, who wore a cap made of grass of different colours, much used by the women.

## CHAP. XIV.

Fort Victoria —Accidental Clover.—Blankets of Dog's Hair.—Aprons of Bark.—A Chief's Inauguration.—Monstrous Sturgeon. —Crows which Feed on Fish. — The Domestic Institution. — The Dead Slave.—Frightening a Native.—Washing the Dead.—The Game of Lehallum.—An Expensive Feast.—Medicine Caps.

*April 8th.* — I LEFT Nasqually this morning with six Indians in a canoe, and continued paddling on the whole day and the following night, as the tide seemed favourable, not stopping till 2 P.M., when we reached Fort Victoria on Vancouver's Island, having travelled ninety miles without stopping. Fort Victoria stands upon the banks of an inlet in the island about seven miles long and a quarter of a mile wide, forming a safe and convenient harbour, deep enough for any sized vessel. Its Indian name is the Esquimelt, or, Place for gathering Camas, great quantities of that vegetable being found in the neighbourhood. On my arrival I was kindly welcomed by Mr. Finlayson, the gentleman in charge. He gave me a comfortable room, which I made my head-quarters during the two months I was occupied in sketching excursions amongst the Indians in the neighbourhood and along the surrounding coasts.

The soil of this locality is good, and wheat is grown in considerable abundance. Clover grows plentifully, and is supposed to have sprung from accidental seeds which had fallen from the packages of goods brought from England; many of which are made up in hay.

The interior of the island has not been explored to any extent except by the Indians, who represent it as badly supplied with water in the summer, and the water obtained from a well dug at the fort was found to be too brackish for use. The appearance of the interior, when seen from the coast, is rocky and mountainous, evidently volcanic; the trees are large, principally oak and pine. The timbers of a vessel of some magnitude were being got out. The establishment is very large, and must eventually become the great depôt for the business of the Company. They had ten white men and forty Indians engaged in building new stores and warehouses. On the opposite side of the harbour, facing the fort, stands a village of Clal-lums Indians. They boast of being able to

P

turn out 500 warriors, armed chiefly with bows and arrows. The lodges are built of cedar like the Chinook lodges, but much larger, some of them being sixty or seventy feet long.

The men wear no clothing in summer, and nothing but a blanket in winter, made either of dog's hair alone, or dog's hair and goosedown mixed, frayed cedar-bark, or wildgoose skin, like the Chinooks. They have a peculiar breed of small dogs with long hair of a brownish black and a clear white. These dogs are bred for clothing purposes. The hair is cut off with a knife and mixed with goosedown and a little white earth, with a view of curing the feathers. This is then beaten together with sticks, and twisted into threads by rubbing it down the thigh with the palm of the hand, in the same way that a shoemaker forms his waxend, after which it undergoes a second twisting on a distaff to increase its firmness. The cedar bark is frayed and twisted into threads in a similar manner. These threads are then woven into blankets by a very simple loom of their own contrivance. A single thread is wound over rollers at the top and bottom of a square frame, so as to form a continuous woof through which an alternate thread is carried by the hand, and pressed closely together by a sort of wooden comb; by turning the rollers every part of the woof is brought within reach of the weaver; by this means a bag is formed, open at each end, which being cut down makes a square blanket. The women wear only an apron of twisted cedar-bark shreds, tied round the waist and hanging down in front only, almost to the knees. They however, use the blankets more than the men do, but certainly not from any feeling of delicacy.

This tribe flatten the head, but their language varies very much from the Chinook; however, the same patois used on the Columbia is spoken by many of them, and I was thus enabled to communicate easily with them. I took a sketch of Cheaclach, their head chief, of whose inauguration I heard the following account from an eye-witness. On his father becoming too old to fulfil the duties of head chief, the son was called upon by the tribe to take his place; on which occasion he left the mountains for the ostensible purpose of fasting and dreaming for thirty days and nights; these Indians, like all other tribes, placing great confidence in dreams, and believing that it is necessary to undergo a long fast whenever they are desirous of inducing one of any importance. At the end of the period assigned, the tribe prepared a great feast. After covering himself with a thick covering of grease and goosedown, he rushed into the midst of the village, seized a small dog, and began devouring it alive, this being a customary preliminary on such occasions. The tribe collected about him singing and dancing in the wildest manner, on which he approached those whom he most regarded and bit their bare shoulders or arms, which was considered by them as a high mark of distinction, more especially those from whom he took the piece clean out and swallowed it. Of the women he took no notice.

I have seen many men on the North-west coast of the Pacific who bore frightful marks of what they regarded as an honourable distinction; nor is this the only way in which their persons become disfigured. I have myself seen a young girl bleeding most profusely from gashes inflicted by her own hand over her arms and bosom with a sharp flint, on the occasion of losing a near relative. After some time spent in singing and dancing, Chea-clach retired with his people to the feast prepared inside a large lodge, which consisted principally of whale's blubber, in their opinion the greatest of all delicacies, although they have salmon, cod, sturgeon, and other excellent fish in great abundance.

All the tribes about here subsist almost entirely upon fish, which they obtain with so little trouble during all seasons of the year, that they are probably the laziest race of people in the world. Sturgeon are caught in considerable numbers, and here attain an enormous size, weighing from four to six hundred weight; this is done by means of a long pointed spear handle seventy to eighty feet in length, fitted into, but not actually fastened to, a barbed spear-head, to which is attached a line, with which they feel along the bottom of the river where the sturgeon are found lying at the spawning season. Upon feeling the fish the barbed spear is driven in and the handle withdrawn. The fish is then gradually drawn in by the line, which being very long, allows the sturgeon to waste his great strength, so that he can with safety be taken into the canoe or towed ashore. Most of their fishing lines are formed of a long seaweed, which is often found 150 feet long, of equal thickness throughout the whole length, and about as thick as a black-lead pencil; while wet it is very strong. Their fish-hooks are made of pine-roots, made something in the shape of our ordinary hooks, but attached differently to the line; the barb is made of bone.

Clams are in great plenty, and are preyed on in great numbers by the crows, who seize them in their claws and fly up with them to some height, and then let them drop on the rocks, which of course smashes the shell to pieces. I have watched dozens of them at this singular employment. A small oyster of a fine flavour is found in the bays in great plenty. Seal, wild ducks and geese, are also in great numbers.

The Indians are extremely fond of herring-roe, which they collect in the following manner:—Cedar branches are sunk to the bottom of the river in shallow places by placing upon them a few heavy stones, taking care not to cover the green foliage, as the fish prefer spawning on anything green. The branches are all covered by the next morning with the spawn, which is washed off into their waterproof baskets, to the bottom of which it sinks; it is then squeezed by the hand into small balls and dried, and is very palatable.

The only other vegetable besides the camas and wappatoos that the Indians use, are the roots of fern roasted, which here grow to a very large size.

Slavery in its most cruel form exists among the

Indians of the whole coast, from California to
Behring's Straits, the stronger tribes making slaves
of all the others they can conquer. In the interior,
where there is but little warfare, slavery does not
exist. On the coast a custom prevails which
authorises the seizure and enslavement, unless ran-
somed by his friends, of every Indian met with at a
distance from his tribe, although they may not be
at war with each other. The master exercises the
power of life and death over his slaves, whom he
sacrifices at pleasure in gratification of any superstitious or other whim of the moment.

One morning while I was sketching, I saw upon
the rocks the dead body of a young woman,
thrown out to the vultures and crows, whom I
had seen a few days previously walking about in
perfect health. Mr. Finlayson, the gentleman in
charge of Fort Victoria, accompanied me to the
lodge she belonged to, where we found an Indian woman, her mistress, who made light of her
death, and was doubtless the cause of it. She
told us that a slave had no right to burial, and
became perfectly furious when Mr. Finlayson told
her that the slave was far better than herself. " I,"
she exclaimed, " the daughter of a chief, no better
than a dead slave!" and bridling up with all the

dignity she could assume, she stalked out, and next morning she had up her lodge and was gone. I was also told by an eye-witness, of a chief, who having erected a colossal idol of wood, sacrificed five slaves to it, barbarously murdering them at its base, and asking in a boasting manner who amongst them could afford to kill so many slaves.

These Indians also flatten their heads, and are far more superstitious than any I have met with. They believe, for instance, that if they can procure the hair of an enemy and confine it with a frog in a hole, the head from which it came will suffer all the torments that the frog endures in its living grave. They are never seen to spit without carefully obliterating all traces of their saliva. This they do lest an enemy should find it, in which case they believe he would have the power of doing them some injury. They always spit on their blankets, if they happen to wear one at the time.

I was indebted to the superstitious fears which they attached to my pictures for the safety and ease with which I mingled amongst them. One of them gave me a great deal of annoyance by continually following and watching me wherever I went, for the purpose of warning the other Indians against my sketching them, telling them that it would expose them to all sorts of ill luck. I repeatedly requested him to desist, but in vain. At last I bethought me of looking steadily at himself, paper and pencil in hand, as if in the act of taking his likeness; when he became greatly alarmed, and asked me what I was about. I replied, " I am taking a sketch of you." He earnestly begged of me to stop, and promised never to annoy me again.

These Indians have a great dance, which is called " The Medicine Mask Dance;" this is performed both before and after any important action of the tribe, such as fishing, gathering camas, or going on a war party, either for the purpose of gaining the goodwill of the Great Spirit in their undertaking, or else in honour of him for the success which has attended them. Six or eight of the principal men of the tribe, generally medicine-men, adorn themselves with masks cut out of some soft light wood with feathers, highly painted and ornamented, with the eyes and mouth ingeniously made to open and shut. In their hands they hold carved rattles, which are shaken in time to a monotonous song or humming noise (for there are no words to it) which is sung by the whole company as they slowly dance round and round in a circle.

Among the Clal-lums and other tribes inhabiting this region, I have never heard any traditions as to their former origin, although such traditions are common amongst those on the east side of the Rocky Mountains. They do not believe in any future state of punishment, although in this world they suppose themselves exposed to the malicious designs of the skoocoom, or evil genius, to whom they attribute all their misfortune and ill luck.

The good spirit is called Hias-Soch-a-la-Ti-Yah, that is, the great high chief, from whom they obtain all that is good in this life, and to whose happy and peaceful hunting-grounds they will all eventually go to reside for ever in comfort and abundance. The medicine-men of the tribe are supposed to possess a mysterious influence with these two spirits, either for good or evil. They form a secret society, the initiation into which is accompanied with great ceremony and much expense. The candidate has to prepare a feast for his friends and all who choose to partake of it, and make presents to the other medicine-men. A lodge is prepared for him which he enters, and remains alone for three days and nights without food, whilst those already initiated keep dancing and singing round the lodge during the whole time.

After this fast, which is supposed to endue him with wonderful skill, he is taken up apparently lifeless and plunged into the nearest cold water, where they rub and wash him until he revives: this they call "washing the dead." As soon as he revives, he runs into the woods, and soon returns dressed as a medicine-man, which generally consists of the light down of the goose stuck all over their bodies and heads with thick grease, and a mantle of frayed cedar bark, with the medicine rattle in his hand. He now collects all his property, blankets, shells, and ornaments, and distributes the whole amongst his friends, trusting for his future support to the fees of his profession. The dancing and singing are still continued with great vigour, during the division of the property, at the conclusion of which the whole party again sit down to feast, apparently with miraculous appetites, the quantity of food consumed being perfectly incredible.

Their lodges are the largest buildings of any description that I have met with amongst Indians. They are divided in the interior into compartments, so as to accommodate eight or ten families, and are well built, considering that the boards are split from the logs with bone wedges; but they succeed in getting them out with great smoothness and regularity. I took a sketch one day while a party were engaged in gambling in the centre of the lodge. The game is called lehallum, and is played with ten small circular pieces of wood, one of which is marked black; these pieces are shuffled about rapidly by the player between two bundles of frayed cedar bark. His opponent suddenly stops his shuffling, and endeavours to guess in which bundle the blackened piece is concealed. They are so passionately fond of this game that they frequently pass two or three consecutive days and nights at it without ceasing.

Saw-se-a the head chief of the Cowitchins, from the Gulf of Georgia, an inveterate gambler, was engaged at the game. He had come to the Esquimelt on a friendly visit. This chief was a great warrior in his younger days, and received an arrow through the cheek in one of his battles. He took many captives, whom he usually sold to the tribes further north, thus diminishing their chance of escaping back through a hostile country to their own people, the northern tribes making slaves only of those living south of them. He possessed much of what is considered wealth amongst the Indians, and it gradually accumulated from tributes which he exacted from his people. On his possessions reaching a certain amount it is customary to make a great feast, to which all contribute. The neighbouring chiefs with whom he is in amity are invited, and at the conclusion of the entertainment, he distributes all he has collected since the last feast, perhaps three or four years preceding, among his guests as presents. The amount of property thus collected and given away by a chief is sometimes very considerable. I have heard of one possessing as many as twelve bales of blankets, from twenty to thirty guns, with numberless pots, kettles, and pans, knives, and other articles of cutlery, and great quantities of beads, and other trinkets, as well as numerous beautiful Chinese boxes, which find their way here from the Sandwich Islands. The object in thus giving his treasures away is to add to his own importance in the eyes of others, his own people often boasting of how much their chief had given away, and exhibiting with pride such things as they had received themselves from him.

I also took a sketch of his son, No. 11, Cul-chillum. He had a medicine cap on, to which he attached great importance. It was made of human hair, taken from the heads of persons killed in battle, and ornamented with feathers. This, he told me, he only wore on great occasions, such as

his present visit to the Clal-lums. On my expressing a wish to purchase it, he told me that
he valued it too highly to part with it; nor would

No. 11. — Portrait of Cul-chil-lum, with Medicine Cap.

he allow me to take it to my tent to finish this
sketch without himself accompanying it, for fear
it might be deprived of some of its magical
properties.

# CHAP. XV.

A Coasting Trip.—Indian Curiosity. — Rather Violent Quacks. — An Awkward Hint. — Fighting for a Whale. — A Warm Siege. — Running a Deadly Muck.—Catching Wild Ducks. — A Great Unknown. — The Fate of the " Tonquin." — Fishing for Money. — Shawstun the Ugly — Caledonian Suttee. — Beautiful Biglips. — Price of a Second Spouse.

As I was desirous to coast round the Straits of De Fuca and visit the tribes on its shores, I employed Chea-clach the head chief and four of his people to take me and the interpreter of the fort round the straits in his canoe ; and on the morning of the 6th of May we started about 10 o'clock, running up the east side of Vancouver's Island, and crossed the canal De Aro to the main land. On nearing an Indian village, which contained, as I afterwards found, between five or six hundred Indians, they came rushing down to the beach in an attitude apparently hostile, and as the boats of the exploring expedition had been attacked the year before at the same place, we naturally felt some apprehensions for our safety.

We had no sooner approached the shore than a dense crowd surrounded us, wading up to their middles in water, and seizing our canoe dragged us all high and dry upon the shore, and inquired what we wanted. I replied, that I would explain my business to their chief, who immediately stepped forward in a friendly manner. Having told him that my business was to visit all the Indians, and to take likenesses of the head chiefs and great warriors, he took me to his lodge, where I seated myself on a mat with him in front of me and commenced my drawing. In a few minutes the place was crowded, and when it could hold no more, the people clambered to the top of the lodge and tore off the mats from the supports, to which they clung, one upon another, like a swarm of bees, peering down upon us. Look which way I could it seemed one solid mass of hideous faces, daubed with red and white mud.

I hastily finished my sketch and hurried away, first giving the chief a plug of tobacco for his civility. His name was Chea-clach, chief of the Clallums. On coming over I found the wind so strong that I thought it advisable to risk an encampment, and pitched my tent about two hundred yards from the village. We were soon surrounded by hundreds of Indians, the chief among the rest. I gave the latter some supper, and all the news, which he eagerly inquired after, and on my telling him I was tired and wished to go to sleep, which I could not do while so many of his people were about, he instantly arose and desired them to retire, which was promptly obeyed, he going away with them.

About 10 o'clock at night I strolled into the village, and on hearing a great noise in one of the lodges I entered it, and found an old woman supporting one of the handsomest Indian girls I had ever seen. She was in a state of nudity. Cross-legged and naked, in the middle of the room sat the medicine-man, with a wooden dish of water before him; twelve or fifteen other men were sitting round the lodge. The object in view was to cure the girl of a disease affecting her side. As soon as my presence was noticed a space was cleared for me to sit down. The officiating medicine-man appeared in a state of profuse perspiration from the exertions he had used, and soon took his seat among the rest as if quite exhausted; a younger medicine-man then took his place in front of the bowl, and close beside the patient. Throwing off his blanket he commenced singing and gesticulating in the most violent manner, whilst the others kept time by beating with little sticks on hollow wooden bowls and drums, singing continually. After exercising himself in this manner for about half an hour, until the perspiration ran down his body, he darted suddenly upon the young woman, catching hold of her side with his teeth and shaking her for a few minutes, while the patient seemed to suffer great agony. He then relinquished his hold, and cried out he had got it, at the same time holding his hands to his mouth; after which he plunged them in the water and pretended to hold down with great difficulty the disease which he had extracted, lest it might spring out and return to its victim.

At length, having obtained the mastery over it, he turned round to me in an exulting manner, and held something up between the finger and thumb of each hand, which had the appearance of a piece of cartilage, whereupon one of the Indians sharpened his knife, and divided it in two, leaving one end in each hand. One of the pieces he threw into the water, and the other into the fire, accompanying the action with a diabolical noise, which none but a medicine-man can make. After which he got up perfectly satisfied with himself, although the poor patient seemed to me anything but relieved by the violent treatment she had undergone.

*May 7th.*—We this morning left our encampment before daylight, without waiting to pay our respects to the chief. In the afternoon we touched at Whitby's Island, which divides the Straits of De Fuca from Puget's Sound. A Catholic mission had been established on the island some few years before, but was obliged to be given up, owing to the turbulent disposition of the Indians, who, though friendly to the Hudson Bay Company as traders, look with great suspicion upon others who attempt to settle there, fearing that the whites would attempt to dispossess them of their lands.

On approaching the village of Toanichum, we perceived two stout bastions of logs, well calculated for defence in Indian warfare, and built with considerable skill. As our canoe neared the land, I observed them hurrying towards these bastions, and shortly afterwards we heard several shots. Supposing this to be intended as a salute, we drew still nearer, and were astonished at hearing more discharges, and seeing the balls fall near our canoe. My Indians immediately ceased paddling, and it was with the utmost difficulty that I could prevail on them to proceed. Had we shown the least inclination to retreat, I have no doubt that the firing would have been continued, and with better aim. However, on my landing and asking what they meant, they said it was only done for the purpose of letting me know that they were in the possession of fire-arms.

They afterwards treated me very hospitably. Lock-hi-num, the chief, offered us all the supplies at his command. It was, however, with the greatest difficulty that I could prevail on him to let me take his likeness; but at last I succeeded, by showing him the likenesses of several other chiefs, and telling him that they were intended to be shown to his Great Mother, the Queen, who no doubt would be much disappointed if his was not amongst the rest. I remained amongst them two or three hours, and sketched the village. I also succeeded in getting a very good-looking woman, the wife of the second chief, to sit for me. She had the flattest head of any I had seen in that vicinity. We then crossed over to the south side of the strait, and encamped for the night.

*May* 8*th.*—Proceeded up the south side of the straits in our canoe, and encamped on a long sand spit, projecting into the straits three or four miles.

*May 9th.*—Made a portage across the spit, and by the evening reached I-eh-nus, a Clallum village or fort. It was composed of a double row of strong pickets, the outer ones about twenty feet high, and the inner row about five feet, enclosing a space of 150 feet square. The whole of this inner space is roofed in, and divided into small compartments, or pens, for the use of each separate family. There were about 200 of the tribe in the fort at the time of my arrival. Their chief, Yates-sut-soot, received me with great cordiality. I remained with them three days, and all the tribe treated me with kindness, with one solitary exception, proceeding from a superstitious fear that the presence of a white man in a lodge would produce sickness in the family. Yates-sut-soot was very apprehensive of an attack from the Macaw Indians, and believing my powers and influence as a medicine-man to be of much importance, eagerly asked me which side I would take, in the event of their coming. I replied, that as long as they treated me well I would be their friend.

A few months before my arrival a great battle had been fought with the Macaws, in which the

Clallums had suffered very severely. It originated in the Clallums having taken possession of the body of a whale which had been killed by the Macaws, but had got away, and was drifted by the current to the village. The Macaws demanded a share of the spoil, and also the return of their spears, some fifteen or twenty in number, which were sticking in the carcase; both demands were refused, and a feeling of animosity sprang up between the tribes.

There are few whales now caught on the coast, but the Indians are most enthusiastic in the hunt, and the blubber is highly prized amongst them; it is cut into strips about four inches wide and two feet long, and eaten generally with dried fish.

Their manner of catching the whale is ingenious, and from the description which I received of the hunt must be very exciting. Upon a whale being seen blowing in the offing, they rush down to their large canoes, and push off with ten or twelve men in each. Each canoe is furnished with a number of strong seal-skin bags filled with air, and made with great care and skill, capable of containing about ten gallons each. To each bag is attached a barbed spear-head, made of bone or iron, when they can get it, by a strong string, eight or nine feet long, and in the socket of the spear-head is fitted a handle, seven or eight feet in length. Upon coming up with the whale, the barbed heads with the bags attached are driven into him and the handles withdrawn. The attack is continually renewed, until the whale is no longer able to sink from the buoyancy of the bags, when he is despatched and towed ashore. They are sometimes led twenty or thirty miles out to sea in the chase, but such is the admirable construction of their canoes, and so skilfully are they managed, that an accident rarely happens.

A few months after the quarrel about the whale, the brother of Yellow-cum, the head chief of the Macaws, went to Fort Victoria to trade for ammunition and other necessaries, and on his return was attacked by the Clallums. He and one of his men were killed, but three others escaped, and succeeded in getting to Cape Flattery, where Yellow-cum resided. Immediately upon hearing of the death of his brother, Yellow-cum fitted out twelve of his largest canoes, with twenty warriors in each, and made a sudden descent upon I-eh-nus; but he soon perceived that he had little chance of success while the Clallums remained within their enclosure completely protected by the logs, while his men were exposed without any shelter to the galling fire which was kept up through the openings between the pickets. He accordingly sent some of his party to the westward side of the fort, who set fire to the grass and wood, which soon communicated with the buildings, while he and the rest of his party kept watch to prevent any from escaping. The Clallums were soon forced to rush out and cover the retreat of their women and children into the mountains. Yates-sut-soot and Yellow-cum fought with great bravery hand to hand, with nothing but their knives, until they were separated in the mêlée. I saw one of the Clallums who had been shockingly gashed in the battle, having had to run through a long line of the Macaws, each of whom made a cut at him as he passed. The buildings were only partly consumed. Yellow-cum took eighteen prisoners, mostly females, who were made slaves, and he had eight heads stuck on poles placed in the bows of the canoes on his return. These heads are carried to their village, and placed in front of the lodge of the warriors who had killed them as trophies. These Indians do not scalp their enemies.

Near the village are numerous singular graves

with different erections over them, on which the Indians place the offerings for the dead.

*May 12th.* — We left with the intention of returning to Vancouver's Island, but the wind being very violent we had to put back to the shore, which we coasted for twelve or fourteen miles, until we came to the mouth of a river. The land to the south of us rises in one continuous range of high mountains far as the eye can reach, the peaks of many of which are covered with snow, even at this period of the year. We ascended the river about a mile to an Indian fishing station called Suck. The whole breadth of the stream is obstructed by stakes and open work of willow and other branches, with holes at intervals leading into wicker compartments, which the fish enter in their way up the river from the sea. Once in they cannot get out, as the holes are formed with wicker work inside shaped something like a funnel or a wire mouse-trap. In this preserve they are speared without trouble when required, and the village has thus a constant supply of food. They were catching great quantities at the time of my arrival, and we obtained an abundant supply for a small piece of tobacco.

These Indians also take a great many ducks by

means of a fine net stretched between two posts about thirty feet high, and fifty or sixty feet apart. This is erected in a narrow valley through which the ducks fly in the evening. A smoky fire is made at the bottom of the net, which prevents the ducks from seeing it, and when they fly against it they become confused and fall down, when they are seized by the Indians.

The wind being still too strong for us to venture, we remained until the 14th. Chaw-u-wit, the chief's daughter, allowed me to take her likeness. Whilst she was sitting a great many of the Indians surrounded us, causing her much annoyance, as their native bashfulness renders all squaws peculiarly sensitive to any public notice or ridicule. She was, perhaps, about the best-looking girl I had seen in the straits, which is certainly no very high compliment to the rest of the female population.

Chea-clack considering that our canoe was too small, succeeded in changing it for a larger one, and at 3 o'clock A. M. we embarked and proceeded to make a traverse of thirty-two miles in an open sea. When we had been out for about a couple of hours the wind increased to a perfect gale, and blowing against an ebb tide caused a heavy swell. We were obliged to keep one man constantly baling to prevent our being swamped.

The Indians on board now commenced one of their wild chants, which increased to a perfect yell whenever a wave larger than the rest approached; this was accompanied with blowing and spitting against the wind as if they were in angry contention with the evil spirit of the storm. It was altogether a scene of the most wild and intense excitement: the mountainous waves roaming round our little canoe as if to engulph us every moment, the wind howling over our heads, and the yelling Indians, made it actually terrific. I was surprised at the dexterity with which they managed the canoe, all putting out their paddles on the windward side whenever a wave broke, thus breaking its force and guiding the spray over our heads to the other side of the boat.

It was with the greatest anxiety that I watched each coming wave as it came thundering down, and I must confess that I felt considerable fear as to the event. However, we arrived safely at the fort at 2 P. M., without further damage than what we suffered from intense fatigue, as might be expected, from eleven hours' hard work, thoroughly soaked and without food; but even this soon passed away before the cheerful fire and "hearty" dinner with which we were welcomed at Fort Victoria. One of the Indians told me he had no fear during the storm, except on my account, as his brethren could easily reach the shore by swimming, even should the distance have been ten miles.

A couple of days after my arrival at the fort, I was engaged in taking the likeness of an Indian. The door of my room was suddenly thrown open, and an Indian entered of a very plain and unprepossessing appearance. As I was unwilling to be disturbed, I rather unceremoniously dismissed the intruder, and closed the door on him, supposing him to be some common Indian; for were I to admit all comers, I should have been annoyed from morning till night. About half an hour afterwards, Mr. Finlayson came in, and told me that the great Yellow-cum, the head chief of the Macaws at Cape Flattery, had arrived at the fort. I had heard so much of this chief, both from his enemies, the Clallums at I-eh-nus, and the Indians at Fort Vancouver, that I had determined to go to Cape Flattery, a distance of sixty miles, to see him. I was therefore very glad of his coming, as it would save me the journey; and I immediately went out in search of him, and was not a little astonished and vexed to find in him the visitor I had so rudely sent out of my room. I of course apologised, by stating my ignorance of who he was, and told him how anxious I had been to see him, and of my intention of going to Cape Flattery for that purpose. He said that he willingly acquitted me of any intentional insult; but he had felt extremely mortified at being treated so before so many Indians.

He accompanied me to my room, where I made a sketch of him, and had from him a recital of much of his private history. Yellow-cum's father was the pilot of the unfortunate "Tonquin," the vessel sent out by John Jacob Astor to trade with the Indians north of Vancouver's Island, mentioned in Washington Irving's " Astoria." He was the only survivor who escaped from the vessel previous to her being blown up, the rest of the unfortunate crew having been butchered on board, or blown up with the ship. It was impossible to obtain a clear narrative of this melancholy event, as no white man lived to tell the tale.

Yellow-cum is the wealthiest man of his tribe. His property consists principally of slaves and ioquas, a small shell found at Cape Flattery, and only there, in great abundance. These shells are used as money, and a great traffic is carried on among all the tribes by means of them. They are obtained at the bottom of the sea, at a considerable depth, by means of a long pole stuck in a flat board about fifteen inches square. From this board a number of bone pieces project, which, when pressed down, enter the hollow ends of the shells, which seem to be attached to the bottom by their small ends. The shells stick on the pieces, and are thus brought to the surface. They are from an inch and a half to two inches in length, and are white, slender, and hollow, and tapering to a point; slightly curved, and about the size of an ordinary tobacco-pipe stem. They are valuable in proportion to their length, and their value increases according to a fixed ratio, forty shells being the standard number to extend a fathom's length; which number, in that case, is equal in value to a beaver skin; but if thirty-nine be found large enough to make the fathom, it would be worth two beavers' skins; if thirty-eight, three skins; and so on, increasing one beaver skin for every shell less than the standard number.

Yellow-cum presented me with a pair of ear

ornaments of these shells, consisting of seventy or eighty shells in each. His wealth also partly consisted of sea otter skins, which are the most valuable fur found on the North American coast, their usual value in the tariff being twelve blankets; two blankets being equal to a gun; tobacco and ammunition and other things in proportion. The blanket is the standard by which the value of all articles on the north-west coast is calculated. Independent of his wealth, he possesses vast influence over all the tribes, and has become head chief from his own personal prowess and ability, and not from any hereditary claim to that dignity. It may be adduced, as a proof of the courage of this chief, and of his personal confidence, that I saw him at the fort surrounded by, and in cheerful conversation with, several of the chiefs of the Clallums, with whom he had often been engaged in deadly conflict. His prudence, however, led him to remain inside the fort after nightfall.

I visited the lodges of the Eus-ā-nich Indians, who were on a visit. The chief was very rich, and had eight wives with him. I made him understand, by showing him some sketches, that I wished to take his likeness. This was, however,

opposed so violently by his ladies, that I was glad
to escape out of reach of their tongues, as they
were all chattering together, while he sat like a
Grand Turk, evidently flattered by the interest
they showed for his welfare. A few days afterwards, I met the chief some distance from his
camp, and alone, when he willingly consented to
let me take his likeness upon my giving him a
piece of tobacco.

In one of my daily excursions, I was particularly struck by the ugliness of an Indian whom I
met. Upon inquiry, I found he was Shawstun,
the head chief of the Sinahōmās. He inquired
very earnestly if my sketching him would not
involve the risk of his dying; and after I had
finished the sketch, and given him a piece of
tobacco, he held it up for some moments, and
said it was a small recompense for risking his life.
He followed me afterwards for two or three days,
begging of me to destroy the picture; and at last,
to get rid of him, I made a rough copy of it,
which I tore up in his presence, pretending that
it was the original.

I remained on Vancouver's Island until the
10th of June; and perhaps it would be as well, before my taking leave of it, to give a general sum-

mary of the information I acquired, from personal observation, and from the gentlemen of the Hudson's Bay Company, respecting the characteristics of the different tribes inhabiting these regions.

The Indians south of the Columbia River tattoo themselves below the mouth, which gives a light blue appearance to the countenance. Those at the mouth of the Columbia, and for a hundred miles up it, as well as those at Puget's Sound, and the Straits of De Fuea, and at the southern part of Vancouver's Island, have their heads flattened down in their infancy, as represented in the sketches of the Chinook tribe. Those inhabiting the north part of the island have their heads compressed into a conical shape during infancy. This is done by means of a bandage, which is wound round the forehead, and gradually tightened, until the head becomes of the required shape.

The next tribe lying north of these on the continent are called by the voyageurs " Babines," or Big-lips, from the fact of the females having their under lips enlarged by the insertion of a piece of wood. A small, slender piece of bone is inserted through the under lip of the infant, from below upwards, and is gradually enlarged, until a flat piece of wood three inches long, and an inch and

R

a half wide, has caused the lip to protrude to a frightful extent, the protrusion increasing with age. Great importance is attached to the size of the lip, as it constitutes the standard of female beauty ; it also marks the difference between native free women and their slaves.

When the stick is removed on any occasion the lip drops down to the chin, presenting one of the most disgusting spectacles imaginable.

The men sometimes wear a ring through the nose, formed of bone, or brass if they can get it ; but the practice is not universal. They wear a cap made of the fibres of cedar-bark, woven very finely together, and a blanket made from the wool of the mountain sheep ; they are very valuable, and take years in making. For one which I procured with great difficulty, I had to pay five pounds of tobacco, ten charges of ammunition, one blanket, one pound of beads, two check shirts, and one ounce of vermilion.

.The next tribes, still more north than the last, insert beads of various colours, two-thirds of their depth, into the whole length of the upper lip, giving it the appearance of so much bead work.

In the interior of New Caledonia, which is east of Vancouver's Island and north of the Columbia, among the tribe called "Taw-wa-tins," who are also Babines, and also among other tribes in their neighbourhood, the custom prevails of burning the bodies, with circumstances of peculiar barbarity to the widows of the deceased. The dead body of the husband is laid naked upon a large heap of resinous wood, his wife is then placed upon the body and covered over with a skin; the pile is then lighted, and the poor woman is compelled to remain until she is nearly suffocated, when she is allowed to descend as best she can through the smoke and flames. No sooner, however, does she reach the ground, than she is expected to prevent the body from becoming distorted by the action of the fire on the muscles and sinews; and whenever such an event takes place she must, with her bare hands, restore the burning corpse to its proper position ; her person being the whole time exposed to the scorching effects of the intense heat. Should she fail in the due performance of this indispensable rite, from weakness or the intensity of her pain, she is held up by some one until the body is consumed. A continual singing and beating of drums is kept up throughout the ceremony, which drowns her cries. Afterwards she must collect the unconsumed pieces of bone and ashes and put them into a bag made for the purpose, which she has to carry on her back for three years ; remaining for the time a slave to her husband's relations, and being neither allowed to wash nor comb herself for the whole time, so that she soon becomes a most disgusting object. At the expiration of the three years, a feast is given by her tormentors, who invite all the friends and relations of her and themselves. At the commencement they deposit with great ceremony the remains of the burnt dead in a box, which they affix to the top of a high pole, and dance around it. The widow is then stripped naked and smeared from head to foot with fish oil, over which one of the by-standers throws a quantity of swan's down, covering her entire person. She is then obliged to dance with the others. After all this is over she is free to marry again, if she have the inclination, and courage enough to venture on a second risk of being roasted alive and the subsequent horrors.

It has often happened that a widow who has married a second husband, in the hope perhaps of not outliving him, committed suicide in the event of her second husband's death, rather than undergo a second ordeal. I was unable to learn any explanation of the motive for these cruel rites, and can only account for them in the natural selfishness, laziness, and cruelty of the Indians, who probably hope by these means to render their wives more attentive to their personal ease and comfort ; whilst, at the same time, it secures them from assassination either by a jealous or an errant spouse.

## CHAP. XVI.

*June 9th.* — THE Company's vessel which annually brings out goods and despatches for the interior having arrived, Mr. Finlayson was anxious to forward the letters on, and knowing that I was soon to start on my return, he asked me if I would take them to Fort Vancouver. I was very anxious to do anything in my power in return for the hospitality and kindness I had received, and accordingly commenced my preparations for starting on the following morning. An old Nasqually chief had come down to the coast to look for a favourite wife who had been carried off by some of his predatory neighbours, and, as he supposed, had been sold somewhere in Vancouver's Island. But not being successful in his search, he was now returning, and I engaged to go with him. He was very glad of my company, as my being the bearer of despatches would be a certain protection for the whole party from whatever Indians we might meet. I asked him how he had managed to escape on coming down, and he showed me an old piece of newspaper, which he said he held up whenever he met with strange Indians, and that they, supposing it to be a letter for Fort Victoria, had allowed him to pass without molestation.

The gentlemen in charge of the various posts, have frequent occasion to send letters, sometimes for a considerable distance, when it is either inconvenient or impossible for them to fit out a canoe with their own men to carry it. In such cases the letter is given to an Indian, who carries it as far as suits his convenience and safety. He then sells the letter to another, who carries it until he finds an opportunity of selling it to advantage ; it is thus passed on and sold until it arrives at its destination, gradually increasing in value according to the distance, and the last possessor receiving the reward for its safe delivery. In this manner letters are frequently sent with perfect security, and with much greater rapidity than could be done otherwise.

*June* 10*th.*—Early in the morning I embarked with the chief, a wife he had brought with him, and two slaves: we paddled on all day, and made good progress. In the evening we encamped under a high rock, where we found some goose eggs, of which we made a hearty supper.

*June* 11*th.*—We came to a rocky island, which was covered with thousands of seal, playing and basking in the sun. We shot several of them, as the Indians highly prize the blubber as food; but it was far too oily for my stomach. I, however, shot a white-headed eagle, and roasted him for my supper, and found him particularly good eating.

*June* 12*th.*—In the evening we arrived at an Indian village, where we stopped for the night; the whole surface of the water at this place seemed to be alive with the gambles of a small silvery fish, dancing and glistening in the rays of the setting sun. This fish is about the size of our sardines, and is caught in immense numbers; it is called there ulé kun, and is much prized on account of its delicacy and extraordinary fatness. When dried this fish will burn from one end to the other with a clear steady light like a candle.

There were several canoes out fishing in the evening, and they caught them with astonishing rapidity : this is done by means of an instrument about seven feet long, the handle is about three feet, into which is fixed a curved wooden blade about four feet, something the shape of a sabre, with the edge at the back. In this edge, at the distance of about an inch and a half, are inserted sharp bone teeth, about an inch long. The Indian stands in the canoe and, holding it as he would a paddle, draws it edgeways with both hands rapidly through the dense mass of fish, which are so thick that every tooth will strike a fish. One knock across the thwarts safely deposits them in the bottom of the canoe. This is done with such rapidity that they never use nets for this description of fishing.

*June* 13*th.*—To-day as we neared the shore we perceived two deer grazing, which the Indians were anxious to go after, but as we had already lost some time on the way I was more anxious to proceed. While at a very long distance I fired my double-barrelled gun at them, more in the hopes of driving them away than of killing them, when, much to the astonishment of both myself and the Indians, one of them fell dead. The chief looked very hard at me and then examined the gun, apparently in doubt whether the magic was in the gun or myself. I said nothing, but took it all as a matter of course, whilst the Indians evidently looked upon me as a person not to be trifled with. We had a splendid supper that evening on our venison, and I took good care not to test the qualities of my gun again before them, although they often asked me.

*June 14th.*—Whilst passing an isolated rock, standing six or seven feet high above the water, and a little more than four feet in circumference, the old chief asked me if I knew what it had originally been. On my replying in the negative, he told me the following legend:—

"It is many moons since a Nasqually family lived near this spot. It consisted of a widow with four sons,—one of them was by her first husband, the other three by the second. The three younger sons treated their elder brother with great unkindness, refusing him any share of the produce of their hunting and fishing; he, on the contrary, wishing to conciliate them, always gave them a share of his spoils. He, in fact, was a great medicine-man, although this was unknown to them, and, being tired of their harsh treatment, which no kindness on his part seemed to soften, he at length resolved to retaliate. He accordingly one day entered the lodge, where they were feasting, and told them that there was a large seal a short distance off. They instantly seized their spears and started in the direction he pointed out, and, coming up to the animal, the eldest drove his spear into it. This seal was 'a great medicine,' a familiar of the elder brother, who had himself created him for the occasion. The foremost of them had no sooner driven in his spear than he found it impossible to disengage his hand from the handle, or to draw it out; the two others drove in their spears with the like effect. The seal now took to the water, dragging them after it, and swam far out to sea. Having travelled on for many miles they saw an island in the distance, towards which the seal made. On nearing the shore they found, for the first time, they could remove their hands from their spears. They accordingly landed, and supposing themselves in some enemy's country, they hid themselves in a clump of bushes from observation. While lying concealed, they saw a diminutive canoe coming round a point in the distance, paddled by a very little man, who, when he came opposite to where they were, anchored his boat with a stone attached to a long line, without perceiving them. He now sprang over the side, and diving down, remained a long time under water. At length he rose to the surface, and brought with him a large fish, which he threw into the boat: this he repeated several times, each time looking in to count the fish he had caught. The three brothers being very hungry, one of them offered to swim out while the little man was under water, and steal one of the fish. This he safely accomplished before the return of the fisherman; but the little fellow no sooner returned with another fish than he discovered that one of those already caught was missing, and, stretching out his hand, he passed it slowly along the horizon, until it pointed directly to their place of concealment. He now drew up his anchor and paddled to the shore, and immediately discovered the three brothers, and being as miraculously strong as he was diminutive, he tied their hands and feet together and, throwing them into his canoe, jumped in and paddled back in the direction from whence he had come. Having rounded the distant point, where they had first descried him, they came to a village inhabited by a race of people as small as their captor, their houses, boats, and utensils being all in proportion to themselves.

" The three brothers were then taken out and thrown, bound as they were, into a lodge, while a council was convened to decide upon their fate. During the sitting of the council an immense flock of birds, resembling geese, but much larger, pounced down upon the inhabitants, and commenced a violent attack. These birds had the power of throwing their sharp quills like the porcupine, and although the little warriors fought with great valour, they soon became covered with the piercing darts and all sunk insensible on the ground. When all resistance had ceased the birds took to flight and disappeared.

" The brothers had witnessed the conflict from their place of confinement, and with much labour had succeeded in releasing themselves from their bonds, when they went to the battle ground, and commenced pulling the quills from the apparently lifeless bodies; but no sooner had they done this, than all instantly returned to consciousness. When all of them had become well again they wished to express their gratitude to their preservers, and offered to grant whatsoever they should desire. The brothers requested to be sent back to their own country. A council was accordingly called to decide on the easiest mode of doing so, and they eventually

determined upon employing a whale for the purpose. The brothers were then seated on the back
of the monster, and proceeded in the direction of
Nasqually. However, when they had reached
about half way, the whale began to think what a
fool he was for carrying them instead of turning
them into porpoises, and letting them swim home
themselves. Now the whale is considered as a
' Soch-a-li-ti-yah,' or Great Spirit, although not
the same as the ' Hias-Soch-a-li-ti-yah,' or Great
High Spirit, possessing greater powers than all
other animals put together, and no sooner had he
thought upon the matter than he carried it into
effect. This, accordingly, is the way that the
porpoises first came into existence, and accounts
for their being constantly at war with the seals,
one of which species was the cause of their misfortunes. After the three brothers had so strangely
disappeared, their mother came down to the beach
and remained there for days, watching for their
return and bewailing their absence with tears.
Whilst thus engaged one day the whale happened
to pass by, and, taking pity on her distress, turned
her into that stone."

I could not observe any very special peculiarity
in the formation of this rock while paddling past.

it in a canoe; and, at least from the points of observation presented to my eye, no resemblance to
the human figure, such as the conclusion of the
legend might lead us to anticipate, appeared to be
traceable. Standing, however, as this rock does,
entirely isolated, and without any other being
visible for miles around, it has naturally become
an object of special note to the Indians, and is not
uncalculated, from its solitary position, to be made
the scene of some of the fanciful creations of their
superstitious credulity.

*June 15th.* — We arrived at Nasqually, where I
procured horses to take me to the Cowlitz River.
I again crossed Prairie de Bute and Mud Mountain,
and arrived at my old friend Kiscox's lodge on the
evening of the third day; but, to my astonishment,
I found him and his family unusually distant in
their manners, and the children even running
away from me and hiding. At last he asked if I
had not taken the likeness of a woman when last
among them. I said that I had, and mentioned her
name, Caw wacham, alluding to the portrait of a
woman and child, No. 10, page 205; a dead silence
ensued, nor could I get the slightest answer to my
inquiries. Upon leaving the lodge, I met a half-
breed, who told me that Caw wacham was dead, and

that I was supposed to be the cause of her death. The silence was occasioned by my having mentioned a dead person's name, which is considered disrespectful to the deceased, and unlucky.

I immediately procured a canoe, and started for Fort Vancouver, down the river, paddling all night, well knowing the danger that would result from my meeting with any of her relations, and arrived safely at Fort Vancouver on the 20th of June, with my budget of news from the civilised world. Here I had to remain until the 1st of July, waiting for the boats, which were daily arriving from New Caledonia and the Upper Columbia with furs, and reloading again with their winter outfits for their posts in the interior. During this time I amused myself in hunting and sketching. I took a sketch of a Chinook boy with a singular headdress of beads; the design seemed to be entirely original with him, as I had never before met with any resembling it.

*July 1st.* — The nine boats composing the brigade had now completed their outfit, and were all prepared for their different destinations. Mr. Lewis was to command until he arrived at his own post, Colville; but we had great difficulty in collecting the men, between sixty and seventy in number: some wanted their allowance of rùm, or regale, before they started, given to the Company's men only preparatory to a long voyage. Others were bidding farewell to their Indian loves, and were hard to be found; in fact, all hesitated to give up the life of idleness and plenty in which they had been luxuriating for the last two or three weeks, for the toils and privations which they well knew were before them. However, towards evening we succeeded in collecting our crews, and Mr. Lewis promised them their regale on the first fitting opportunity. The fort gave us a salute of seven guns, which was repeated by the Company's ship lying at the store-house. The occupants of the fort crowded round us; and at last, amidst cheers and hearty wishes for our safety, we pushed off. Owing to the lateness of the hour at which we started, we only got to the Company's mills, eight miles from the fort, that evening.

*July 2nd.* — We started very early this morning, and the men plied their oars with unusual vigour, as they were to get their regale this evening. By 2 o'clock P.M. we had reached the Prairie de Thé, a distance of twenty-eight miles. Here we landed to let the men have their customary debauch. In the Hudson's Bay Company's service no rations of liquor are given to the men, either while they are stopping in fort or while travelling, nor are they allowed to purchase any; but when they are about commencing a long journey, the men are given what is called a regale, which consists of a pint of rum each. This, however, they are not allowed to drink until they are some distance from the post, where those who are entitled to get drunk may do so without interfering with the resident servants of the establishment.

Immediately on landing, the camp was made, fires lit, and victuals cooked; in short, every preparation for the night was completed before the liquor was given out. As soon as the men got their allowance, they commenced all sorts of athletic games; running, jumping, wrestling, &c. We had eight Sandwich Islanders amongst the crews, who afforded great amusement by a sort of pantomimic dance accompanied by singing. The whole thing was exceedingly grotesque and ridiculous, and elicited peals of laughter from the audience; gradually, as the rum began to take effect, the brigades, belonging to different posts, began to boast of their deeds of daring and endurance. This gradually led on to trying which was the best man. Numberless fights ensued; black eyes and bloody noses became plentiful, but all terminated in good humour. The next day the men were stupid from the effects of drink, but quite good-tempered and obedient; in fact, the fights of the previous evening seemed to be a sort of final settlement of all old grudges and disputes. We did not get away until 3 o'clock P. M., and only made a distance of about fourteen miles. We encamped at the foot of the Cascades, where the first portage in ascending the Columbia commences.

*July 4th and 5th.* — We were engaged both days in carrying the parcels of goods across the portage, and dragging the empty boats up by lines. This is a large fishing station, and immense numbers of fish are caught by the Hudson's Bay Company and the Cascade Indians, who congregate about here in great numbers at the fishing season, which happened at the time of our passing. They gave us a good deal of trouble and uneasiness, as it was only by the utmost vigilance that we could keep them from stealing. On the evening of the 5th we got over the portage; and, although the men were tired, we proceeded seven miles further up the river before we encamped, so as to get clear of the Indians.

In strolling about while the men were engaged

in carrying the goods across the Cascades, I discovered a large burying-ground of Flatheads, and I was very anxious to procure a skull. To do this, however, I had to use the greatest precaution, and ran no small risk, not only in getting it, but in having it in my possession afterwards; even the voyageurs would have refused to travel with me, had they known that I had it in my collection, not only on account of the superstitious dread in which they hold these burial-places, but also on account of the danger of discovery, which might have cost the lives of the whole party. I, however, took advantage of the men being busy watching the Indians to keep them from stealing, and the Indians being equally busy in watching for an opportunity to steal, and succeeded in getting a very perfect skull smuggled in among my traps without the slightest suspicion.

At the place where we encamped on the evening of the 5th, there were a great many stumps of trees standing in the river; it is supposed to be a landslip. I made a sketch of it.

During the night, two of our Sandwich Islanders deserted. A boat was immediately unloaded, and sent back, with the view of intercepting them at the Cascades. They had received 10l. sterling

each in goods as their outfit, and, in passing the
Cascades, had hid their bags in the woods, and
hoped to get back again to the coast with their
booty. Their pursuers, however, discovered their
track, and found the goods, though they did not
find the men; but knowing they must be near the
place, they got Tomaquin to look after them. The
next morning, Tomaquin with three of his tribe,
brought them in: each of the Indians, while paddling, carried his knife in his mouth, ready to
strike should the Islanders make any resistance.
It appeared that they had visited his camp in
the night, on which he assembled his tribe and
surrounded them; when the Islanders, thinking
they were going to be killed, surrendered and
begged for mercy. Tomaquin was rewarded with
four blankets and four shirts. The next thing
was to punish the deserters, and very little time
was wasted in either finding a verdict or carrying
it out. Our guide, a tall powerful Iroquois, took
one of them, and Mr. Lewis seized the other, as
they stepped from the canoe: the punishment consisted in simply knocking the men down, kicking
them until they got up, and knocking them down
again until they could not get up any more, when
they finished them off with a few more kicks. Mr.

Lewis, although a very powerful man, had only his left hand, a gun having exploded in his right, shattering it so dreadfully that he was obliged to have it cut off at the wrist ; but the operation having been performed in the roughest backwood fashion, it often pained him, and the doctors wanted him to let them cut it off again, so as to make a good stump, but he would not let them. On this stump he usually wore a heavy wooden shield, but, luckily for the poor Islanders, it was not on when they landed, or, as he said himself, he might have killed them. The punishment of those men must of course appear savage and severe to persons in civilised life, but it is only treatment of this kind that will keep this sort of men in order; and desertion or insubordination, on journeys through the interior, is often attended by the most dangerous consequences to the whole party.

*July 6th.* — It rained heavily all day, and the wind became so high, that we were obliged to put ashore, although the ground was very low and swampy, and the mosquitoes were in myriads.

*July 7th.* — Passed a Methodist mission, and came to the Portage of the Dalles. We employed the Indians here to make the portage, thirty to each boat, for which each man receives five balls and powder. The Indians at the Dalles do not distort the head. The country begins to look barren, and is entirely destitute of wood. Salmon in great abundance is caught in these rapids.

*July 8th.* — Arrived at the Chutes: we found no difficulty as to the carriage of our boats, as the Indians were very numerous and willing to be employed. In former times these people were more troublesome than any other tribes on the Columbia River. In making this portage, it was then necessary to have sixty armed men for the protection of the goods. It was here that the man with the tin box was shot, mentioned in Washington Irving's "Astoria." We were on the present occasion obliged to buy wood from the Indians, to cook our supper, not a tree nor even a bush being visible in any direction. The Indians, who obtain drift-wood for their own use when the river is high and brings it within their reach, of course prize it highly from its scarcity. The Indians who reside and congregate about the Chutes for the purpose of fishing, are called the Skeen tribe; they do not flatten their heads, and appear to be a hardy, brave people, at this time particularly friendly to the Hudson's Bay Company people, and at peace with their Flathead neighbours. The

s 4

Indians hereabouts catch a few deer and some other game, out of whose skins they make whatever dresses they wear, which are, however, very scanty. I give, in Sketch No. 12, the likeness of Mancemuckt, the chief; he wore a fox-skin cap and a leather deerskin shirt at the time.

*July 9th.* — Left the Chutes with a strong fair wind, running up the rapids under sail, while the water curled over the bows of the boats, which we only prevented from filling by shortening the sail. We encamped in the neighbourhood of a very thievish tribe of Indians, according to report, and were obliged to make use of one of the burial canoes for fuel, taking the bones out and depositing them carefully near some of the others. We had not got our pot to boil, before some of the tribe made their appearance, and gave us to understand that we had destroyed the grave of a relative of one of the men. After a great deal of arguing and trouble, and our party being too strong for the Indians to attempt any open violence, this man consented, at last, to receive some tobacco, ammunition, and other little presents, as an indemnity for our sacrilege. This we willingly gave him, as, had we not done so, in all probability they would have killed the first white man they could have laid their

PORTRAIT OF MAN-CE MUCKT.

hands on with impunity; having, however, received compensation for the insult, there was no fear of anything further being done about it.

*July* 10*th.* — Saw great quantities of rattlesnakes to-day, some few of which we killed ; the men, while tracking (that is hauling the boats along the edge of the shore by a line, in places where the river is too rapid to row), were in great dread of them as they had no shoes, but fortunately no one was bitten. It is said by the Indians, that salt applied plentifully and immediately to the wound will effect a cure, also that drinking copiously of ardent spirits as soon as the bite has been inflicted will avert the danger. I have, however, never seen either of them tried, and should much suspect the latter cure to be merely a piece of Indian cunning, to overcome the great difficulty of getting liquor, on any terms, from the Company's servants and officers.

*July* 11*th.*—Many Indians followed us for a long distance on horseback along the shore. I obtained one of their horses, and, accompanied by an Indian, took a gallop of seven or eight miles into the interior, and found the country equally sterile and unpromising as on the banks of the stream. The bend in the river, which the boats were, of course,

obliged to follow, enabled me to come up with them
a very few miles further; the ride, although un-
interesting as regarded landscape—for not a tree
was visible as far as the eye could reach—was still
a delightful change to me from the monotony of

No. 13. — Chimney Rock.

the boats.   As we approached the place where the
Walla-Walla debouches into the Columbia river,
we came in sight of two extraordinary rocks projecting from a high steep cone or mound about

700 feet above the level of the river. These are called by the voyageurs the Chimney Rocks, and from their being visible from a great distance, they are very serviceable as landmarks. Sketch No. 13 represents one of them and the cone, but, owing to the position in which I stood while taking the sketch, the other rock or chimney is not visible, being immediately in rear of the one represented.

The Walla-Walla Indians call these the "Rocks of the Ki-use girls," of which they relate the following legend, which was told to me by an Indian, whilst I was sketching this extraordinary scene. It must be borne in mind that all Indian tribes select some animal to which they attribute supernatural, or, in the language of the country, *medicine* powers: the whale, for instance, on the north-west coast; the kee-yeu, or war eagle, on the east side of the Rocky Mountains, supposed to be the maker of thunder; and the wolf on the Columbia River. Now the great medicine wolf of the Columbia River—according to the Walla-Walla tradition, the most cunning and artful of all manitous— having heard that a great medicine grasshopper was desolating the whole of the country which of right belonged to himself, and was especially under his protection, immediately resolved to trace him out, and have a personal encounter with him. With this view, he proceeded down the banks of the river, and soon fell in with the object of his search. Each of these formidable manitous thought it best to resort to stratagem to overcome his opponent. Being afraid of each other's "medicine" powers, they accordingly commenced by exchanging civilities, and then, with a view of terrifying each other, began boasting of their wonderful exploits, and the numbers they had killed and eaten. The grasshopper said to the wolf that the best way to ascertain who had devoured the largest numbers would be to vomit up the contents of their respective stomachs, and he who threw up the most hair — that being an indigestible substance — by showing who had swallowed the most animals, should be considered as the superior. To this proposal the wolf consented, and they commenced retching and vomiting up all in their stomachs. The grasshopper, in the violence of his exertions, naturally closed his eyes, and the wolf, perceiving this, adroitly drew a great part of his opponent's share over to his own side without being detected. The grasshopper, when he perceived how much larger the pile before the wolf was than his own, gave up the contest, and proposed to the wolf an exchange of shirts in token of amity and forgiveness. To this also the wolf consented, but requested the grasshopper to take off his shirt first as he was the first proposer; but the grasshopper refused, and wished the wolf to commence the ceremony.

The wolf finally even agreed to this, and striking himself suddenly on the breast, his shirt immediately flew off; the grasshopper was greatly astonished, and not being possessed of any charm by which he could strip himself so expeditiously, was obliged to take off his shirt in the common way of drawing it over his head; the wolf now watched his opportunity, and while the grasshopper had his head and arms entangled in the shirt, he killed him.

The wolf having thus got rid of his troublesome and dangerous rival, commenced his return home. On arriving within a few miles of the Walla-Walla, he saw three beautiful Ki-use girls, with whom he fell desperately in love: they were engaged in carrying stones into the river, in order to make an artificial cascade or rapid, to catch the salmon in leaping over it. The wolf secretly watched their operations through the day, and repaired at night to the dam and entirely destroyed their work: this he repeated for three successive evenings. On the fourth morning, he saw the girls sitting weeping on the bank, and accosted them, inquiring what was the matter: they told him they were starving, as they could get no fish for want of a dam. He then proposed to erect a dam for them, if they would consent to become his wives, to which they consented sooner than perish from the want of food. A long point of stones running nearly across the river is to this day attributed to the magic of the wolf-lover.

For a long time he lived happily with the three sisters (a custom very frequent amongst Indians, who marry as many sisters in a family as they can, and assign as a reason that sisters will naturally agree together better than strangers); but at length the wolf became jealous of his wives, and, by his supernatural power, changed two of them into the two basalt pillars, on the south side of the river, and then changed himself into a lark rock, somewhat similar to them, on the north side, so that he might watch them for ever afterwards. I asked the narrator what had become of the third sister. Says he, " Did you not observe a cavern as you came up?" I said that I had. " That," he replied, " is all that remains of her!"

# CHAP. XVII.

Fort Walla-Walla. — Salmon the Staff of Life. — Burrows for the Winter. — Ride to see a Cataract. — Splendid Fall of Water. — Desert of burning Sand. — A jealous Spouse. — Respect to a dead Chief.

*July 12th.* — I ARRIVED at Walla-Walla. It is a small fort, built of *dobies*, or blocks of mud baked in the sun, which is here intensely hot. Fort Walla-Walla is situated at the mouth of the river of the same name, in the most sandy and barren desert that can be conceived, and is about 500 miles from the mouth of the Columbia. Little or no rain ever falls here, although a few miles lower down the river it is seen from hence to pour down in torrents. Owing to its being built at the mouth of a gully, formed by the Columbia River through high mountainous land leading to the Pacific Ocean, it is exposed to furious gales of wind, which rush through the opening in the hills with inconceivable violence, and raise the sand in clouds so dense and continuous as frequently to render travelling impossible. I was kindly received by Mr. M'Bain, a clerk in the Hudson's Bay Company's service, who, with five men, had charge of the fort. The establishment is kept up solely for trading with the Indians from the interior, as those about the post have few or no peltries to deal in.

The Walla-Walla Indians live almost entirely upon salmon throughout the whole year. In the summer season they inhabit lodges made of mats of rushes spread on poles. Owing to the absence of trees in their vicinity, they have to depend for the small quantity of fuel which they require, upon the drift-wood, which they collect from the river in the spring. In the winter they dig a large circular excavation in the ground, about ten or twelve feet deep, and from forty to fifty feet in circumference, and cover it over with split logs, over which they place a layer of mud collected from the river. A hole is left at one side of this roofing, large enough for one person to enter at a time. A stick with notches reaches to the bottom of the excavation, and serves as a ladder, by means of which they ascend and descend into the subterranean dwelling. Here twelve or fifteen persons burrow through the winter, having little or no occasion for fuel ; their food of dried salmon being most frequently eaten uncooked, and the place being excessively warm from the numbers congregated together in so small and confined a space. They are frequently obliged, by the drifting billows of sand, to close the aperture, when the heat and stench become insupportable to all but those accustomed to it. The drifting of the sand is a frightful feature in this barren waste. Great numbers of the Indians lose their sight, and even those who have not suffered to so great an extent have the appearance of labouring under intense inflammation of these organs. The salmon, while in the process of drying, also become filled with sand to such an extent as to wear away the teeth of the Indians, and an Indian is seldom met with over forty years of age whose teeth are not worn quite to the gums.

*July* 13*th.* — Procured three horses and a man, and left for the Palucc or Pavilion River; traversed a sandy country, where we could find no water until we arrived at the Fouchay River, when we met with Pere José, a Jesuit missionary, who had left Walla-Walla on the night before, on the way to his mission of the Cœur de Laine. Here we encamped.

*July 14th.*—Started at five o'clock in the morning. Weather intensely hot, and no water procurable all day. Found some Indians, who ferried ourselves and baggage over the Nezperees River, in a canoe, which is here about 250 yards wide. We swam our horses at the mouth of the Pelouse River, where it empties itself into the Nezperees. The Chief of this place is named Slo-ce-ac-cum. He wore his hair divided in long masses, stuck together with grease. The tribe do not number more than seventy or eighty warriors, and are called Upputuppets. He told me that there was a fall up the Pelouse that no white man had ever seen, and that he would conduct me up the bed of the river, as it was sufficiently shallow for our horses. I accepted his proposal, and rode eight or ten miles through a wild and savage gorge, composed of dark brown basaltic rocks, heaped in confusion one upon another to the height of 1000 and 1500 feet, sometimes taking the appearance of immense ruins in the distance. At one place the strata assumed the circular form, and somewhat the appearance, of the Colosseum at Rome. Our path, at the bottom of this gorge, was very difficult, as it lay through masses of tangled brush and fallen rocks.

The chief now halted, and refused to go further unless I gave him a blanket in payment; but as this was unreasonable I urged on my horse, desiring my own man, who accompanied me, to follow with the jaded nag. I had not advanced more than a mile when the chief came up to us and guided us to the falls through one of the boldest and most sublime passes the eye ever beheld. At the foot of the falls we made our encampment, and our guide left us, quite satisfied with his present of tobacco and ammunition. The water falls in one perpendicular sheet of about 600 feet in height, from between rocks of a greyish-yellow colour, which rise to about 400 feet above the summit of the fall. The water tumbles into a rocky basin below, with a continuous hollow echoing roar, and courses with great velocity along its bed, until it falls into the Nezperees. There was a constant current of air around our encampment, which was delightfully cool and refreshing. When I was there it was low water, and the Indian told me, that during the rainy season the falls were much increased in volume, and of course in grandeur of effect.

*July 15th.* — Having finished my sketches of this magnificent scene, we left our encampment for a fall fifteen or twenty miles higher up the river, and it was necessary for us to leave the bed of the river and attain the top of the banks, which being at least 1000 feet above us, would have been impracticable, had we not found a ravine, which, although steep and difficult, we managed to lead our horses up. In this hollow we found great quantities of wild currants, of delicious flavour, which proved most refreshing.

At length we gained the summit. The country around, as far as the eye could reach, seemed to be a perfect desert of yellow, hot sand, with immense masses of broken rock jutting up abruptly here and there over the surface. No trees or shrubs of any kind relieved the monotony of the barren waste. A few patches of tuft-grass, thinly scattered here and there, were the only representatives of vegetation, while animal life seemed to be entirely extinct, and during my whole journey through this place I never met with an animal or bird, — not even a mosquito or a snake.

We now followed the course of the river, and en-camped at the upper fall, where I remained until the 17th sketching, much gratified with the surrounding magnificent scenes. The fall of water is only about fifteen feet. Along the margin of the river high bushes and grass grow, whose bright green contrasts vividly with the high hills of yellow sand which enclose them.

I was anxious to have remained in this neighbourhood for a week or ten days longer, to have made some more sketches of the curious and strange region in which I found myself, but the half-breed whom I had with me became so anxious to return, and so importunate and sulky about it, that he made me quite uncomfortable, and I consented to return. I found out afterwards that it was on account of his wife, of whom he was jealous, being left at the fort. Had I known this sooner I would have chosen another man; as it was, it was with great regret that I commenced retracing my steps down the river on the 17th, and in the evening again encamped on the banks of the Nezperees.

During the day we saw a large band of fine horses running wild; they had belonged to a chief who was much honoured by his tribe, and as a mark of respect, at his death, they determined not to use or touch his horses, which had, accordingly, kept increasing in numbers. I took a sketch of the Nezperees, near the mouth of the Pelouse River, showing the singular formation of the basaltic rocks.

T 3

# CHAP. XVIII.

*July* 18*th*.—STARTED for Dr. Whitman's mission, a
distance of sixty miles, neither myself nor my man
knowing anything of the road. I inquired of one
of the Indians here: he pointed out the direction,
but told us that we would be sure to die before we
reached it for want of water; nor could we prevail
on any of them to guide us. However, we started
in the direction pointed out: the weather was intensely hot, and we had nothing to shelter us from
the scorching rays of the sun, which were reflected
back by the hot yellow sand. Towards the middle
of the day we observed a bush in the distance, and
in our line of march; we eagerly rushed forward,
hoping to find water, for want of which both ourselves and our horses were now suffering severely;

but had the mortification to find the stream dried up, if ever there had been one there. Our only hope was now to struggle on as fast as possible, but our horses soon began to fail, and we were obliged to lead them many a weary mile tottering with exhaustion, before we arrived at the mission house. This we at length accomplished about 6 o'clock in the evening, and I was received very kindly by the missionary and his wife.

Dr. Whitman's duties included those of superintendent of the American Presbyterian missions on the west side of the Rocky Mountains. He had built himself a house of unburnt clay, for want of timber, which, as stated above, is here extremely scarce. He had resided at this locality, on the banks of the Walla-Walla River, upwards of eight years, doing all in his power to benefit the Indians in his mission. He had brought forty or fifty acres of land in the vicinity of the river under cultivation, and had a great many heads of domestic cattle, affording greater comfort to his family than one would expect in such an isolated spot. I remained with him four days, during which he kindly accompanied me amongst the Indians. These Indians, the Kye-use, resemble the Walla-Wallas very much. They are always allies in war, and

their language and customs are almost identical,
except that the Kye-use Indians are far more
vicious and ungovernable.

Dr. Whitman took me to the lodge of an Indian
called To-ma-kus, that I might take his likeness.
We found him in his lodge sitting perfectly naked.
His appearance was the most savage I ever beheld,
and his looks, as I afterwards heard, by no means
belied his character.  He was not aware of what
I was doing until I had finished the sketch.  He
then asked to look at it, and inquired what I
intended doing with it, and whether I was not
going to give it to the Americans, against whom
he bore a strong antipathy, superstitiously fancy-
ing that their possessing it would put him in their
power.  I in vain told him that I should not give
it to them; but not being satisfied with this assurance, he attempted to throw it in the fire, when I
seized him by the arm and snatched it from him.
He glanced at me like a fiend, and appeared greatly
enraged, but before he had time to recover from his
surprise I left the lodge and mounted my horse,
not without occasionally looking back to see if he
might not send an arrow after me.

Usually, when I wished to take the likeness of
an Indian, I walked into the lodge, sat down, and

commenced without speaking, as an Indian under these circumstances will generally pretend not to notice.   If they did not like what I was doing they would get up and walk away; but if I asked them to sit they most frequently refused, supposing that it would have some injurious effect upon themselves. In this manner I went into the lodge of Til-au-kite, the chief, and took his likeness without a word passing between us.

Having enjoyed the kind hospitality of Dr. Whitman and his lady for four days, on

*July* 22nd I left for Walla-Walla, after breakfast, taking with me, at the Doctor's desire, a dog belonging to Mr. M'Bain.   The weather continued intensely hot, and I had not ridden more than an hour when I observed the poor animal in a state of such extreme exhaustion that I requested my man to place him on his horse, but the man, feeling inconvenienced by him, put him down on the ground, and in a few minutes afterwards the poor brute lay down and died, actually scorched to death by the burning sand.

On the day after my arrival at the fort, a boy, one of the sons of Peo-Peo-mox-mox, the chief of the Walla-Wallas, arrived at the camp close to the fort.   He was a few days in advance of a war party headed by his father, and composed of Walla-Walla and Kye-use Indians, which had been absent eighteen months, and had been almost given up by the tribes. This party, numbering 200 men, had started for California for the purpose of revenging the death of another son of the chief, who had been killed by some Californian emigrants; and the messenger now arrived bringing the most disastrous tidings, not only of the total failure of the expedition, but also of their suffering and detention by sickness. Hearing that a messenger was coming in across the plains, I went to the Indian camp and was there at his arrival. No sooner had he dismounted from his horse than the whole camp, men, women, and children, surrounded him, eagerly inquiring after their absent friends, as they had hitherto received no intelligence, beyond a report, that the party had been cut off by hostile tribes. His downcast looks and silence confirmed the fears that some dire calamity must have happened, and they set up a tremendous howl, while he stood silent and dejected, with the tears streaming down his face. At length, after much coaxing and entreaty on their part, he commenced the recital of their misfortunes.

After describing the progress of the journey

up to the time of the disease (the measles) making its appearance, during which he was listened to in breathless silence, he began to name its victims one after another. On the first name being mentioned, a terrific howl ensued, the women loosening their hair and gesticulating in a most violent manner. When this had subsided, he, after much persuasion, named a second and a third, until he had named upwards of thirty. The same signs of intense grief followed the mention of each name, presenting a scene which accustomed as I was to Indian life, I must confess, affected me deeply. I stood close by them on a log, with the interpreter of the fort, who explained to me the Indian's statement, which occupied nearly three hours. After this the excitement increased, and apprehensions were entertained at the fort that it might lead to some hostile movement against the establishment. This fear, however, was groundless, as the Indians knew the distinction between the Hudson's Bay Company and the Americans. They immediately sent messengers in every direction on horseback to spread the news of the disaster among all the neighbouring tribes, and Mr. M'Bain and I both considered that Dr. Whitman and his family would be in great danger. I, therefore, determined to go and warn him of what had occurred. It was six o'clock in the evening when I started, but I had a good horse, and arrived at his house in three hours. I told him of the arrival of the messenger, and the excitement of the Indians, and advised him strongly to come to the fort, for a while at least, until the Indians had cooled down; but he said he had lived so long amongst them, and had done so much for them, that he did not apprehend they would injure him. I remained with him only an hour, and hastened back to the fort, where I arrived at one o'clock, A.M. Not wishing to expose myself unnecessarily to any danger arising from the superstitious notions which the Indians might attach to my having taken some of their likenesses, I remained at Fort Walla-Walla four or five days, during which the war party had returned, and I had an opportunity of taking the likeness of the great chief Peo-Peo-mox-mox, or, "the Yellow Serpent," who exercises great influence, not only over his own people, but also among the neighbouring tribes.

While at the fort one of the gentlemen of the establishment, who had been amongst the Indians for forty years, and who had resided for the most part of that time amongst the Walla-Wallas, re-

lated to me the following story, which I shall
introduce, as nearly as possible, in the manner in
which it was told to me; as it is strongly illustrative of the Indian character, of their love for
their children, and the firmness with which they
meet the approach of death, and their belief in a
future state.

Several years back, when the Walla-Wallas used
to go in annual buffalo hunts, and herds of these
immense animals frequented the west side of the
mountains, though now rarely seen, the tribe was
governed by a chief adored by his own people,
and respected and feared by all the surrounding
tribes for his great wisdom and courage. This
chief had many sons, who, in childhood, all
promised to resemble their father both in mind
and body, but one by one, as they arrived at
manhood, and as the proud father hoped to see
them take their place amongst the warriors and
leaders of the tribe, they withered and sank into
untimely graves, and as each loved one passed
away, the stern chief soothed his silent sorrow
with hopes of those still left. At last his hair
grew white with sorrow and with age, and he had
but one boy left — his youngest — but apparently
the strongest, the bravest, and the best: at least to

the old warrior's heart he was all this ; for in him
still seemed to live all the most cherished virtues
of his dead brothers.

The old man now devoted his whole time to the
instruction of this boy : he taught him to hunt the
buffalo and the moose, to snare the lynx and trap
the bear, to draw the bow and poise the spear with
unerring aim.   Young as the boy was, he yet made
him head the warriors of his tribe, and led him on
himself, the foremost to surprise the enemy and
secure the bloody trophies of victory ; already had
he become the theme of the war-chant, and his
name was known far and wide for all the virtues
that could adorn an Indian brave.

But the Great Spirit took this one too ; and the
lonely and desolate father shut himself up in the
solitude of his lodge, and no one saw him nor spoke
to him, nor was there any sound of wailing or of
grief heard from that sad abode.   At length the
appointed day arrived upon which the body was to
be laid in its last resting-place, where the chief had
ordered a large grave to be made ; and the funeral
procession being formed, the chief came forth and
placed himself at their head, but, to the astonishment of all, instead of being dressed in the shabby
garments indicative of mourning, he came forth

arrayed in full war costume, fully equipped as if
for some distant hostile excursion, painted with
the most brilliant war paints, and hung round
with the trophies of his many bloody and successful wars.

Calmly and sternly he marched to the grave,
and the body of his loved son having been laid
in it, with all the Indian treasures supposed to
be useful to him in the next world, the bereaved
father stood on the verge, and addressed his tribe :
" From my youth upwards I have ever sought
the honour and welfare of my tribe, and have
never spared myself either in the battle or the
chase. I have led you from victory to victory,
and, instead of being surrounded by hostile tribes,
you are now feared by all, and your friendship is
sought, and your enmity dreaded, wherever the
hunters of the tribe may roam. I have been a
father to you, and ye have been as children
to me, for more moons than I am able to count,
until my hairs have become as hoar frost upon
the mountains. You have never withheld your
obedience from me, nor will you deny it to me
now. When the Great Spirit was pleased to call
my children one by one, to His blessed hunting
grounds, I saw them borne to the sepulchre of

their fathers without murmuring against His will,
so long as one was left me.   I toiled on for him,
taking pride in his pride, glorying in his glory,
and living in his life, fondly hoping that when I
should go to join his loved brothers in the other
world that I should leave him to perpetuate my
deeds amongst you ; but the Great Spirit hath
called him also, — this last prop of my declining
years, — this hope of my old age, — endeared to
me by so many fond recollections of his worth, his
manly strength, his courage, skill, and prowess in
war.   Alas ! he lies in the cold ground, and I am
left alone, like the sapless trunk of a tree whose
branches have been scathed by the lightning.   I
tracked that loved form, now cold, from its childhood's gambols to its manly acts of daring.   I it
was who first placed in his hands the bow and the
tomahawk, and taught him how to use them ; and
often have you witnessed and praised his skill and
courage in wielding them.   And shall I now for-
sake him, and leave him alone and unaided, to
take the long and toilsome journey in the Spirit's
hunting grounds ?   No ! his spirit beckons me
to follow, and he shall not be disappointed ; the
same grave shall contain us, the same earth shall
cover us ; and as in this world, his father's arm

was ever near to assist him in every toil and danger, so shall his spirit find him by his side in the long and toilsome journey to the plenteous and everlasting hunting grounds of the Great Spirit. You, my people, have never disobeyed me, and will not fail to fulfil my last commands. I now leave you, and when I lie extended at his side; heap the earth over us both : nothing can change my purpose." He then descended into the grave, and clasped the corpse in his arms. His people, after in vain endeavouring to change his resolution, obeyed his commands, and buried the living and the dead. A stick, with a piece of ragged red cloth, was the only monument erected over the warriors, but their names will form the theme of many an Indian *talk* as long as the Walla-Walla tribe exists.

*July* 29*th.*—I had determined to go to Colville by the Grand Coulet: this, from the appearance of the two extremities, seemed to have been a former bed of the Columbia River, but no person could tell me anything about it, nor could I hear of any one, either Indian or White, who had penetrated any considerable distance up it; the place was, however, so much talked of as the abode of evil spirits and other strange things, that I could

U

not resist the desire of trying to explore it. I accordingly sent on everything by the boats, except what I usually carried about my own person, but I could not get an Indian guide, as none of them would venture an encounter with the evil spirits.

At last a half-breed, called Donny, although ignorant of the route, agreed to accompany me. We procured two riding horses, and one to carry our provisions, consisting of two fine hams, which had been sent to me from Fort Vancouver, and a stock of dried salmon, cured by the Indians. About ten miles from the fort, we swam our horses across the Nezperees River, where it enters the Columbia, and then proceeded along the banks of the Columbia, about ten miles further, where we encamped for the night.

During the day we passed a large encampment of Nezperees, who were very kind to us, but stole a tin cup (a valuable article in that part of the world) I suppose as a souvenir of my visit. I took a sketch of a man, and might have frightened the chief into getting the cup restored to me by means of this sketch, but I had been so warned of the treachery and villany of these Indians, that I considered it too dangerous an experiment.

*July 30th.*—Proceeded along the shore for eight

or ten miles, when I discovered that I had left my
pistols and some other articles at our last night's
encampment. I had, therefore, to send my man
back for them, while I sat by the river, with horses
and baggage, under a burning sun, without the
slightest shelter. Whilst sitting there, a canoe
approached with four Indians, streaked all over
with white mud (the ordinary pipe-clay). On
landing, they showed much surprise, and watched
very cautiously at a distance, some creeping close
to me, and then retreating. This continued for
about three hours, during which not a sound broke
through the surrounding stillness. I had commenced travelling very early, and this, combined
with the heat and silence, made me intensely
drowsy. Even the danger I was in scarcely suf-
ficed to keep my eyes open, but the Indians were
evidently at fault as to what to make of me.

As I sat upon the packs taken from the horse,
nodding in silence, with a fixed stare at them
whichever way they turned, my double-barrelled
gun, cocked, across my knees, and a large red
beard (an object of great wonder to all Indians)
hanging half way down my breast, I was, no
doubt, a very good embodiment of their ideas of
a scoocoom, or evil genius. To this I attributed

my safety, and took good care not to encourage
their closer acquaintance, as I had no wish to have
my immortality tested by them.

At length my man returned with the missing
articles, and the Indians hastily took to their canoe
and crossed the river. We now continued our
course along the river until evening, when we encamped, and as we were very hungry, and expected
a hard journey next day, we determined upon
attacking one of our hams. I accordingly seized
hold of the bone to pull it from the bag with
which it was covered, when, alas! the bare bone
slipped out, leaving a living mass of maggots, into
which the heat had turned the flesh, behind. Upon
examination, we found the other in the same state,
and had to satisfy our hunger on the salmon,
which, as usual, was full of sand.

## CHAP. XIX.

*July 31st.* — OWING to the great bend which the Columbia takes to the northward, I thought I should save a considerable distance by striking across the country, and intersecting the Grand Coulet at some distance from its mouth. We accordingly left the river early in the morning, and travelled all day through a barren, sandy desert, without a drop of water to drink, a tree to rest under, or a spot of grass to sit upon. Towards evening, we saw in the distance a small lake, and to this we accordingly pushed forward: as soon as our horses perceived it, wearied and exhausted as they were, they rushed forward and plunged bodily into the water. No sooner, however, had they tasted it, than they drew their

υ 3

heads back, refusing to drink. On alighting, I
found the water was intensely salt, and never shall
I forget the painful emotion which came over me,
as it became certain to my mind that I could not
satisfy my thirst. Our horses were too weary,
after our long and rapid ride, to proceed further;
and though it was tantalising to look at the water
which we could not drink, the vegetation which
surrounded it was refreshing to the horses, and
we remained here all night, though we enjoyed
scarcely any sleep owing to our thirst.

*August* 1st. — We started at 4 o'clock this
morning, and travelled steadily on without getting
water, until about noon, when we fell in with a
narrow lake, about a mile long, very shallow, and
swarming with pelicans, whose dung had made the
water green and thick. Bad as this was, added to its
being also rather salt, yet our thirst was so great,
that we strained some through a cloth and drank
it. Leaving this Lake of Pelicans, we now entered
upon a still more discouraging route: the country,
as far as the eye could reach, was covered with loose
fine sand, which the violent winds of this region
had drifted into immense mounds, varying from
80 to 120 feet in height. This was very toilsome to us, as our horses had become so exhausted

that we were obliged to lead them, and we sank deep at every step in the hot sand. Had the wind risen while we were crossing this place, we must have been immediately buried in the sand. Towards evening we arrived at a rock, and in a small cleft we discovered three or four gallons of water almost as black as ink, and abounding in disgusting animalcula. The horses no sooner saw it, than they made a spring towards it, and it was with the greatest difficulty we drove them back, fearing that they would drink all, and leave us to our misery. After satisfying our thirst, we strained a kettleful for our supper, and allowed the horses to drink up the remainder, which they did to the last drop, showing how necessary was the precaution we had taken. Here we passed the night.

*Aug. 2nd.*—I awoke in the morning, and felt something cold and clammy against my thigh, and on throwing off my blanket, perceived a reptile of the lizard species, eight or ten inches long, which had been my companion during the night. I cannot say whether it was venomous or not, but I found no ill effects from it. We proceeded on, and about noon emerged from these mountains of sand; the country was still sandy and barren, but here and there we found tufts of **grass** sufficient to support our horses.   The country **was** intersected with immense walls of basaltic **rock,** which continually threw us out of our **direct** course, or rather the course I had **determined** on, for of the actual route I had no **information.** These interruptions added considerably to our **diffi-** culties, as I had no compass, and it was only **by** noticing the sun at mid-day by my watch, and fix- ing on some distant hill, that I guided my course. We still suffered from the want of water, and my man was getting disheartened at our wandering thus almost at random through this trackless desert.

*Aug. 3rd.* — After riding a few hours, we came to an immense gully or dried-up water-course crossing our route.   The banks rose seven or eight hundred feet high from the bottom on each side, and its width was nearly half a mile.   At first it seemed impossible to pass it; however, after many difficulties, we succeeded in leading our horses to the bottom, which we crossed, and clambered up the rocks on the opposite side for about 200 feet, when we came to one of the most beautiful spots that can well be conceived: at least, it appeared to us all that was beautiful, amongst the surround- ing desolation.

It was a piece of table land, about half a mile in circumference, covered with luxuriant grass, and having in its centre a small lake of exquisitely cool fresh water. The basaltic rock rose like an amphitheatre, from about three-quarters of its circuit to the height of about 500 feet, while the precipice up which we had toiled sank down at the other side. We remained here three hours, luxuriating in the delicious water, so sweet to us after suffering the torments of thirst for so long. My man seemed as if he never could have enough of it, for when he could swallow no more, he walked in, clothes and all, and actually wallowed in it, the horses following his example. How much longer we might have been tempted to stay here, it is impossible to say, but we accidentally set fire to the grass and were obliged to decamp; this was accomplished with considerable difficulty, and in getting up the precipitous rocks, the pack-horse lost his footing and fell to the bottom, but pitching, fortunately, on his back with the packs under him, he escaped with a few cuts on his legs only. Had he been anything but an Indian horse, he would doubtless have paid the forfeit of his life for the insecurity of his feet.

As soon as I arrived at the level of the country

once more, I saw in the distance another vast
wall of rock, and leaving my man to bring up
the unfortunate pack-horse, I rode briskly forward
to endeavour to find a passage over this formidable
barrier, considering it to be like many others
that we had already passed, an isolated wall of
basalt. I therefore rode backwards and forwards
along its front, exploring every part that presented any opening, but without finding one that
our horses could traverse. At last I came to the
conclusion that we must go round it, but my man
not having come up, it was necessary for me to return and seek him, which proved for several hours
unavailing, and I began to fear that he and my
provisions were inevitably lost; however, after
riding a long way back, I fell upon his track,
which I followed up with care.

I soon perceived that he had taken a wrong direction. After some time, I saw him mounted on
a high rock in the distance, shouting and signalling
with all his might till I got up to him: he was very
much frightened, as he said that if he had lost me
he never could have got on. Though the day was
by this time pretty far advanced, we succeeded in
making a circuit of the basaltic wall, and struck a
deep ravine which in the distance so much resembled

the banks of the Columbia, that I at first thought I had missed my way, and had come upon the river.

When we reached the edge, I saw that there was no water at the bottom, and that there could be no doubt of my having at last arrived at the Grand Coulet. With great difficulty we descended the bank, 1000 feet; its width varies from one mile to a mile and a half; and there can be no doubt of its having been previously an arm of the Columbia, which now flows four or five hundred feet below it, leaving the channel of the Coulet dry, and exposing to view the bases of the enormous rocky islands that now stud its bottom, some of them rising to the elevation of the surrounding country.

This wonderful gully is about 150 miles long, and walled-in in many places with an unbroken length twenty miles long of perpendicular basalt 1000 feet high. The bottom of this valley is perfectly level, and covered with luxuriant grass, except where broken by the immense rocks above mentioned: there is not a single tree to be seen throughout its whole extent, and scarcely a bush; neither did we see any insects, reptiles, or animals. Having found a beautiful spring of water gushing from the rocks, we encamped near it. After we had rested ourselves, we commenced an examination of our provisions of dried salmon, for we saw no chance of adding anything to our larder, and of course what we had was of great importance. Much to our regret, we found that it was perfectly alive with maggots, and every mouthful had to be well shaken before eaten; so full of life indeed had the fish become, that my man proposed tying them by the tails to prevent their crawling away. Bad as the salmon was, our prospects were made still more gloomy by the fact that there was but a very small supply left, and that we had a long and unknown road to travel before we could hope for any help. A thunderstorm came on during the night, and in the whole course of my life I never heard anything so awfully sublime as the endless reverberations amongst the rocks of this grand and beautiful ravine. There is hardly another spot in the world that could produce so astounding an effect.

*August 4th.* — We followed the course of the Coulet, lost in admiration of its beauty and grandeur assuming a new aspect of increased wildness and magnificence at every turn. I shot the first bird we had seen since leaving Walla-Walla, except the pelicans, which are never eaten, even by the Indians, who are far from particular. This bird proved to be what is here called a wild turkey, but resembling in nothing the wild turkeys of the south. Its plumage resembles that of a pheasant, it is not larger than a domestic hen, and its flesh, though very white, is dry and unpalatable; to us, however, it proved a great treat, as we were enabled to make one meal without the usual accompaniments of sand and maggots. Our journey now would have been delightful, if we had anything like good food. We had plenty of grass of the best quality for our horses, delicious springs gushing from the rocks at every mile or two, and camping grounds which almost tempted us to stay at the risk of starvation.

*August 5th.* — Towards evening we began to see trees, principally pine, in the heights and in the distance, and I concluded that we were now approaching the Columbia River. I now pressed forward and before sundown emerged from the gorge of this stupendous ravine, and saw the mighty river flowing at least 500 feet below us, though the banks rose considerably more than that height above us on each side. This river exceeds in grandeur any other perhaps in the world, not so much from its volume of water, although that is immense, as from the romantic wildness of its stupendous and ever-varying surrounding scenery, now towering into snow-capped mountains thousands of feet high, and now sinking in undulating terraces to the level of its pellucid waters.

Two Indians were floating down the river, on a few logs tied together. They were the first we had encountered for many days; and on our hailing them, they landed, and climbed up to us. They told me we were ten days' journey from Colville. This I did not believe, although I could not tell why they wished to deceive me. I gave them a little tobacco, and hoped to get some provisions from them, but they said they had none, so we were obliged to make our supper on the salmon as usual. We descended the bank, and camped for the night on the margin of the river.

## CHAP. XX.

A Dangerous Path. — Incredible Sagacity.—Levying Black Mail.— Fort Colville. — Hiding-Places of the Indians. — Indian Baptism. — The Kettle Falls. — Tilting at the Ring. — Chief of the Waters. —Dead Salmon by Thousands.—Dislike to Salt Meat.—A Widow's Consolation. — A Wife for the Woods.

*August 6th.* — WE continued along the shore for twelve or fifteen miles, under the rocky banks, which towered over our heads fourteen or fifteen hundred feet. In some places, immense ledges hung over our path, seemingly ready to crush all beneath them. At length we came to a high perpendicular rock jutting out into the river; and as the water was too deep and too rapid to allow us to wade round its base, we attempted to ascend the bank over loose rocks and stones that slipped from under us at every step, and rolled thundering to the bottom. Having led our horses up about three hundred feet, I stopped, and sent Donny a-head on foot to seek for an opening to the top. The pack-horse could with great difficulty preserve his footing under his load. One of the other **horses**, with incredible sagacity, now walked up **past me**, until he reached his burdened companion; **and**, putting his shoulder under one side of the **load**, actually assisted him in sustaining it, until **the** man's return. Finding that we could not **possibly** ascend, we were obliged to turn back; and we **did** not find a practicable place to ascend until we **had** nearly reached the place from which we had **started** in the morning.

At last, with great difficulty, we succeeded **in** gaining the upper bank, and entered upon **a** wild and romantic district, studded here and **there** with small clumps of trees, which gradually in- creased in thickness, until we became surrounded with dense woods, having made a circuit of about twenty-five miles, traversing gullies of prodigious depth and steepness. We again struck the river opposite the mouth of a small stream, on whose banks we saw a couple of Indians. As soon as we were perceived, they sent a canoe over to us, offering to assist in swimming the horses across, as they assured us that the shortest and best route to Colville was on the other side. We accepted their friendly offer, and camped alongside them on the other side. Both Donny and myself were dreadfully fatigued from the length of our day's travel, the labour we had gone through, and the weakness under which we suffered from the want of sufficient food. These Indians, as I afterwards learned, were generally very unfriendly to the whites, and had often given trouble to small parties passing, generally levying a pretty heavy toll for a free passage through their territory. But to me they were all kindness, presenting me with plenty of fresh salmon and dried berries, which were most acceptable, after the disgusting fare on which we had been so long struggling to support life; and one of them proposed to accompany me as a guide to Colville. My last day's experience made me gladly accept of this offer; and long before darkness set in, I found myself as sound asleep as the most weary of dyspeptic patients could wish himself to be.

*August 7th.* — Started very early in the morning with the guide, and made, what is called in those parts, a long day. We were continually ascending and descending, and found it very fatiguing. It was quite dark when we encamped on the banks of the river.

*August 8th.* — Started again very early for the purpose of reaching Colville before night. Came

x

to a high hill overlooking the Columbia for many miles of its course, and sat down on its summit to enjoy the magnificent prospect, and give a short rest to the horses. As I was lying under the trees, the wind sprang up, and, much to my astonishment, I felt the whole sod moving under me. At first I imagined it to be an earthquake, and expected to see the whole hillside move off; but on examination, I found that it proceeded from the roots of the immense trees being interlaced one within another in the shallow soil. This alone prevented their being blown over, as the rocks are everywhere close to the surface; and as the wind bends the tops of the trees, the roots rise and fall with the surface in a rolling motion like a dead swell. We proceeded on until we were within a mile of Kettle Falls, where we swam across in the usual way, holding on by the tails of our horses; and just at dusk we were kindly received by Mr. Lewis.

Fort Colville stands in the middle of a small prairie, about one mile and a half wide by about three miles long, surrounded by high hills. This little prairie is extremely valuable for agricultural purposes, as it is, in fact, an island of fertility, surrounded by barren rocks, sandy plains, and arid mountains, to the distance of three or four hundred miles along the river, the Spokan valley to the south being the nearest land fit for cultivation. I remained here until the 9th of September, when I made an excursion of sixty miles, accompanied by Mr. Lewis, to Walker and Eales' Presbyterian mission, where I was most hospitably received by these worthy people.

Each of the missionaries had a comfortable log-house, situated in the midst of a fertile plain, and, with their wives and children, seem to be happily located. There are numerous Indian *caches* of dried salmon in the vicinity, which are very seldom robbed, although left in isolated spots for months without any person in charge. I enjoyed for a week the kind hospitality of my hosts, who were most attentive in accompanying me in my visits to the Spokan River and the Indians in the vicinity.

The Spokan Indians are a small tribe, differing very little from the Indians at Colville either in their appearance, habits, or language. They all seemed to treat the missionaries with great affection and respect; but as to their success in making converts, I must speak with great diffidence, as I was not sufficiently acquainted with the language to examine them, even had I wished to do so. I have

no doubt that a great number have been baptised;
but I also am aware that almost all Indians will
take a name from a man whom they esteem, and
give him one in return; and the more ceremony
there is about the transaction, the more importance
will be attached to it, and the greater the induce-
ment to others to be equally honoured.   No influence, however, seems to be able to make agri-
culturists of them, as they still pursue their hunting and fishing, evincing the greatest dislike to
anything like manual labour.

On the 17th of September I returned again to
Colville.   The Indian village is situated about two
miles below the fort, on a rocky eminence overlooking the Kettle Falls.   These are the highest in the
Columbia River.   They are about one thousand
yards across, and eighteen feet high.   The immense
body of water tumbling amongst the broken rocks
renders them exceedingly picturesque and grand.
The Indians have no particular name for them,
giving them the general name of Tum-tum, which
is applied to all falls of water.   The voyageurs call
them the "Chaudière," or "Kettle Falls," from the
numerous round holes worn in the solid rocks by
loose boulders.   These boulders, being caught in
the inequalities of rocks below the falls, are con-

stantly driven round by the tremendous force of
the current, and wear out holes as perfectly round
and smooth as in the inner surface of a cast-iron
kettle.   The village has a population of about
five hundred souls, called, in their own language,
Chualpays.   They differ but little from the Walla-
Wallas.   The lodges are formed of mats of rushes
stretched on poles.   A flooring is made of sticks,
raised three or four feet from the ground, leaving
the space beneath it entirely open, and forming a
cool, airy, and shady place, in which to hang their
salmon to dry.

These people are governed by two chiefs, Allam-
māk-hum Stole-luch, the "Chief of the Earth."  This
chief exercises great power over the tribe except as
regards the fishing, which is under the exclusive
control of See-pays, the "Chief of the Waters."  He
dispenses justice strictly, and punishes with rigour
any cheating or dishonesty among his subjects.
He opposes the gambling propensities of his tribe
to the utmost, even depriving the victorious gamblers of their share of the fish received annually
from the Chief of the Waters; but still the passion
for gambling continues, and an instance occurred
during my stay here of a young man committing
suicide by shooting himself, having lost everything

he possessed by indulging in this habit.  I may here remark that suicide prevails more among the Indians of the Columbia River than in any other portion of the continent which I have visited.

A curious case occurred, about a year before my visit, of two sisters, wives of one man, each jealous of the other, who went into the woods and hung themselves, as was supposed, unknown to each other, as they were found dead a long distance apart.

The principal game played here is called Al-kol-lock, and requires considerable skill.  A smooth level piece of ground is chosen, and a slight barrier of a couple of sticks placed lengthwise, is laid at each end of the chosen spot, being from forty to fifty feet apart and only a few inches high.  The two players, stripped naked, are armed each with a very slight spear about three feet long, and finely pointed with bone; one of them takes a ring made of bone, or some heavy wood, and wound round with cord; this ring is about three inches in diameter, on the inner circumference of which are fastened six beads of different colours at equal distances, to each of which a separate numerical value is attached.  The ring is then rolled along the ground to one of the barriers, and is followed at the distance of two or three yards by the players, and as the ring strikes the barrier and is falling on its side, the spears are thrown, so that the ring may fall on them. If only one of the spears should be covered by the ring, the owner of it counts according to the coloured bead over it. But it generally happens, from the dexterity of the players, that the ring covers both spears, and each counts according to the colour of the beads above his spear; they then play towards the other barrier, and so on until one party has attained the number agreed upon for game.

The other chief is called See-pays, the "Chief of the Waters," or the "Salmon Chief." No one is allowed to catch fish without his permission. His large fishing basket or trap is put down a month before anyone is allowed to fish for themselves. This basket is constructed of stout willow wands woven together, and supported by stout sticks of timber, and is so placed that the salmon, in leaping up the falls strike against a stick placed at the top, and are thrown back into the confined space at the bottom of the trap, which is too narrow to allow them to attempt another jump.

The salmon commence their ascent about the

15th of July, and continue to arrive in almost incredible numbers for nearly two months; in fact, there is one continuous body of them, more resembling a flock of birds than anything else in their extraordinary leap up the falls, beginning at sunrise and ceasing at the approach of night. The chief told me that he had taken as many as 1700 salmon, weighing on an average 30 lbs. each, in the course of one day. Probably the daily average taken in the chief's basket is about 400. The chief distributes the fish thus taken during the season amongst his people, everyone, even to the smallest child, getting an equal share.

By the time the salmon reach the Kettle Falls, after surmounting the numerous rapids impeding their journey from the sea, a distance of between 700 and 800 miles, they become so exhausted, that in their efforts to leap these falls, their strength often proves unequal to the task, and striking against the projecting rocks they batter their noses so severely, that they fall back stunned and often dead, and float down the river, where they are picked up some six miles below by another camp of Indians, who do not belong to the Salmon Chief's jurisdiction, and of course have no participation in the produce of his basket.

None of these salmon coming up from the sea ever return, but remain in the river and die by thousands; in fact, in such numbers that in our passage down the river in the fall, whenever we came to still water, we found them floating dead or cast up along the shore in such vast numbers as literally to poison the atmosphere.

The young fish return to the sea in the spring. Strange to say, nothing has ever been found in the stomachs of the salmon caught in the Columbia River; and no angler, although frequent trials have been made by the most expert in the art, has yet succeeded in tempting them to take any description of fly or other bait.

After the expiration of one month, the Salmon Chief abandons his exclusive privilege, as the fish are then getting thin and poor, and allows all who wish it to take them. For this purpose some use smaller baskets made like the chief's; others use the spear, with which they are very expert, and an ordinary spearsman will take easily as many as 200 in a day; others use a small hand-net in the rapids, where the salmon are crowded together and near the surface. These nets are somewhat like our common landing-nets, but ingeniously contrived, so that when a fish is in them, his own

struggles loosen a little stick which keeps the
mouth of the net open while empty; the weight
of the salmon then draws the mouth close like
a purse, and effectually secures the prey.

Salmon is almost the only food used by the Indians
on the Lower Columbia River, the two months'
fishing affording a sufficient supply to last them
the whole year round.   The mode in which they
cure them is by splitting them down the back,
after which each half is again split, making them
sufficiently thin to dry with facility, a process
occupying in general from four to five days.*
The salmon are afterwards sewed up in rush mats,
containing about ninety or one hundred pounds,
and put up on scaffolds to keep the dogs from
them.   Infinitely greater numbers of salmon could
be readily taken here, if it were desired; but, as
the chief considerately remarked to me, if he were to
take all that came up, there would be none left for
the Indians on the upper part of the river; so that
they content themselves with supplying their own
wants.

A few days before leaving Colville I was in-

* I have never seen salt made use of by any tribe of Indians
for the purpose of preserving food, and they all evince the
greatest dislike to salt meat.

formed that the Chualpays were about to celebrate
a scalp dance, and accordingly I took my sketch-
book and went down to their encampment, where
I learned that a small party had returned from
a hunting expedition to the mountains, bringing
with them, as a present from a friendly tribe, the
scalp of a Blackfoot Indian. This to them was a
present of inestimable value, as one of their tribe
had been killed by a Blackfoot Indian two or three
years before, and they had not been able to obtain
any revenge for the injury. This scalp, however,
would soothe the sorrows of his widow and friends.
Accordingly, it was stretched upon a small hoop,
and attached to a stick as a handle, and thus carried
by the afflicted woman to a place where a large
fire was kindled: here she commenced dancing and
singing, swaying the scalp violently about and
kicking it, whilst eight women, hideously painted,
chanted and danced round her and the fire. The
remainder of the tribe stood round in a circle,
beating drums, and all singing.

Having witnessed the performance for about four
or five hours, seeing no variation in it, nor any
likelihood of its termination, I returned, deeply
impressed with the sincerity of a grief which could
endure such violent monotony for so long a period.

My kind host, Mr. Lewis, was now obliged to give
up rambling about with me, as he had to see to the
preparations for the further progress of the return
brigade.   Both himself and his Cree wife were most
attentive in adding every little thing to my outfit
which they could supply.   Mrs. Lewis was a most
excellent wife for a trader, possessing great energy
and decision, combined with natural kindness of
disposition.   Several years before I became acquainted with her she had amputated her husband's arm, a little below the elbow, with a common
knife, and tied it up so well, that he soon recovered
without any other assistance.   Her surgical aid
had been called in requisition by the accidental
discharge of his gun, which had shattered the limb
so much that it was hopeless to try and save it.

## CHAP. XXI.

Dreadful Tidings. — Horrible Tragedy. — A devoted Husband.— A joyful Surprise. — Perilous Pass. — Walk on Shore. — The Rapid of the Dead. — The detected Cannibal. — A Western Honeymoon. — The Last Embrace. — Capote Blanc. — Boat Encampment. — A bothered Steed. — Forest swept away. — The Flooded Athabasca. — Shoes long as yourself. — Crossing Jasper's Lake. — — In for it everyway. — Rising of the River. — Starving of the Dogs. — Waiting for a Frost-Bridge. — Too Thin to be Eaten. — Fort Assiniboine. — Pleasure after Pain.

*Sept. 21st.* — THIS evening two men arrived from Walla-Walla, and my grief and horror can be well imagined when they told me the sad fate of those with whom I had so lately been a cherished guest. It appeared that the war party before mentioned had brought the measles back with them, and that it spread with fearful rapidity through the neighbouring tribe, but more particularly among the Kye-uses. Dr. Whitman, as a medical man, did all he could to stay its progress; but owing to their injudicious mode of living, which he could not prevail on them to relinquish, great numbers of them died. At this time the doctor's family consisted of himself, his wife, and a nephew, with two or three servants, and several children whom he had humanely adopted, left orphans by the death of their parents who had died on their way to Oregon, besides a Spanish half-breed boy, whom he had brought up for several years. There were likewise several families of emigrants staying with him at the time, to rest and refresh themselves and cattle.

The Indians supposed that the doctor could have stayed the course of the malady had he wished it; and they were confirmed in this belief by the Spanish half-breed boy, who told some of them that he had overheard the doctor say to his wife after they had retired for the night, that he would give them bad medicine, and kill all the Indians, that he might appropriate their land to himself. They accordingly concocted a plan to destroy the doctor and his wife, and all the males of the establishment. With this object in view, about sixty of them armed themselves and came to his house. The inmates, having no suspicion of any hostile intention, were totally unprepared for resistance or flight. Dr. and Mrs. Whitman and their nephew, a youth about seventeen or eighteen years of age, were sitting in their parlour in the afternoon, when Til-au-kite, the chief, and To-ma-kus entered the room, and, addressing the doctor, told him very coolly that they had come to kill him. The doctor, not believing it possible that they could entertain any hostile intentions towards him, told them as much; but while in the act of speaking, To-ma-kus drew a tomahawk from under his robe and buried it deep in his brain. The unfortunate man fell dead from his chair. Mrs. Whitman and the nephew fled up stairs, and locked themselves into an upper room.

In the meantime Til-au-kite gave the war whoop, as a signal to his party outside to proceed in the work of destruction, which they did with the ferocity and yells of so many fiends. Mrs. Whitman, hearing the shrieks and groans of the dying, looked out of the window, and was shot through the breast by a son of the chief, but not mortally wounded. A party then rushed up stairs, and, despatching the nephew on the spot, dragged her down by the hair of her head, and, taking her to the front of the house, mutilated her in a shocking manner with their knives and tomahawks.

There was one man who had a wife bedridden. On the commencement of the affray he ran to her room, and, taking her up in his arms, carried her, unperceived by the Indians, to the thick bushes that skirted the river, and hurried on with his burden in the direction of Fort Walla-Walla. Having reached a distance of fifteen miles, he became so exhausted, that, unable to carry her further, he concealed her in a thick hummock of bushes on the margin of the river, and hastened to the fort for assistance. On his arrival, Mr. M'Bain immediately sent out men with him, and brought her in. She had fortunately suffered nothing more than fright. The number killed, including Dr. and Mrs. Whitman, amounted to fourteen. The other females and children were carried off by the Indians, and two of them were forthwith taken as wives by Til-au-kite's son and another. A man, employed in a little mill, forming a part of the establishment, was spared to work the mill for the Indians.

The day following this awful tragedy, a Catholic priest, who had not heard of the massacre, stopped, on seeing the mangled corpses strewn round the house, and requested permission to bury them, which he did with the rites of his own church. The permission was granted the more readily as these Indians are friendly towards the Catholic missionaries. On the priest leaving the place, he met, at a distance of five or six miles, a brother missionary of the deceased, a Mr. Spalding, the field of whose labours lay about a hundred miles off, at a place on the River Coldwater. He communicated to him the melancholy fate of his friend, and advised him to fly as fast as possible, or in all probability he would be another victim. He gave him a share of his provisions, and Mr. Spalding hurried homeward full of apprehensions for the safety of his own family; but unfortunately his horse escaped from him in the night, and, after a six days' toilsome march on foot, having lost his way, he at length reached the banks of the river, but on the opposite side to his own house.

In the dead of the night, and in a state of starvation, having eaten nothing for three days, everything seeming to be quiet about his own place, he cautiously embarked in a small canoe and paddled across the river. But he had no sooner landed than an Indian seized him and dragged him to his house, where he found all his family prisoners, and the Indians in full possession. These Indians were not of the same tribe with those who had destroyed Dr. Whitman's family, nor had they at all participated in the outrage; but having heard of it, and

Y

fearing that the whites would include them in their vengeance, they had seized on the family of Mr. Spalding for the purpose of holding them as hostages for their own safety. The family were uninjured, and he was overjoyed to find that things were no worse.

Mr. Ogden, the chief factor of the Hudson's Bay Company on the Columbia, immediately on hearing of the outrage, came to Walla-Walla, and, although the occurrence took place in the territory of the United States, and of course the sufferers could have no further claim to the protection of the Company than such as humanity dictated, he at once purchased the release of all the prisoners, and from them the particulars of the massacre were afterwards obtained. The Indians, in their negotiations with Mr. Ogden, offered to give up the prisoners for nothing, if he would guarantee that the United States would not go to war with them; but this, of course, he could not do.

On the 22nd September our two boats, with their crews of six men each, being all ready, we bade farewell to our kind host and his family and again embarked on the river. As usual, on leaving a fort, we did not start till evening, and stopped again for the night at ten miles distant, at Day's

Encampment. We had no regale, as these men were not going into the interior. They only carried the express to Boat Encampment, where they exchange boxes with the express from the east side of the mountains, with whom I was to recross.

*Sept. 23rd.* — To-day we succeeded in getting past the Little Dalles in safety. They are about twenty miles from Kettle Falls, and are the narrowest part of the Columbia River for full one thousand miles. It is here contracted into a passage of one hundred and fifty yards by lofty rocks on each side, through which it rushes with tremendous violence, forming whirlpools in its passage capable of engulphing the largest forest trees, which are afterwards disgorged with great force. This is one of the most dangerous places that the boats have to pass. In going up the river the boats are all emptied, and the freight has to be carried about half a mile over the tops of the high and rugged rocks. One man remains in each boat with a long pole to keep it off from the rocks, whilst the others drag it by a long tow-rope up the torrent.

Last year a man, who was on the outside of the rope, was jerked over the rocks by some sudden strain, and was immediately lost. In coming down, however, all remain in the boats; and the

guides in this perilous pass, display the greatest
courage and presence of mind at moments when
the slightest error in managing the frail bark
would hurl its occupants to certain destruction.
On arriving at the head of the rapids, the guide
gets out on to the rocks and surveys the whirlpools.  If they are filling in "or making," as
they term it, the men rest on their paddles until
they commence throwing off, when the guides instantly re-embark, and shove off the boat, and shoot
through this dread portal with the speed of lightning.  Sometimes the boats are whirled round in
the vortex with such awful rapidity that it renders
the management impossible, and the boat and its
hapless crew are swallowed up in the abyss.

*Sept. 24th.*—We had fine weather and made
good progress.  I shot the largest wolf to-day I
had ever seen; he was swimming away from us
across the river.

*Sept 25th.*—The morning broke dark and cloudy,
and soon turned to heavy rain; but the wind was
fair, so we hoisted our sail, and soon scudded into
an open lake, about three miles wide and twelve
long.

*Sept. 26th.*—It continued raining heavily all
night, and heavy mists hung over us during the

day; but we continued our journey and got into what is called another lake.

*Sept.* 27*th.*—Still in the lakes. The day was clearer, and we could distinguish the surrounding scenery, which seemed to consist of immense mountains, towering peak on peak above the clouds. The land appeared barren and unfit for cultivation. The cedars are of enormous magnitude, some of them measuring not less than thirty or forty feet in circumference. I was told of one fifty feet, but did not see it. I attempted to reach the upper side of one which had been uprooted and lay on the ground, with the end of my gun stretched out at arm's length, and could but just attain it.

*Sept.* 28*th.*—We had an exciting chase after a mountain goat, which showed himself in the distance, on a point of land jutting out into the lake. Putting the boat ashore, I started in pursuit, accompanied by three or four Indians, and after a long hunt succeeded in killing him. He afforded us a most delicious repast. In size and shape he somewhat resembled the domestic goat, but was covered with white wool resembling that of a sheep; the horns are straight, small, pointed, and black.

*Sept.* 29*th.*—Got through the lakes by 5 o'clock P.M., and again entered into what may be more

properly called the river. The rain was pouring heavily on us almost all day, whilst in the distance we could see the tops of the mountains
becoming white with snow down to a well-defined
line, where it seemed to change to rain.

*Sept. 30th.* — Started at 6 A.M., during a pouring rain, which soon soaked us to the skin. We
stopped here to make some paddles, in a forest
abounding with birch, the only wood fit for this
purpose, and which is not met with lower down
the Columbia ; large cedar-trees were also very
abundant.

*Oct. 1st.* — The morning was fine and clear,
and the temperature was agreeable : I was enabled
to leave the boat for a walk for a few miles along
the shore, much to the relief of my legs. The place
is a sandbank, extending for miles in a direction
parallel with the shore, and generally but a few
furlongs from it ; it is called the " Grand Batteur."
The steepness of the banks of the river, and the
density of the under-brushwood, had confined us to
the boats for the last three days ; it was therefore
no wonder that I should enjoy a walk. We saw
some very large piles of drift-wood, called by the
Canadians " Aumbereaux." These piles consist of
trees of all sizes, but usually very large, which are

drifted down the river, and are piled high up upon one another by the force of the ice when they meet with any obstruction. I amused myself by setting fire to some of them *en passant*, and leaving an immense fire burning, the smoke of which we could see for days in our rear.

*Oct. 2nd.* — It again rained heavily all day. Towards the evening we encamped. It is difficult to imagine the pleasure of an encampment round a large fire, after sitting in an open boat on the Columbia River, with the rain pouring down in torrents all day; but though the rain may not have ceased, yet the cheerful warmth of the fire dispels all the annoyance of mere moisture in this uncivilised state of life. We passed the Upper Little Dalle, a very long and rapid shoot of three or four miles. One of the Indians brought in some white berries, which he ate eagerly, but which I found very nauseous. I never saw any berry in the course of my travels which the Indians scruple to eat, nor have I seen any ill effect result from their doing so.

*Oct. 3rd.* — Saw four carriboos, a species of deer of the ordinary size, which we followed, but without success, as they got the wind of us before we could approach them within gunshot. We fell in

with the Indian chief of the lakes, and procured
some bear's and deer's meat from him, of which
he seemed to possess a plentiful supply. A small
species of dog was tied to the bushes near his
lodge, to prevent them from hunting on their own
account, and driving away all the deer. The chief
told me that when disposed to hunt with them,
he had only to find a fresh deer-track, set his
dogs on it and lie down to sleep, as they never
fail to find the deer, and turn them back to the
place where they had left him lying. We saw
some of these dogs, apparently on the track of
some deer, full twelve or fifteen miles from the
chief's lodge.

*Oct. 4th.* — The chief, with wife and daughter,
accompanied us in their canoe, which they paddled
with great dexterity, from ten to fifteen miles.
They make their canoes of pine bark, being the only
Indians who use this material for the purpose;
their form is also peculiar and very beautiful.
These canoes run the rapids with more safety for
their size, than those of any other shape. The
chief and his ladies breakfasted with us, and then
bid us good bye.

We camped at night below the " Dalle des
Morts," or the Rapid of the Dead, so called from

the following circumstance. About twenty-five or thirty years ago, an Iroquois, a half-breed, and a French Canadian, having charge of a boat, had to descend this frightful rapid. Fearful of running it, they affixed a long line to the bow, and being themselves on the shore, they attempted to lower her gradually by means of it down the foaming torrent. The boat took a sheer and ran outside of a rock, and all their efforts to get her back, or reach the rock themselves through the boiling surge were unavailing. The rope, chafing on the sharp edge of the rock, soon broke, and she dashed down among the whirling eddies, and broke to pieces, with their whole stock of provisions on board.

They then continued to follow on foot, along the rugged and difficult banks of the river, without food, guns, or ammunition; nor had they been able to save even a blanket, to protect them from the inclement weather. At night they encamped in a shivering and famishing condition, not having been able to surmount more than three miles of the obstacles that obstructed their passage at every step along the banks. The next day they proceeded with no better success. They well knew that if they constructed a raft it would not live an hour in this part of the Columbia River, owing to the quick succession of rapids that here beset the navigation. In this starving condition they continued their slow progress till the third day, when the half-breed, fearing his companions would kill him for their food, left them, and was never after heard of, falling, in all probability, a prey to the wolves. The other two lay down, and the Iroquois watching his opportunity, got up at night, and beat his companion's brains out with a stick, and going to work in a methodical manner, after first satisfying his craving hunger with a portion of the body, cut the remainder into thin slices and dried them in the sun, after the manner in which buffalo meat is prepared. Here he remained three days drying his meat, which he made into a pack, and continued his journey with it down the river bank, until he came to the commencement of the Upper Lake, where he made a raft, on which he placed his dried meat, and covered it over with pine-bark, seating himself upon it, and paddling down the lake.

He had not proceeded very far, before he met a canoe, which had been sent from one of the forts below, on the Spokan River, in quest of them, owing to their long absence. The new comers immediately inquired what had become of his two companions ; he replied, that they had deserted him, giving at the same time an account of the loss of the boat. They took him on board their canoe, and one of the men seeing the bark on the raft, and desirous of getting it to place under him in the canoe, the Iroquois shoved off the raft, with evident signs of confusion, on which the man, who noticed his embarrassment, paddled up to it, and lifting the bark, discovered the dried meat beneath it, among which was a human foot. He was asked how he had obtained the dried meat, and replied, that he had killed a wolf, swimming across the river.

The foot with the meat was slyly deposited in a bag, belonging to one of the men, but not without the act being perceived by the murderer, who, while they were asleep during the night, threw the bag and its contents into the river. Appearing not to notice its loss, they went on to Fort Spokan, and delivered him up to Mr. M'Mullan, the person in charge, detailing the particulars. The Indian was shortly afterwards sent to a distant post in New Caledonia, both as a punishment, and also in order to get rid of him, as no voyageur will willingly associate with any one known to have eaten human flesh. I had previously travelled several hundreds of miles with the son of this very man, who always behaved well, although there certainly was something repulsive in his appearance, which would have made me dislike to have had him for a companion in a situation such as above described.

*Oct. 5th.*—It rained so hard throughout the day and night, and the river was swollen so much, that we despaired of hauling the boats up the rapids, and therefore remained until the following morning at our encampment.

*Oct. 6th.*—It was a lovely morning. Saw some carriboos, but could not approach them near enough for a shot. We had a magnificent view of the Rocky Mountains in the distance, in all their azure grandeur. The flood soon subsided sufficiently to allow our ascending the rapids, although it took us the whole day to haul the boats up—the distance is not more than three miles—but the boats were so strained and tossed about in the operation, that we were obliged to haul them ashore and grease their bottoms with the resin which exudes from the pine.

Whilst the men were engaged in these operations, I took advantage of the delay, and made a sketch, looking down the rapids. As I was sketching, our steersman, who was present at the time, told me a melancholy occurrence, which

took place at this spot, and which I will give as
nearly as possible in his own words. "About four
years ago," said he, "I crossed the Rocky Mountains
with a party of forty. When we got to Boat Encampment, we embarked in two boats; the one
which I was steering had twenty-two on board,
amongst whom was a gentleman sent into the interior for the purpose of botanical research. On his
way to Saskatchawan, he had fallen in with a young
lady, a half-breed, who was travelling to cross the
mountains and go down the Columbia on a visit
to some of her friends. They had not travelled
far, before a mutual attachment induced them to
become man and wife, at Edmonton, though few
couples, I think, in the world would choose a trip
across the mountains for a honeymoon excursion;
but they bore all their hardships and labours cheer-
fully, perfectly happy in helping each other, and
being kind to their companions.

"We had two or three other women with us, and
I had my own daughter, about ten years old, whom
I was taking home to my wife at Fort Vancouver.
I had left her two or three years before, on the
east side of the mountains, with some of her rela-
tions, as I was unable to bring her over at the time
I had come with my wife. We had also a young

man of the name of M'Gillveray, belonging to the Company, with a small dog; the remainder were principally voyageurs.

" When I came to the head of the rapids, I found that the other boat, which contained the principal guide, had passed on, and I thought, therefore, that the rapids were in a proper state for running them, that is, that the whirlpools were throwing out and not filling, which they do alternately. I therefore went on without stopping, and when in the midst of the rapids, where there was no possibility of staying the downward course of the boat, I discovered to my dismay that the whirlpools were filling. One moment more and the water curled over the sides of the boat, immediately filling her. I called out for all to sit still and hold on steadily to the seats, as the boat would not sink entirely owing to the nature of the cargo, and that I could guide them to shore in this state. We ran more than a mile in safety, when the boat ran close by a ledge of rocks. The botanist, who held his wife in his arms, seeing the boat approach so near the rock, made a sudden spring for the shore; but the boat filled with water, yielded to the double weight of himself and wife, and they sank clasped in each other's arms. The boat was

suddenly turned completely bottom upwards; but I
and another man succeeded in getting on the top of
her, and were thus carried down safely. We thought
we heard some noise inside the boat, and the man
who was with me, being a good swimmer, dived
under, and soon, to my unexpected joy, appeared
with my little daughter, who almost miraculously
had been preserved by being jammed in amongst the
luggage, and supported by the small quantity of air
which had been caught by the boat when she
turned over. We soon got ashore: M'Gillveray
and four others saved themselves by swimming,
the remaining fourteen were drowned; we immediately commenced searching for the bodies, and
soon recovered all of them, the unfortunate botanist
and his wife still fast locked in each other's arms,
—an embrace which we had not the hearts to un-
clasp, but buried them as we found them, in one
grave. We afterwards found M'Gillveray's little
dog thrown up dead on a sandbank, with his
master's cap held firmly between his teeth."

*Oct. 7th.*—We embarked in the morning, and
continued our journey through a continual drizzle
of rain, which was anything but pleasant.

*Oct. 8th.*—The weather cleared up, and we saw
carriboos in great numbers; but, as usual, they

were too wary for us to get a shot at them. Passed the rapids of St. Martin before night.

*Oct. 9th.*—Travelled but a short distance to-day, having to cut our way through the numerous fallen trees which, projecting into the stream, obstructed the course close to the shore, which we were obliged to take owing to the violence of the current in mid-channel.

*Oct. 10th.*—In the forenoon we perceived tracks of human feet in the sand on the shore, which astonished us very much, as no Indians come near these parts; and on approaching Boat Encampment, which we did about 2 P.M., we perceived smoke rising, which made us hope that the brigade from the east with the express had arrived, but were much disappointed at finding that it was only my old friend Capote Blanc, the Sho-shawp chief from Jasper's House, and two Indians who had come over to hunt. Here we made a suitable encampment, and hauled up our boats high and dry on the sand. Capote Blanc had been very successful in his hunt, and had a large stock of dried moose meat and beavers' tails, with which he supplied us abundantly, receiving a few small articles and ammunition in exchange.

We now had nothing to do but to try and pass the

time pleasantly as we could under the circumstances, until the arrival of the brigade from the east side of the mountains. The men spent the day principally in gambling, and performing charms which they supposed would hasten the arrival of the brigade, such as erecting crosses, with one of the arms pointing to the direction from which it was expected. They also prepared what they call a " lobstick." For this purpose a high tree is chosen which has thick branches at the top, and all the lower limbs are carefully trimmed off; a smooth surface is then cut on one side of the tree, on which the person in whose honour it has been trimmed is invited to cut his name; this being done, three rounds of blank-charges are fired, and three cheers given, and the spot afterwards bears the name of his encampment. On this occasion I had the honour of carving my name upon the " lobstick." We had almost constant rain, accompanied by immense snow-flakes, which obscured our view of the mountains nearly the whole time of our remaining here. I, however, managed to pick out some few bright hours for sketching.

We found very little game about here; the men only succeeded in trapping a few martens, and we began to be very uneasy, fearing that some disaster

z

must have befallen the brigade which was to meet
us.   I endeavoured to prevail on some of the men
to accompany me across the mountains; but they
would not go with me, so that I was forced to
stay with the rest.   Boat Encampment derives its
name from its being the head of the navigable
water.   Three rivers here unite, forming the commencement of the north branch of the Columbia,
so that the enlargement of the river is very sudden.

*Oct. 28th.* — About three o'clock in the afternoon
a clerk in the company's service arrived, and
announced that he had come in advance of the
eastern brigade, which would arrive next day
under the command of Mr. Low: this was indeed
joyful news to us, as we were all heartily tired of
our gloomy situation.

*Oct. 29th.* — Mr. Low and party arrived this
morning with between fifty and sixty horses loaded
with provision, and the furs destined for Russia.
They had been nine days crossing from Jasper's
House.   Mr. Low seemed doubtful about our being
able to recross with the horses; but I cared little
whether we had horses or not, so that I got
away, for I was completely wearied with my long
inaction.   My provisions, too, were getting short,
and the person in charge did not offer to re-

plenish my stock, so that I had no choice but to cross as quickly as possible.

*Oct. 30th.* — This day Mr. Low left for Fort Vancouver with the boats which had brought me up, leaving me with four Indians who had accompanied him from the east side for the purpose of taking the horses back, and of guiding me over the mountains.

*Oct. 31st.* — It was a beautiful morning, and we started about ten o'clock, after loading fifteen horses out of the fifty-six which Mr. Low had brought with him, and got the first day as far as the Grande Batture, where we encamped.

*Nov. 1st.* — We passed through the Pointe des Bois, a distance of ten miles, by about the worst road I had ever travelled, it being cut up by so many horses having passed it a short time previously. My horse stuck in a mud hole until he sank up to his head, and it was with the greatest difficulty that one of the men and myself extricated him alive. What with the horses sticking in the mud, the packs falling off, the shouting to the animals in Cree, and swearing at them in French, there being no oaths in the Indian languages, I never passed such a busy, tiresome, noisy, and disagreeable day in my life. This was in a

great measure owing to having so few men to look
after so large a number of horses, which would not
keep the road, but ran helter skelter through the
thick woods.    At last we arrived at the bottom of
the Grande Côte, and there encamped for the night,
thoroughly wearied out and disgusted with horse-
driving.

*Nov. 2nd.*—We started an hour before daybreak
to ascend the stupendous Grande Côte, and soon
found the snow becoming deeper at every step.
One of our horses fell down a declivity of twenty-
five to thirty feet with a heavy load on his back,
and, strange to say, neither deranged his load nor
hurt himself.  We soon had him on the track
again as well as ever, except that he certainly
looked a little *bothered.*  The snow now reached
up to the horses' sides as we slowly toiled along,
and reached the summit just as the sun sank
below the horizon; but we could not stop here, as
there was no food for the horses, we were therefore obliged to push on past the Committee's Punch
Bowl, a lake I have before described.

It was intensely cold, as might be supposed, in
this elevated region. Although the sun shone during
the day with intense brilliancy, my long beard became one solid mass of ice.  It was long after dark

before we arrived at the Campment de Fusei, having met with no other place which afforded any food for the horses, and even here they had to dig the snow away with their hoofs to enable them to get at it.

A distressing occurrence took place here some years previously. Whilst a party were ascending this mountain, a lady, who was crossing to meet her husband, was in the rear, and it was not noticed until the party had encamped that she was not come up. Men were instantly sent back to seek her. After some hours' search, they found her tracks in the snow, which they followed until they came to a perpendicular rock overhanging a roaring torrent; here all traces of her were lost, and her body was never found, notwithstanding every exertion was made to find it. Little doubt, however, could exist but that she had lost her way, and had fallen over the precipice into the torrent, which would have quickly hurried her into chasms where the foot of man could not reach.

*Nov. 3rd.*—Last night was the coldest (according to my feelings) that I had ever experienced; but not having a thermometer with me, I do not know what was the intensity. I am, however, confident that it was colder on that night than it was on a subsequent night, when the spirit thermometer indicated 56° below zero, a temperature at which mercury would have become frozen and useless. I endeavoured to thaw myself by melting some snow over the fire; but the water froze upon my hair and beard, although I stood as close as I well could to a blazing fire, and I actually had to scorch my face before I could thaw the ice out. We now passed through the Grande Batture, and, much to our relief, found the snow decreasing in depth as we descended. We succeeded in reaching the Campment de Regnalle in the evening, and camped there for the night.

*Nov. 4th.* — We got our breakfast and started long before day. We made good progress until about noon, when we came to a wild tract of country which appeared to have been visited years before by some terrible hurricane, which had uprooted the whole forest for miles round, not leaving a tree standing; a younger growth of trees were now pushing their heads up through the fallen timber of the ancient forest. We all got so hungry with our violent exercise in such a cold clear atmosphere, that we could not resist the temptation of stopping and cooking something to eat, before we entered the tangled maze before us. This was the first time we had done so, as daylight was too valuable to be wasted in sitting down, and the danger of being caught in one of the tremendous snow storms, which are so frequent in these regions, was too imminent for us not to push on to the utmost of our power. The snow often lies here to the depth of twenty or thirty feet, and one storm might have caused us the loss of the horses and baggage at least, even if we had been able to save ourselves by making snow shoes. It was, therefore, no slight temptation which could induce the men who knew the country to stop for dinner; but hunger is a good persuader, and carried the question. After dinner we pushed on with renewed strength; but it was with great difficulty that we were enabled to get the horses through the fallen and tangled woods, and it was not until after nightfall that we reached the " Grand Traverse," where we found three men, who had been sent out to meet us and assist in driving in our sixty horses, which were as yet all safe.

*Nov. 5th.* — In the morning we found the Athabasca River in a flooded state, and a heavy snow storm had set in; we, however, proceeded to ford the rapid stream, although the snow was driving with such fury in our faces that we could not distinguish the opposite bank. The water almost covered the backs of the horses, and my pack, containing sketches and curiosities, &c., had to be carried on the shoulders of the men riding across, to keep them out of the water.   After fording the river we crossed La Rouge's Praire, and encamped on the very spot that I had slept at exactly a year previously, to the very day.

*Nov. 6th.* — The wind blew intensely cold, and we had to pass along the margin of a frozen lake, seven or eight miles long, over which the snow drifted furiously in our faces.   It became so cold that we could no longer sit on the horses, but were obliged to dismount and drive them on before us.   My beard, the growth of nearly two years, gave me great trouble, as it became heavy with ice from the freezing of my breath; even my nostrils became stopped up, and I was forced to breathe through my mouth.

Fortunately I fell in with an Indian lodge, and had an opportunity of thawing myself, so that I rode the remainder of the way to Jasper's House with comparative comfort.   There we soon forgot our trouble over a good piece of mountain sheep, which is really delicious, even when not seasoned by such hardships as we had undergone.

This place is completely surrounded by lofty mountains, some of them close to the house, others many miles distant, and is subject to violent tornadoes, which sweep through the mountain gorges with terrific fury. A great number of mountain sheep had been driven down into the valleys by the intensity of the cold, which had set in this winter with unusual severity. I have counted as many as five large flocks of these animals grazing in different directions from the house at one time, and the Indians brought them in every day, so that we fared most sumptuously. These sheep are those most commonly called the " big horn."

I made a sketch of a ram's head of an enormous size; his horns were similar in shape to those of our domestic ram, but measured forty-two inches in length. They are considerably larger than our domestic sheep; their coat somewhat resembles in texture and colour the red deer, but a little darker. We were now obliged to set our men to work to make snow shoes, as our further journey had to be made over deep snow. The birch wood of which they are made does not grow near Jasper's House, and the men had to go twenty miles off to get it. At last, by the 14th, our snow shoes and a sledge were completed, and with much difficulty I obtained two

wretched dogs from the Indians, and one Mr. Colin
Frazer lent me, to drag the sledge with my packs,
provisions, and blankets.   I had two men, one an
Indian, the other a half-breed.  They had come with
Mr. Low from Edmonton, with seven others, and
ought to have waited for me; but we had been so
long coming, and the weather had got so cold, that
the seven got afraid of waiting any longer, and
departed without me.   Had these two followed
the example of their companions, I should have
been obliged to spend a most dreary winter in
the wretched accommodation which Jasper's House
afforded.

*Nov. 15th.* — Early in the morning we equipped
ourselves for the journey, putting on snow shoes
between five and six feet long, — the pair I wore
were exactly my own height, five feet eleven inches.
Owing to our having so few dogs, we could not carry
many provisions, but trusted to our guns to provide
more on the way.

About fifteen or sixteen miles from Jasper's
House, we came to an Indian lodge, which we
found tenanted by a woman and her five children,
her husband being out on a hunt.   She was so
civil and kind, and the lodge was so comfortable,
that we were induced to stop, particularly as it

was our first day on snow shoes, and stopping there saved us the trouble of making a camp for ourselves. The hunter returned late in the evening, having killed four sheep, one of which he brought home on his back. This we all set to work to cook, the squaw boiling as much as her kettle would hold, and the men sticking the rest upon sticks and roasting it. The whole party then set resolutely to work, and ate the whole sheep, and it was not a small one either. The hunter told us that he had seen thirty-four sheep that day, and that he never remembered a winter in which so many sheep had come down from the mountains. He proved a most agreeable host, and entertained me with stories of his hunting exploits during the whole evening. My kind hostess prepared me a bed of sheep skins for the night, the most comfortable bed I had slept in for many months.

*Nov.* 16*th.* — At an early hour before daylight we got our breakfast and harnessed our dogs, and made our way through some very thick woods. We entered on Jasper's Lake, twelve miles long, the wind blowing a perfect hurricane, as it always does here when it blows at all. Fortunately the wind always comes from the mountains: had it been otherwise, we should not have been able to pass

along the lake on the glare ice against such a
storm of wind and sleet; as it was, we were blown
along by the wind, and could only stop ourselves
by lying down ; our sledge sometimes flying in
front of the dogs, while we were enveloped in a
cloud of snow that prevented our seeing more than
a few yards before us.

When we were about half way over the
lake, we perceived two Indians, who were making
their way across in a course intersecting our
own route, and evidently had hard work to keep
in the right direction.   On coming up to them, we
all sat down and had a smoke.   The Indians,
when they come to ice or hard frozen snow,
where the snow shoe has to be taken off, always
take off their moccasins also, and travel barefooted; by this means they preserve their moccasins, and when they sit down they put them on
dry and wrap their feet in their furs.   This walking barefooted on ice in such intense cold would
seem dangerous to the inexperienced, but, in fact,
the feet of those who are accustomed to it suffer
less in this way than they do from the ice which
always forms on the inside of the moccasin in long
and quick travelling, as the ice thus formed cracks
into small pieces and cuts the feet.   After we had

crossed the lake, we proceeded about five miles down the river, and encamped.

*Nov. 17th.* — The night had been intensely cold, but all felt well and in high spirits when we started in the morning. These feelings were, however, soon damped by the painful difficulties which we soon encountered. Where the river is rapid, the ice becomes rough, craggy, and unsafe, and is raised in hillocks to a considerable height, by the masses being forced by the current on the top of each other. Some of those hillocks we met were so formidable, that we at first doubted the possibility of surmounting them; even in the hollows we were obliged to move slowly, feeling our way with long sticks, to ascertain if the ice was solid. This was rendered necessary by the frequent occurrence of flat fields of ice, which, being formed high above the usual level of the water, and having nothing to support them underneath, easily give way, and the traveller falls either into the torrent far below, or upon another layer of ice. These dangerous places are formed by the large masses of ice getting jammed together against the rocks, or in some bend of the river, and damming the water up, on the top of which a thin coating is formed. As soon as the weight of water becomes too heavy for the dam, it is carried away, and the water sinks, leaving the coat formed on the top without support from beneath, which, when covered with snow, it is impossible to distinguish from good ice, except by feeling it with a stick.

We had not proceeded very far, before one of the men fell through one of these places; luckily he did not come to water, and we soon got him out. Our dogs were now almost useless, as they were unable to drag the sledge over the uneven surface, and we were obliged to push the sledge after them with our poles, and often to lift the dogs, sledge, and baggage up and down the perpendicular ice ridges (or *bourdigneaux*, as the voyageurs call them) with which our path was constantly intersected. At this place it was impossible to leave the river, as the ground on both sides was so broken, and the forest was so dense and tangled, that we should have starved long before we could have made our way through it. About an hour before sundown I unfortunately broke through, and it was with the utmost difficulty that I saved myself from being carried under by the current, which here ran with the velocity of a mill race: happily, I neither lost my pole nor my presence of mind, so the men had time to come up and help me out; but the moment I was out of the water my clothes became perfectly stiff, and we were obliged to make a fire and encamp for the night.

*Nov. 18th.* — Our trials seemed now to be increasing at every step, but the struggle was not optional now; so cheering ourselves with the idea that none know what they can bear until they are tried, we prepared for an early start. Our first trouble was that the dog Mr. Frazer lent me (the best dog we had) was gone; he had gnawed the cord asunder with which he was tied, and bolted off home. This was a serious loss, as besides his use in drawing the sledge, we did not know but that we might want to eat him, our provisions were getting so scarce, and we met with very few rabbits, the only thing to be found on the route at this season.

Our next difficulty was to pass the Grand Rapid, where we found the river obstructed for nearly four miles by bourdigneaux, from ten to fourteen feet high. Over this continuous mass of icy pinnacles we scrambled with incredible labour, our limbs bruised with repeated falls, and our feet wounded and cut by treading on the sharp edges of fractured ice. At last, overpowered by fatigue and pain,

we made our camp for the night, almost disheartened with our slow progress, as we had not made
more than ten or twelve miles through the whole
day.

During the night we were awoke by a tremendous
roaring amongst the masses of ice, caused by a
rising in the river. I could not help feeling apprehensive lest we should be crushed amongst
it, from our camp being so near; but the men were
too tired to move, and I was too tired to argue
with them; so we slept on.

*Nov. 19th.* — When we got up in the morning,
we found that the water had overflowed the ice,
and we were compelled to make a circuit through
the woods. We found the brush and fallen timber
so thick, that we had to cut a road through it to
enable our two dogs and the sledge to get along.
It took us three hours to make an advance of one
mile, before we again got back to the bourdigneaux,
glad even to get to them, in preference to the
tangled and almost impassable growth of trees and
underwood which follows the course of the river
through its whole length. This day I suffered a
great deal; my feet were so severely cut by the
frozen strings of my snow-shoes, that I left a track
of blood behind me on the snow at every step.

At night, when we encamped, it became so cold that we could only sleep for a few minutes at a time: no matter how large we made the fire, it would only keep that part warm which was immediately next to it, so that we were obliged to keep turning round and round to save ourselves from freezing.

*Nov. 20th.*—This morning I found I had what the voyageurs call *mal de racquet*. This complaint attacks those who are unaccustomed to the use of snow-shoes, if they walk far on them at first. It is felt at the instep. I do not know how to convey an idea of the intense pain, except by saying that it feels as if the bones were broken, and the rough edges were grinding against each other at every motion.

*Nov. 21st.*—In the morning we found that the river had become dammed up a short distance below our encampment, and was throwing the ice up in mountainous heaps with tremendous noise. This forced us again to make a short détour through the woods, which we effected with a great deal of trouble. By the time we got to the river again it snowed very hard, and continued without intermission all day; notwithstanding all this, and the mal de racquet, from which I suffered very severely, we pushed on, and, impelled by dire necessity, for our supply of food was fast diminishing, we made rather a good day's journey. We had, up to this, always given our dogs food every day, but my guide advised us not to do so any more, as he had known dogs travel twenty days without food, and every ounce we now had was too precious to give to them, even if they died; so the poor brutes were tied up supperless, and we tried to content ourselves with about half of what was our usual allowance.

*Nov. 22nd.* — The snow still continued, and was getting very deep and light, adding considerably to the labour of our journey; but we toiled on manfully, and succeeded in getting across Baptiste River before we stopped for the night, which did not seem to me as cold as usual, I suppose on account of the falling snow and stillness of the atmosphere.

*Nov. 23rd.* — The snow had ceased falling, but lay very deep and feathery on the ground, so that it fell over on to the snow-shoes, adding to their weight. This to me became very distressing, after two or three hours' walking, owing to the state of my ankles; but the weather was clear and fine, and the bright sun, while it lasted, seemed to cheer us

on, so that at night, when we stopped, we calculated that we had made at least thirty-five miles.
Not having met with any rabbits, we were obliged
to stint ourselves in food, and starve our dogs.

*Nov. 24th.* — To-day we again came to open
water, and had to make another détour through
the woods of about a mile and a half, but it was
not such a bad place as we had encountered before,
the woods being a little more open. When we
came to the river again, we found ourselves on the
top of a high bank, down which we lowered our
sledge and baggage, and then pitched the poor
dogs after. As for ourselves, we scrambled at
the commencement of the descent, then rolled
a little by way of variety, and fell the rest of the
way; however, the snow was so deep, that we did
not get hurt, and after some trouble in unburying
ourselves at the bottom, we continued our route
along the river.

*Nov. 23rd.* — We had not travelled more than
twenty miles, when we came to a part of the river
in which the current was so rapid, that the ice
was all tumbling about in broken masses. On each
side we were encompassed by high banks rising
into hills, which it was impossible for us to ascend;
and as it is a rule, in travelling in the interior,

never to go back, we had nothing for it but to
encamp under the shelter of the hill, in hopes that
the intense cold of the night would sufficiently
unite the masses of ice to enable us to cross in
the morning.

After our camp was made, the men, seeing me
suffer so much from the mal de racquet, recom-
mended me to scarify my insteps, and kindly offered
to perform the operation, which is done with a
sharp gun-flint; but I was afraid of the frost getting into the wounds, and refused, although I had
every confidence in their knowledge of what would
be the best remedy in a case like mine. We had
not succeeded in shooting a single animal on our
route, and it was with melancholy forebodings we
looked at our diminished stock of provisions. Our
poor dogs looked so savage and starved, that we
had to tie their heads close up to the trees,
fearing lest they might gnaw the strings, and make
off.

*Nov.* 26*th.*—In the morning we found the ice
sufficiently strong to induce us to proceed, but we
had to use great caution, as it was still very weak.
Our long snow shoes covering such a large surface,
supported us safely; but the ice was so thin, that
the dogs and sledge went through, and we should

have lost everything we had, had not the Indian held a string fastened to the sledge, and by this means hauled them up. When we surmounted this difficulty, we found the ice better than usual, and were enabled to make in all forty miles before we encamped.

*Nov. 27th.*—We got on to-day very well till about noon, when the mal de racquet became so painful to me, that I thought I would try to walk without my snow-shoes. But I had not waded through the snow very far before I fell through the ice. Luckily, I got out easily enough, but I was wet through; and as our provisions were nearly all gone, and we were all hungry, I pushed on in my wet clothes, trusting to the violent exercise to keep me warm. I certainly did not suffer from cold, but the freezing of my leathern trowsers chafed my legs and made me very uncomfortable. We encamped after a very hard day's work, and as we were in great hopes of reaching Fort Assiniboine next day, we finished the last of our provisions.

*Nov. 28th.*—We started early in the morning, about three o'clock: this was an hour earlier than we usually got away, but we had nothing to cook and no breakfast to eat. I began to feel that my hardships were telling seriously on me. The mal de racquet tortured me at every step; the soles of my feet were terribly cut and wounded from the ice, which formed inside of my stockings as much as an eighth of an inch thick every day, occasioned by the freezing of the perspiration. It breaks in small pieces, and is like so much sharp gravel in the shoes; and I was weak from the want of food: but the hope of reaching a place of safety kept me up, and I toiled on over the bourdigneaux, which were very numerous to-day, steadily but slowly. At last, overcome with fatigue and weakness we had to encamp still far from the fort. We had a long consultation over our camp fire, as to whether we should eat the dogs or not, but their thinness saved them—the two would not have furnished us with a sufficient meal; besides, they could draw the sledge still, and that was a great consideration to us in our weak state; and we knew that if we met with no accident, we must reach the fort next day; still, if the dogs had been young, and in anything like condition, they would most assuredly have gone into the pot.

*Nov. 29th.*—We again started very early in the morning, hunger waking us up earlier than usual. It is the general rule of travelling in these

northern regions, to start as soon as awake, and
to continue until fagged out. Daylight is of such
short duration (not more than four or five hours)
at this time of the year, that it is taken little into
account, the light of the snow and the Aurora
enabling the traveller to see at all hours. Our
way was not very bad, in comparison with what
we had come over; still we had to move on slowly
from weakness, and it was not until four o'clock
P.M., that we arrived at Fort Assiniboine, having
travelled 350 miles in fifteen days.

No sooner had we arrived, than all hands set
to work cooking; luckily for us, this post is plentifully supplied with white fish—indeed, it is almost
the only thing they ever have to eat here—which
are caught in immense numbers in a small lake
near the fort, called M'Leod's Lake. I never saw
such large ones as those caught here. They average
six and seven pounds; and one of them which I
saw weighed had actually attained to the enormous
weight of eighteen pounds.

Whether it was the hunger from which I was
suffering, or the real goodness of the fish, I know
not now; but certainly they seemed to be the most
delicious I had ever tasted, and the memory of
that feast hung over me, even in my dreams, for

many a day afterwards. One of the women devoted herself to the rather arduous task of satisfying my appetite, whilst my two men cooked on their own account, thinking that nobody else would do it quick enough; and no cook who cared for his reputation would have dished-up fish in the raw state in which they devoured the first two or three. I, however, controlled myself, and gave the woman a little time to prepare mine. Having wrapped my feet up in clean pieces of blanket (the only stockings worn in the interior) and put on a pair of clean dry moccasins, I bethought me of the poor dogs, and taking down some raw fish, went out to feed them. It was almost miraculous to see the big lumps of fish which they gulped down, without even an attempt at mastication. Their appearance after the repast was singularly ridiculous, as their bellies were paunched out like full bladders, whilst the rest of their bodies retained still all the scraggy symptoms of prolonged hunger.

On returning from my charitable errand, I found that the good woman had lost no time, and soon, seated on a pile of buffalo skins before a good fire, I commenced the most luxurious repast of which it had ever been my fate to partake. I had

no brandy, spirits, nor wine, neither had I tea,
or coffee—nothing but water to drink.  I had no
Harvey's sauce, or catsup, or butter, or bread,
or potatoes, or any other vegetable.  I had nothing but fish; no variety, save that some were
broiled on the hot coals and some were boiled.
But I had been suffering for days from intense
cold, and I now had rest; I had been starving,
and I now had food; I had been weary and in
pain, without rest or relief, and I now had both
rest and ease.  But, to sum up all, I had come
through a long and serious peril, where for days
I had been haunted with the idea that I must
camp alone in that solitary forest, and let the men
go on, with no food to support me but what I
might obtain by the chance snaring of rabbits.
It was, in fact, the dread of this almost hopeless
alternative, that urged me to exertions upon which
I cannot look back except with wonder, and thus
brought me at last to the safety and comfort in
which I now luxuriated.  How many fish the men
ate, I do not know; but having satiated themselves, they all lay down to sleep.  In the middle
of the night they woke me up, to ask me if I
would not join them in another feast, but I did
not; much to their astonishment, as the woman had

told them that she was afraid I was sick, as I only
ate four fish out of the seven she had prepared for
me. However, in the morning, about five o'clock,
I commenced again, and made another hearty
meal; and then how happy I was when I lay down
and slept again, instead of clambering over the
rugged bourdigneaux !

## CHAP. XXII.

An easy Time. — Clever Rabbit-snare. — Fort Edmonton. — Buffalo Ice-pits. — The Horse and its Keeper. — A tame Battue. — Saving the Credit of the Herd. — Harnessing the Dogs. — My Big Head. — Sober Mirth. — Christmas-day in the Wilds. — Our Fare. — The Feast and the Dance.—" One that looks at the Stars."—Fighting to the Death. — The better part of Valour. — Making a Calf. — An affectionate Bull. — The Aurora Borealis.

*Nov. 30th and Dec. 1st.* — I REMAINED at Fort Assiniboine to allow my feet to recover, which they did rapidly, as I did little but sleep before the fire and eat fish. On the evening of the 1st we all felt so well, that we prepared to proceed next morning to Edmonton, which we calculated to reach easily in four days.

*Dec. 2nd.* — We started early in the morning on snow-shoes, taking with us very little provisions, as we were assured that we should find plenty of rabbits on the road. Our route lay through the woods, which were very thick and encumbered with fallen trees: this rendered our progress slow and very fatiguing; but our renewed strength, and the certainty of a good supper when we stopped kept up our spirits and enabled us to make a very good day's journey. When we encamped for the night, we set to work cooking the rabbits which we had killed on the way, of which we had more than enough. The whole evening they were running across our path. This year they were much more numerous than had been remembered for a long time previously, and the woods were filled with traps set by the Indians, from which we might have helped ourselves if we pleased; but this would not have been considered right as long as we had our guns to shoot them. These snares are fastened to the top of young saplings in such a manner as to spring up when the rabbit is caught, and so suspend him in the air; if this was not done, the wolves and the lynxes, who always follow the rabbits in great numbers, and whose tracks we perceived all round us, would eat them as fast as they were caught.

The lynx is caught by a slip noose made of sinew, simply fastened to a small movable log, which the ensnared animal can drag with difficulty after him. Strange to say, they never attempt to gnaw the string which holds them, although, from the shape of their teeth, they evidently could do so with the greatest ease.

*Dec. 3rd, 4th, and 5th.* — Our route was mostly through woods, but the weather was pleasant, and we had abundance of rabbits, so that the journey seemed like a mere pleasure trip in comparison with what we had gone through.

On the evening of the 5th we arrived at Fort Edmonton, where I was most kindly received by Mr. Harriett, and provided with a comfortable room to myself—a luxury I had not known for many months. This was to be my head-quarters for the winter; and certainly no place in the interior is at all equal to it, either in comfort or interest. All the Company's servants, with their wives and children, numbering about 130, live within the palings of the fort in comfortable log-houses, supplied with abundance of fire-wood.

Along the banks of the river in the vicinity of the fort, about twenty feet below the upper surface, beds of hard coal are seen protruding, which is, however, not much used, except in the blacksmith's forge, for which purpose it seems to be admirably adapted. The want of proper grates or furnaces in those distant regions, where iron is at present so scarce, prevents its general use as fuel.

Provisions are in the greatest plenty, consisting
of fresh buffalo meat, venison, salted geese, magnificent white fish, and rabbits in abundance,
with plenty of good potatoes, turnips, and flour.
The potatoes are very fine, and the turnips do
well here.    Of wheat, they can of course have only
one crop; but with very indifferent farming they
manage to get from twenty to twenty-five bushels
per acre.    The crop, however, is sometimes destroyed by early frost.    The corn is ground in
a windmill, which had been erected since my last
visit, and seemed to make very good flour.    Indian
corn has been tried, but it did not succeed, owing
to the very short summer.

Outside, the buffaloes range in thousands close
to the fort; deer are to be obtained at an easy
distance; rabbits run about in all directions, and
wolves and lynxes prowl after them all through
the neighbouring woods.    As for seeing aborigines,
no place can be more advantageous.    Seven of the
most important and warlike tribes on the continent are in constant communication with the fort,
which is situated in the country of the Crees and
Assiniboines, and is visited at least twice in the
year by the Blackfeet, Sur-cees, Gros-Vents, Pay-
gans, and Blood Indians, who come to sell the

dried buffalo meat and fat for making pemmi-kon, which is prepared in large quantities for the supply of the other posts.

The buffaloes were extremely numerous this winter, and several had been shot within a few hundred yards of the fort. The men had already commenced gathering their supply of fresh meat for the summer in the ice-pit. This is made by digging a square hole, capable of containing 700 or 800 buffalo carcases. As soon as the ice in the river is of sufficient thickness, it is cut into square blocks of a uniform size with saws; with these blocks the floor of the pit is regularly paved, and the blocks cemented together by pouring water in between them, and allowing it to freeze solid. In like manner, the walls are solidly built up to the surface of the ground. The head and feet of the buffalo, when killed, are cut off, and the carcase, without being skinned, is divided into quarters, and piled in layers in the pit as brought in, until it is filled up, when the whole is covered with a thick coating of straw, which is again protected from the sun and rain by a shed. In this manner the meat keeps perfectly good through the whole summer, and eats much better than fresh killed meat, being more tender and better flavoured.

Shortly after my arrival, Mr. Harriett, myself, and two or three gentlemen of the establishment, prepared for a buffalo hunt. We had our choice of splendid horses, as about a dozen are selected and kept in stables for the gentlemen's use from the wild band of 700 or 800, which roam about the fort, and forage for themselves through the winter, by scraping the snow away from the long grass with their hoofs. These horses have only one man to take care of them, who is called the horsekeeper; he follows them about and encamps near them with his family, turning the band should he perceive them going too far away. This would appear to be a most arduous task; but instinct soon teaches the animals that their only safety from their great enemies, the wolves, is by remaining near the habitations of man; and by keeping in one body they are enabled to fight the bands of wolves, which they often drive off after severe contests. Thus they do not stray far away, and they never leave the band. These horses are kept and bred there for the purpose of sending off the pemmi-kon and stores to other forts during the summer; in winter they are almost useless, on account of the depth of snow.

In the morning we breakfasted most heartily

on white fish and buffalo tongues, accompanied by tea, milk, sugar, and *galettes*, which the voyageurs consider a great luxury. These are cakes made of simple flour and water, and baked by clearing away a place near the fire; the cake is then laid on the hot ground, and covered with hot ashes, where it is allowed to remain until sufficiently baked. They are very light and pleasant, and are much esteemed. We then mounted our chosen horses, and got upon the track the men had made on the river by hauling wood. This we followed for about six miles, when we espied a band of buffaloes on the bank; but a dog, who had sneaked after us, running after them, gave the alarm too soon, and they started off at full speed, much to our disappointment. We caught the dog, and tied his legs together, and left him lying in the road to await our return.

After going about three miles further, we came to a place where the snow was trodden down in every direction, and on ascending the bank, we found ourselves in the close vicinity of an enormous band of buffaloes, probably numbering nearly 10,000. An Indian hunter started off for the purpose of turning some of them towards us; but the snow was so deep, that the buffaloes were either

B B

unable or unwilling to run far, and at last came to
a dead stand. We therefore secured our horses,
and advanced towards them on foot to within
forty or fifty yards, when we commenced firing,
which we continued to do until we were tired of
a sport so little exciting ; for, strange to say, they
never tried either to escape or to attack us.

Seeing a very large bull in the herd, I thought I
would kill him, for the purpose of getting the skin of
his enormous head, and preserving it. He fell ; but
as he was surrounded by three others that I could
not frighten )away, I was obliged to shoot them
all before I could venture near him, although they
were all bulls, and they are not generally saved
for meat. The sport proving rather tedious, from
the unusual quietness of the buffaloes, we determined to return home, and send the men for the
carcases, and remounted our horses. But, before
we came to the river, we found an old bull standing right in our way, and Mr. Harriett, for the
purpose of driving him off, fired at him and
slightly wounded him, when he turned and made
a furious charge. Mr. Harriett barely escaped by
jumping his horse on one side. So close, indeed,
was the charge, that the horse was slightly struck
on the rump. The animal still pursued Mr. Har-

riett at full speed, and we all set after him, firing ball after ball into him, as we ranged up close to him, without any apparent effect than that of making him more furious, and turning his rage on ourselves. This enabled Mr. Harriett to reload, and plant a couple more balls in him, which evidently sickened him. We were now all close to him, and we all fired deliberately at him. At last, after receiving sixteen bullets in his body, he slowly fell, dying harder than I had ever seen an animal die before. )

On our return, we told the men to get the dog-sledges ready to go in the morning to bring in the cows we had killed, numbering twenty-seven, with the head of the bull I wanted; whereupon the squaws and half-breed women, who have always this job to do, started off to catch the requisite number of dogs. About the fort there are always two or three hundred who forage for themselves like the horses, and lie outside. These dogs are quite as valuable there as horses, as it is with them that everything is drawn over the snow. Two of them will easily draw in a large cow; yet no care is taken of them, except that of beating them sufficiently before using them, to make them quiet for the time they are in harness.

It would be almost impossible to catch these animals, who are almost as wild as wolves, were it not for the precaution which is taken in the autumn of catching the dogs singly by stratagem, and tying light logs to them, which they can drag about. By this means the squaws soon catch as many as they want, and bring them into the fort, where they arc fed — sometimes — before being harnessed. This operation is certainly (if it were not for the cruelty exhibited) one of the most amusing scenes I had witnessed. Early next morning I was roused by a yelling and screaming that made me rush from my room, thinking that we were all being murdered; and there I saw the women harnessing the dogs. Such a scene! The women were like so many furies with big sticks, threshing away at the poor animals, who rolled and yelled in agony and terror, until each team was yoked up and started off.

During the day the men returned, bringing the quartered cows ready to be put in the ice-pit, and my big head, which, before skinning, I had put in the scales, and found that it weighed exactly 202 lbs. The skin of the head I brought home with me.

The fort at this time of the year presented a most

pleasing picture of cheerful activity : every one was busy ; the men, some in hunting and bringing in the meat when the weather permitted, some in sawing boards in the saw-pit, and building the boats, about thirty feet long and six feet beam, which go as far as York Factory, and are found more convenient for carrying goods on the Sascatchawan and Red River than canoes. They are mostly built at Edmonton, because there are more boats required to take the peltries to York Factory than is required to bring goods back; and more than one-half of the boats built here never return. This system requires them to keep constantly building.

The women find ample employment in making mocassins and clothes for the men, putting up pemmi-kon in ninety-pound bags, and doing all the household drudgery, in which the men never assist them. The evenings are spent round their large fires in eternal gossiping and smoking. The sole musician of the establishment, a fiddler, is now in great requisition amongst the French part of the inmates, who give full vent to their national vivacity, whilst the more sedate Indian looks on with solemn enjoyment.

No liquor is allowed to the men or Indians ; but the want of it did not in the least seem to impair

their cheerfulness.    True, the gentlemen of the
fort had liquor brought out at their own expense;
but the rules respecting its use were so strict and
so well known, that none but those to whom it belonged either expected, or asked, to share it.

On Christmas-day the flag was hoisted, and all
appeared in their best and gaudiest style, to do
honour to the holiday.  Towards noon every chimney
gave evidence of being in full blast, whilst savoury
steams of cooking pervaded the atmosphere in all directions.  About two o'clock we sat down to dinner.
Our party consisted of Mr. Harriett, the chief, and
three clerks, Mr. Thebo, the Roman Catholic missionary from Manitou Lake, about thirty miles off,
Mr. Rundell, the Wesleyan missionary, who resided
within the pickets, and myself, the wanderer, who,
though returning from the shores of the Pacific,
was still the latest importation from civilised life.

The dining-hall in which we assembled was the
largest room in the fort, probably about fifty by
twenty-five feet, well warmed by large fires, which
are scarcely ever allowed to go out.  The walls and
ceilings are boarded, as plastering is not used,
there being no limestone within reach; but these
boards are painted in a style of the most startling
barbaric gaudiness, and the ceiling filled with

centre-pieces of fantastic gilt scrolls, making altogether a saloon which no white man would enter for the first time without a start, and which the Indians always looked upon with awe and wonder.

The room was intended as a reception room for the wild chiefs who visited the fort; and the artist who designed the decorations was no doubt directed to "astonish the natives." If such were his instructions, he deserves the highest praise for having faithfully complied with them, although, were he to attempt a repetition of the same style in one of the rooms of the Vatican, it might subject him to some severe criticisms from the fastidious. No table-cloth shed its snowy whiteness over the board; no silver candelabra or gaudy china interfered with its simple magnificence. The bright tin plates and dishes reflected jolly faces, and burnished gold can give no truer zest to a feast.

Perhaps it might be interesting to some dyspeptic idler, who painfully strolls through a city park, to coax an appetite to a sufficient intensity to enable him to pick an ortolan, if I were to describe to him the fare set before us, to appease appetites nourished by constant out-door exercise in an atmosphere ranging at 40° to 50° below zero. At the head, before Mr. Harriett, was a

large dish of boiled buffalo hump; at the foot
smoked a boiled buffalo calf. Start not, gentle
reader, the calf is very small, and is taken from
the cow by the Cæsarean operation long before it
attains its full growth. This, boiled whole, is one
of the most esteemed dishes amongst the epicures
of the interior. My pleasing duty was to help a
dish of mouffle, or dried moose nose; the gentleman
on my left distributed, with graceful impartiality,
the white fish, delicately browned in buffalo marrow.
The worthy priest helped the buffalo tongue,
whilst Mr. Rundell cut up the beavers' tails. Nor
was the other gentleman left unemployed, as all
his spare time was occupied in dissecting a roast
wild goose. The centre of the table was graced
with piles of potatoes, turnips, and bread conveniently placed, so that each could help himself
without interrupting the labours of his companions.
Such was our jolly Christmas dinner at Edmonton;
and long will it remain in my memory, although
no pies, or puddings, or blanc manges, shed their
fragrance over the scene.

In the evening the hall was prepared for the
dance to which Mr. Harriett had invited all the inmates of the fort, and was early filled by the gaily
dressed guests. Indians, whose chief ornament

consisted in the paint on their faces, voyageurs with bright sashes and neatly ornamented mocassins, half-breeds glittering in every ornament they could lay their hands on; whether civilised or savage, all were laughing, and jabbering in as many different languages as there were styles of dress. English, however, was little used, as none could speak it but those who sat at the dinner-table. The dancing was most picturesque, and almost all joined in it. Occasionally I, among the rest, led out a young Cree squaw, who sported enough beads round her neck to have made a pedlar's fortune, and having led her into the centre of the room, I danced round her with all the agility I was capable of exhibiting, to some highland-reel tune which the fiddler played with great vigour, whilst my partner with grave face kept jumping up and down, both feet off the ground at once, as only an Indian can dance. I believe, however, that we elicited a great deal of applause from Indian squaws and children, who sat squatting round the room on the floor. Another lady with whom I sported the light fantastic toe, whose poetic name was Cunne-wa-bum, or "One that looks at the Stars," was a half-breed Cree girl; and I was so much struck by her beauty, that I prevailed upon her to promise to sit for her likeness, which she afterwards did with great patience, holding her fan, which was made of the tip end of swan's wing with an ornamental handle of porcupine's quills, in a most coquettish manner.—(*Frontispiece.*)

After enjoying ourselves with such boisterous vigour for several hours, we all gladly retired to rest about twelve o'clock, the guests separating in great good humour, not only with themselves but with their entertainers.

A few days afterwards, when we had recovered from the effects of our Christmas festivities, I went out with François Lucie, the half-breed voyageur, of whom Sir George Simpson, in his "Journey round the World," tells the following story:—

"A band of Assiniboines had carried off twenty-four horses from Edmonton, and, being pursued, they were overtaken at the small river Boutbière. One of the keepers of the animals, a very courageous man, of the name of François Lucie, plunged into the stream, grappling in the midst with a tall savage, and, in spite of his inferiority of strength, he kept so close that his enemy could not draw his bow; still, however, the Indian continued to strike his assailant on the head with the weapon in question, and thereby knocked him off his horse into

the water. Springing immediately to his feet,
Lucie was about to smite the Assiniboine with his
dagger, when the savage arrested his arm by seizing a whip, which was hanging to his wrist by a
loop, and then turning round the handle, with a
scornful laugh, he drew the string so tight as to
render the poor man's hand nearly powerless.
François continued nevertheless to saw away at
the fellow's fingers with his dagger till he had
nearly cut them off, and when at length the Assiniboine of necessity relaxed his grasp, François,
with the quickness of thought, sheathed the weapon
in his heart." François told me the story himself,
much as related above, except, he said, that the
savage did not die immediately, although he had
ripped his breast so open that he could see his
heart throbbing, and that he never let go the lasso
of the stolen horses until it ceased, which was for
some minutes, though he tried to pull it from his
hand.

We had not left the fort more than five or six
miles behind us, when we fell in with an enormous
grisly bear, but François would not fire at him,
nor allow me to do so, although I told him I had
helped to kill one before. A younger man than
he, who had his character to make, might have

been foolish enough to have run the risk, for the
sake of the standing it would have given him
amongst his companions; but François had a character established, and would not risk attacking so
formidable an animal with only two men. In fact,
their enormous strength, agility, and wonderful
tenacity of life, make them shunned even by large
numbers, and few are killed, except by young
men, for the sake of proudly wearing the claws —
one of the most esteemed ornaments to an Indian
chief — round their necks.

The bear walked on, looking at us now and then,
but seeming to treat us with contempt. My fingers
were itching to let fly at him: it seemed so easy,
and his skin was in such fine condition. But
though my gun had two barrels, and François was
by my side, with the almost certainty of putting
three balls well in; yet we well knew that it was
ten chances to one that three balls would kill him
quick enough to prevent a hand-to-hand encounter,
a sort of amusement that neither were Quixotic
enough to desire. After we had proceeded a few
miles further, we fell in with a small band of buffaloes, and François initiated me into the mysteries
of "making a calf."

This ruse is generally performed by two men,

one covering himself with wolf skin, the other
with buffalo skin. They then crawl on all fours
within sight of the buffaloes, and as soon as
they have engaged their attention, the pretended
wolf jumps on the pretended calf, which bellows
in imitation of a real one. The buffaloes seem
to be easily deceived in this way. As the bellowing is generally perfect, the herd rush on to
the protection of their supposed young with such
impetuosity that they do not perceive the cheat
until they are quite close enough to be shot; indeed, François' bellowing was so perfect, that we
were nearly run down. As soon, however, as we
jumped up, they turned and fled, leaving two of
their number behind, who paid the penalty of their
want of discernment with their lives.

We shortly afterwards fell in with a solitary
bull and cow, and again "made a calf." The
cow attempted to spring towards us, but the bull
seeming to understand the trick, tried to stop her
by running between us: the cow, however, dodged
and got round him, and ran within ten or fifteen
yards of us, with the bull close at her heels, when
we both fired and brought her down. The bull
instantly stopped short, and bending over her, tried
to raise her up with his nose, evincing the most

persevering affection for her in a rather ridiculous
manner; nor could we get rid of him so as to cut
up the cow, without shooting him also, although
bull flesh is not desirable at this season of the year,
when the female can be procured.

Having loaded our horses with the choice parts of
the three cows we had killed, we proceeded home,
François having taken particular care to secure the
mesenteries or monyplies, as he called them, a part
much esteemed in the interior, although I must
confess I did not like it myself.

Another mode of hunting buffaloes, which we
often practised with great success at Edmonton,.
was accompanied however with considerable fatigue:
it consisted in crawling on our bellies and dragging
ourselves along by our hands, being first fully certain that we were to the leeward of the herd, however light the wind, lest they should scent us until
we came within a few yards of them, which they
would almost invariably permit us to do. Should
there be twenty hunters engaged in the sport, each
man follows exactly in the track of his leader,
keeping his head close to the heels of his predecessor: the buffaloes seem not to take the slightest
notice of the moving line, which the Indians account for by saying that the buffalo supposes it

to be a big snake winding through the snow or grass.

Tired as I was at night after my day's hunt, I was kept long from my bed, fascinated by the appearance of the heavens, which presented to the view one of the most splendid meteoric phenomena I had ever witnessed. Soon after dark a zone of light began to appear, increasing rapidly in brilliancy until about nine or ten o'clock, when it attained its greatest intensity. It was about four degrees in breadth, and extended from the east to the west across the zenith. In its centre, immediately overhead, appeared a blood-red ball of fire, of greater diameter than the full moon rising in a misty horizon; from the ball emanated rays of crimson light, merging into a brilliant yellow at the northern edges. The belt also on the northern side presented the same dazzling brightness; while the snow and every object surrounding us was tinted by the same hues. I continued lost in admiration of this splendid phenomenon until past one in the morning, when it still shone with undiminished, if not increased, brilliancy. Tired out at last, I was compelled to retire to bed, but those who still sat up told me that it faded away about three o'clock in the morning, without varying its position or form.

The Indians have a poetical superstition in regard to the Aurora Borealis, which is in this high latitude remarkably brilliant, shooting up coruscations of surprising splendour.    These, they think, are " the spirits of the dead dancing before the Manitou, or Great Spirit."

# CHAP. XXIII.

A pleasant Wedding.—Sledges and Carioles.—Useful but Dangerous Dogs. — The Hunter's Bravado. — Journey through the Snow. — An unwilling Chase. — A Tumble in a Drift. — Indian Etiquette. — The Spotted Leg. — The Indian in Heaven.—Battle of the Dogs. — Arrival at Fort Pitt. — The Medicine Pipe-stem and its Carrier. — Ceremony of opening Pipe-stems. — Exhibition of Medicine Dresses.—Digging up the Hatchet.—Crying for War. —Invoking the Great Spirit. — Preparing for the March. — Eating a Warrior's Heart.

On the 6th of January 1848, we had a wedding at Edmonton; the bride was the daughter of the gentleman in charge, the bridegroom Mr. Rowand, junior, who resided at Fort Pitt, a distance of 200 miles from the establishment. After the ceremony, which was performed by the Rev. Mr. Rundell, the Methodist missionary, we spent a pleasant evening, feasting and dancing until midnight. Having received an invitation to accompany the happy pair on the journey home, I gladly accepted it, as I began to find my amusements rather monotonous. Next morning I was awoke by the yelping of the dogs and the ringing of the bells on the dog-collars, accompanied by the shouts of the men thrashing the brutes into something like discipline, as they harnessed them to the sledges and carioles. On coming out into the yard, I found our party nearly ready to start. It consisted of Mr. Rowand and his

No. 14. — Winter-travelling in Dog-sleds.

bride, with nine men. We had three carioles and six sledges, with four dogs to each, forming when on route a long and picturesque cavalcade: all the dogs gaudily decorated with saddle-cloths of various colours, fringed and embroidered in the most fantastic manner, with innumerable small bells and feathers, producing altogether a pleasing and en-livening effect (sketch No. 14).

Our carioles were also handsomely decorated, the bride's more particularly, which had been made expressly for the occasion, and was elaborately painted and ornamented, and was drawn by a set of dogs recently imported from Lower Canada by Mr. Rowand. The cariole is intended for carry-ing one person only; it is a thin flat board, about eighteen inches wide, bent up in front, with a straight back behind to lean against; the sides are made of green buffalo hide, with the hair scraped completely off and dried, resembling thick parchment; this entirely covers the front part, so that a person slips into it as into a tin bath.

We started as the day dawned, the dogs running at a furious rate, as they invariably do at first starting, and require all the strength and agility of the men to keep the sledges and carioles from upsetting, which they manage to do as well as they can by holding on to a cord attached to each side from behind. Two men go before on the run in snow shoes to beat a track, which the dogs instinctively follow: these men are relieved every two hours, as it is very laborious. The dogs generally used are of a breed peculiar to the country, and partake largely of the character and disposition of the wolf, which they often so resemble in appearance as sometimes to have been shot in mistake. Their ferocity is so great that they are often dangerous. Some of them this winter attacked a horse belonging to Mr. Harriett, harnessed to a sledge. Mr. Harriett had tied him to a stake and left him; on his return, in about half an hour, he found the dogs tearing him to pieces; nor would the dogs leave their prey until he had shot five of them: the horse died almost immediately.

Mr. Rundell was himself attacked one evening, while walking a short distance from the fort, by a band of these brutes belonging to the establishment; they got him down, and, but for his cries bringing the assistance of a squaw, they would have served him in a similar manner.

Immediately on leaving the fort, we got on the ice of the Saskatchawan River, and travelled down it all day, having, in the true voyageur style, trusted to our prowess as hunters for a supply of food on our journey, although of 200 miles; and, having literally brought nothing with us but the kettles, we were unable to break our fast until we had killed a fat cow, which was soon demolished by ourselves and the dogs. This apparent absence of foresight is, in reality, often affected by the voyageurs out of bravado, for they are quite as much disinclined to hunger and abstinence as other people. In our case we might certainly have brought plenty of food if we liked, but, on the other hand, buffaloes were plentiful, and there was almost a certainty of obtaining them.

*Jan. 9th.*—Left our encampment three hours before day, and about daylight we killed two buffaloes and stopped to breakfast. The wind blew very cold and strong all day, with continued snow. After breakfast we left the circuitous windings of the river, and the friendly shelter of its banks and woods, to cut across the bleak and open plains, where we were exposed to the full fury of the chill blast; but this shortened our journey by many miles. In the evening we killed two more buffaloes, and encamped in a clump of pines, the last sheltered spot we might expect on our journey.

*Jan. 10th.*—Our spirit thermometer stood this morning at 47° below zero, Fahr. Finding it impossible to keep myself warm in my cariole, in spite of plenty of skins and blankets, I put on a pair of snow shoes and walked all day. The snow was three feet deep on an average, and was drifted by the wind with such violence in our faces as to nearly blind us; notwithstanding which our guides seemed to find no difficulty in pursuing their course—such is the instinctive faculty of these men in tracing their way over this trackless desert, where not a stick or a shrub is to be met with to guide them. Towards evening we arrived at a sort of enclosure, which had evidently been erected by the Blackfoot Indians as a protection from the Crees, whose country this is, but where the Blackfeet sometimes come to steal horses. In the evening we only got one cow, which seemed barely to satisfy our dogs.

*Jan.* 11*th.*—Started as usual this morning three hours before daylight, the days being short: this early starting is necessary to allow the men to stop and make the encampment before dark. We met two of the Company's men on their way from Carlton to the place we had so recently left. We killed only one buffalo to-day, and were obliged to sleep on the snow, no pine branches being within reach to make our beds. These we missed much, as they add much to the comfort of an encampment.

*Jan.* 12*th.*—We again got on the river. Having

brought a small quantity of meat from our last night's supper with us, but not sufficient for all, some of our party went on in advance to hunt, whilst we stopped to take a scanty breakfast. About two hours afterwards we came up to them, sitting round a good fire cooking a fine . fat cow, the delicate pieces of which they were demolishing with considerable rapidity, owing to the lateness of their meal.

During the day a diverting occurrence took place, although it might have turned out very serious. A herd of buffaloes had come down the bank on to the ice, and did not perceive our approach until the foremost sledge was so near them as to excite the dogs, who rushed furiously after them, notwithstanding all the efforts of the men to stop them. The spirit of the hunt was at once communicated through the whole line, and we were soon all, carioles and sledges, dashing along at a furious rate after the buffaloes. The frightened animals made a bold dash at last through a deep snow bank, and attempted to scramble up the steep bank of the river, the top of which the foremost one had nearly reached, when, slipping, he rolled over and knocked those behind, one on top of another, down into the deep snow-drift amongst the men and dogs, who were struggling in it. It would be impossible to describe the wild scene of uproar and confusion that followed. Some of our sledges were smashed, and one of the men was nearly killed; but at last we succeeded in getting clear and repairing damages. We continued on our wedding tour.

*Jan.* 13*th.* — Started at half-past 1 A.M. We followed a buffalo track along the river, in the deep ruts of which our carioles were frequently upset, rolling us into the snow. Having killed three buffaloes on the banks of the river, we stopped to breakfast; two calves, evidently belonging to the slaughtered animals, remained within a hundred yards of our fire the whole time.

Leaving the river, we passed over a succession of hills and valleys until dark, when we arrived at a camp of Cree Indians, consisting of about forty lodges. We went to the lodge of the chief named " Broken Arm," who received us very kindly, spreading buffalo robes in the best part of his tent for us to sit on, and placing before us the best his stock afforded. After supper, the chief having cut some tobacco and filled a handsome stone pipe, took a few whiffs from it himself, and then presented it to me. On my doing the same, and offering it to him again, as is the custom, he told me that he wished me to accept it as a gift.

The lodge was soon filled with Indians, anxious to learn the news, which they are always eager to hear from strangers. Amongst our visitors was the son-in-law of the chief; and, according to the Indian custom, he took his seat with his back towards his father and mother-in-law, never addressing them but through the medium of a third party, and they preserving the same etiquette towards him. This rule is not broken through until the son-in-law proves himself worthy of personally speaking to him, (by having killed an enemy with white hairs; they then become entitled to wear a dress trimmed with human hair, taken from the scalps of their foes. I remarked that one of the leggings of the young man was spotted with some red earth, and the other not: on inquiring the reason, I was told that the spotted leg had been wounded, and the red earth was intended to indicate blood.

We sat up very late, talking to the chief, who seemed to enjoy our society very much. Amongst other topics of discourse, he began talking about the efforts of the missionaries amongst his people, and seemed to think that they would not be very successful; for though he did not interfere with the religious belief of any of his tribe, yet many thought as he did; and his idea was, that as Mr. Rundell had told him that what he preached was the only true road to heaven, and Mr. Hunter told him the same thing, and so did Mr. Thebo, and as they all three said that the other two were wrong, and as he did not know which was right, he thought they ought to call a council amongst themselves, and that then he would go with them all three; but that until they agreed he would wait. He then told us that there was a tradition in his tribe of one of them having become a Christian, and was very good, and did all that he ought; and that when he died he was taken up to the white man's heaven, where everything was very good and very beautiful, and all were happy amongst their friends and relatives who had gone before them, and where they had everything that the white man loves and longs for; but the Indian could not share their joy and pleasure, for all was strange to him, and he met none of the spirits of his ancestors, and there was none to welcome him, no hunting nor fishing, nor any of those joys in which he used to delight, and his spirit grew sad. Then the Great Manitou called him, and asked him, "Why art thou sad in this beautiful heaven which I have made for your joy and happiness?" and the Indian told him that he sighed for the company of the spirits of his relations, and that he felt lone and sorrowful. So the Great Manitou told him that he could not send him to the Indian heaven, as he had, whilst on earth, chosen this one, but that as he had been a very good man, he would send him back to earth again, and give him another chance.

*Jan. 14th.*—We travelled to-day through a hilly country until we arrived at another encampment of about thirty lodges. Our dogs rushed down amongst the lodges, dragging the sledges and carioles after them, and were immediately attacked by all the dogs in the Indian camp, barking, howling, and fighting, until all the sledges were upset, and some of them broken to pieces. It was half an hour before we could separate the enraged brutes.

These Indians had a buffalo pound within a short distance of their encampment, which was literally crammed with the dead frozen carcases they had slaughtered in it. On nearing Fort Pitt we fell in with two buffaloes, immediately in our track, and as we did not want the meat, they might have been allowed to escape, but for the large development of the bump of destructiveness in our men's heads.

We reached the fort soon after dark, having been seven days on our route from Edmonton. We had killed seventeen buffaloes in this journey, for feeding ourselves and dogs. The animals had, we were told, never appeared in such vast numbers, nor shown themselves so near the Company's establishments; some have even been shot within the gates of the fort. They killed with their horns twenty or thirty horses in their attempt to drive them off from the patches of grass which the horses had pawed the snow from with their hoofs for the purpose of getting at the grass, and severely gored many others, which eventually recovered.

These remarks convey but a faint idea of the astonishing numbers of these animals: within the whole distance we had travelled on this journey we were never out of sight of large herds of them, and we had not found it necessary to go a step out of our direct course to find more than we required for our use. They were probably migrating northwards, to escape from the human migrations which are so rapidly filling up the southern and western regions, which were formerly their pasture grounds.

I spent a very pleasant and interesting month at

Fort Pitt, surrounded by Cree Indians, this being one of their principal places of resort, and had ample opportunity of studying their habits and manners. I took an elaborate sketch of a pipe-stem carrier with his medicine pipe-stem. The pipe-stem carrier is elected every four years by the band of the whole tribe to which he belongs, and is not allowed to retain the distinction beyond that period, all being eligible for the situation who have sufficient means to pay for it. But the expense is considerable, as the new officer elect has to pay his predecessor for the emblems of his dignity, which frequently are valued at from fifteen to twenty horses. Should he not possess sufficient means, his friends usually make up the deficiency, otherwise the office would in many cases be declined. It is, however, compulsory upon the person elected to serve if he can pay. The official insignia of the pipe-stem carrier are numerous, consisting of a highly ornamental skin tent, in which he is always expected to reside; a bear's skin upon which the pipe-stem is to be exposed to view when any circumstance requires it to be taken out from its manifold coverings in which it is usually wrapped up, such as a council of war, or a medicine pipe-stem dance, or on a quarrel taking

place in the tribe, to settle which the medicine-
man opens it for the adverse parties to smoke
out of,—their superstitions leading them to fear
a refusal of the reconciling ceremony, lest some
calamity should be inflicted on them by the Great
Spirit for their presumption;—a medicine rattle,
which is employed in their medicine dances, and a
wooden bowl, from which the dignitary always
takes his food,—this he always carries about his
person, sometimes in his hand, and often on his
head;—besides numerous small articles.

It requires two horses to carry them when on the
move. The pipe-stem itself is usually carried by
the favourite wife of the official, and should it under
any circumstances fall on the ground, it is regarded
as a bad omen, and many ceremonies must be gone
through to reinstate it. A young man, a half-
breed, assured me that he had once a pipe-stem committed to his charge by an official who had gone out
on a hunting excursion, and that being well aware
of the sanctity attributed to it by the Crees, he was
determined to try himself the effect of throwing it
down and kicking it about, and that shortly after
this act of desecration, as it would be considered,
the pipe-stem carrier was killed by the Blackfeet.
From that time he became a firm believer in the

sanctity of the pipe-stem, and, as may be supposed,
told me this story as a great secret.

A pipe-stem carrier always sits on the right side
of his lodge as you enter, and it is considered a great
mark of disrespect to him if you pass between him
and the fire, which always occupies the centre of the
lodge.   He must not condescend to cut his own
meat, but it is always cut for him by one of his
wives, of whom he usually has five or six, and placed
in his medicine bowl, which, as before said, he has
always with him.   One of the greatest incon-
veniences attached to the office, particularly to an
Indian, who has always innumerable parasitical
insects infesting his person, is, that the pipe-stem
carrier dares not scratch his own head without
compromising his dignity, without the intervention
of a stick, which he always carries for that purpose.
The pipe-stem, enclosed in its wrappers, always
hangs in a large bag, when they can procure it, of
party-coloured woollen cloth, on the outside of
the lodge, and is never taken inside either by night
or by day, nor allowed to be uncovered when any
woman is present. ·

About a fortnight after my arrival, Kee-a-kee-ka-
sa-coo-way, " the Man who gives the War-whoop,"
whom I mentioned before as having met on the Sas-

katchawan on my journey out, arrived at Fort Pitt with his sub-chief, Muck-e-too, "Powder."

Kee-a-kee-ka-sa-coo-way is the head chief of all the Crees, and was now travelling through all their camps to induce them to take up the tomahawk and follow him on a war excursion in the following spring. He had eleven medicine pipe-stems with him, ten of which belonged to inferior chiefs, who had already consented to join in the expedition. Being curious to witness the opening of these pipe-stems and see the ceremonial accompanying it, I travelled with him to the camp, situated a few miles from Fort Pitt. On our arrival, the wrappers of the stems were removed and carried in procession, headed by the chief in person, through the camp. The procession halted in front of nearly every lodge, where he delivered a continuous harangue, the burden of which was to rouse them to take up arms and revenge the death of the warriors who had been killed in former wars. During the whole of this address the tears continued to stream down his face as if at his entire command. This the Indians call crying for war.

The weather was most intensely cold, notwithstanding which, and his being half naked, so strongly was every feeling concentrated on the subject, that he appeared altogether insensible to its severity, although the thermometer must have indicated at least thirty to forty degrees below zero. ( On the day following, I endeavoured to prevail on him to open the pipe-stems, in order that I might sketch some of them; this he at first declined, until he had been told that I was a great medicine-man, and that my sketching them would very much increase their efficiency when opened on the field of battle. He thereupon opened them with the following ceremonies. He first took a coal from the fire, and sprinkled upon it the dried leaves of a plant collected on the Rocky Mountains, the smoke of which filled the place with a fragrant odour resembling that of the incense burned in Catholic churches; while this was burning, he filled the bowls of these pipes with tobacco and some other weed, after which he took off all his clothes, with the exception of the breechcloth.

On my looking rather suspiciously at the clothes he had taken off, seeing they were rather old and filthy, he took notice of my doing so, and remarked, that although he possessed better, he was not allowed by the customs of his tribe to wear them, as he was then mourning the death of four

of his relations who had been killed by the Blackfeet the year before. (He, however, put on his
good clothes for me afterwards, when I took
sketch No. 15, as I told him that the picture would
be shown to the queen.) He then threw over his
shoulders the skin of a wolf highly ornamented
after the Indian fashion, and immediately removed
the wrappers of leather, &c., that covered one of
the stems, and inserting it into one of the bowls
he had previously filled with tobacco, commenced
a song which I could not understand.

On finishing, he lighted the pipe, and inhaled a
mouthful of smoke; then turning his face upwards
and pointing in the same direction with the stem,
he blew upwards a long stream of smoke, and
called on the Great Spirit to give them success in
war, to enable them to take many scalps, and set
their enemies asleep whilst they carried off their
horses; that their own wives might continue vir-
tuous and never grow old. He then turned the
stem to the earth, after blowing out another puff
of smoke, and called upon the earth to produce
abundance of buffalo and roots for the coming
season. He then pointed the stem towards me,
and requested that, if I possessed any influence
with the Great Spirit, I would intercede with him

Paul Kane, del.                              Vincent Brooks, Lith

PORTRAIT OF KEE-AKEE-KA-SAA-KA-WOW WITH PIPE-STEM.

for the supply of all their wants. A half-breed woman happening to look into the lodge at this moment, the ceremony was instantly suspended, and she as instantly shrunk back; a woman never being allowed to be present when the medicine pipe-stem is exposed to view.

After some little prolonged ceremony, consisting principally of all present smoking from each stem as it was opened, he permitted me to sketch them, but never left the lodge until I had finished and he had carefully recovered and removed them. He told me he had been on this war mission to nearly every camp in his tribe, and intended to visit the whole of them; the distance he would have to travel in snow shoes to accomplish this would not be less than six or seven hundred miles. It is the custom of the Indians after such a call to assemble at a place appointed on the Saskatchawan River, where they continue feasting and dancing three days previously to their starting for the enemy's country. Here all their pipe-stems and medicine dresses are exhibited, and they decorate themselves with all the finery they can command, in which they continue their advance until they reach the enemy. But no sooner are they in view, than their ornaments and their whole clothing are hastily thrown aside, and they fight naked.

A year before my arrival amongst them, a war party of 700 left for the Blackfeet country, which nation the Crees regard as their natural enemies, and are never at peace with them. After travelling for some fifteen or twenty days, a sickness broke out among them, affecting numbers and carrying off a few. This was considered by some of their great men a judgment upon them from the Great Spirit for some previous misconduct, and they, therefore, returned home without having accomplished anything. On another occasion a similar party fell in with a great warrior among the Blackfeet, named "Big Horn," and six of his tribe, who were out on the legitimate calling of horse stealing,—for the greater the horse thief the greater the warrior. This small band, seeing their inferiority to their enemies, attempted flight; but finding escape impossible, they instantly dug holes sufficiently deep to intrench themselves, from which they kept up a constant fire with guns and arrows, and for nearly twelve hours held at bay this large war party, bringing down every man who ventured within shot, until their ammunition and arrows were entirely exhausted, when they of course fell an easy prey to their enemies, thirty of whom had fallen before their fire. This so enraged the Crees that they cut them in pieces, and mangled the dead bodies in a most brutal manner, and carried their scalps back as trophies.

It is said that Big Horn frequently sprang out from his intrenchment, and tried to irritate his foes by recounting the numbers of them he had destroyed, and boasting his many war exploits, and the Cree scalps that then hung in his lodge. So exasperated were they against him, that they tore out his heart from his quivering body, and savagely devoured it amongst them.

I returned to Edmonton by the same route, and in the same manner I had come from it, and as nothing material occurred in the route, I omit the details.

# CHAP. XXIV.

I REMAINED at Edmonton until the 12th of April,
when, having heard that a large band of Blackfeet
were shortly expected to visit Rocky Mountain
House, situated about 180 miles south-west of
Edmonton, on the Saskatchawan, for the purpose
of trading, and being anxious to see them, I started
with a small party of six men and about twenty
horses, ten of which were loaded with goods. The
snow had not left the ground, and our horses were
in very bad condition, from living out all the
winter, except the one which I rode, which had
been kept in, and was the most vicious brute I
ever met. When I dismounted from him the first

evening, he tried to get away from me, and when he found that I held on to the lasso, he attacked me with open mouth, and had not one of the men knocked him down with a stick, he might have seriously injured me. Our progress was, therefore, necessarily slow, as I would not ride away from the party.

We found buffaloes in places where the Indians said they had never been seen before, and remained two days at a place called Battle River, to rest our horses, as we had plenty of food for ourselves and grass for the horses. I went out with an Indian and killed a cow, which was followed by her calf. Wishing to take the calf alive, so that it might carry itself to the camp, I pursued and caught it, and, tying my sash round its neck, endeavoured to drag it along; but it plunged and tried so violently to escape that I was about to kill it, when the Indian took hold of its head, and turning up its muzzle, spat two or three times into it, when, much to my astonishment, the animal became perfectly docile, and followed us quietly to the camp, where it was immediately cooked for supper.

Finding three of the rivers in our route much flooded, we were obliged to make rafts to cross upon, so as to keep the goods dry. At the fourth river we were fortunate to find a raft formed by nature, in the shape of a large mass of floating ice, which one of the men swimming out dragged ashore. It was sufficiently buoyant to support two or three men, and by attaching our lassoes to it, and drawing it backwards and forwards, we soon got all our goods over dry. The horses we made swim.

Some of the men suffered severely from what is called "snow blind," which is a species of inflammation, brought on by the strong glare of the sun reflected from the snow. The pain in the eyeballs is excessive, and resembles the feeling produced by having sand in the eyes ; the sufferers are sometimes blinded by it for weeks. This can be prevented by wearing a veil, which I did, and is generally adopted when they can be procured.

We arrived at Rocky Mountain Fort on the 21st of April. This fort is beautifully situated on the banks of the Saskatchawan, in a small prairie, backed by the Rocky Mountains in the distance. In the vicinity was a camp of Assiniboine lodges, formed entirely of pine branches. It was built for the purpose of keeping a supply of goods to trade with the Blackfoot Indians, who come there every winter, and is abandoned and left empty every summer. It is built like most of the other forts, of wood, but with more than ordinary regard to strength, which is thought necessary on account of the vicious disposition of the Blackfoot tribe, who are, without exception, the most warlike on the northern continent. I may state that beds of coal are seen protruding here along the banks of the river, similar to that of Edmonton.

There is also a small band of Assiniboines in the neighbourhood of the fort. The Blackfeet attacked them last year, and carried off two girls captives. One of them, after having been carried away a long distance, was stripped naked, and told to find her way back as best she could, and as she was never heard of afterwards, it was supposed that she perished from cold and hunger; the other girl was taken charge of by a chief, who sent her relations word that she should be returned safe, which promise he fulfilled.

We found a man at the establishment, called Jemmy Jock, a Cree half-breed, who had temporary charge of it; he had obtained much Blackfoot celebrity. He was sent out when a clerk of Hudson's Bay Company, by them, to the Blackfoot

Indians, in order to learn their language, for the purpose of facilitating the trade with them. He then married a daughter of one of their chiefs, and taking a fancy to their mode of life, he left the Company's service, and stayed with them. He afterwards became one of their chiefs, and being a man of singular acuteness, soon acquired great influence. The missionaries entertained very little respect for him, and have spoken very badly of him throughout the whole country; but as far as my intercourse with him went, I always found him trustworthy and hospitable. I learned much from him relative to the customs of the Blackfoot tribe, of which, owing to his long residence amongst them, thirty or forty years, he possessed a greater knowledge probably than any other man with the same education.

Shortly after my arrival a report was brought in that the Blackfoot Indians had killed a party of Crees, and that amongst the slain was a pipe-stem carrier, whom they had skinned and stuffed with grass; the figure was then placed in a trail which the Crees were accustomed to pass in their hunting excursions. The Assiniboines, who reside in the vicinity of this fort, I found the most kind and honourable of any tribe that I met with. They constitute a very small part (say forty or fifty families) of a very large tribe who live in a more easterly direction. Mah-Min, " The Feather," their head chief, permitted me to take his likeness, and after I had finished it, and it was shown to the others, who all recognised and admired it, he said to me, " You are a greater chief than I am, and I present you with this collar of grizzly bear's claws, which I have worn for twenty-three summers, and which I hope you will wear as a token of my friendship." This collar I have, of course, brought home with me.

The second chief, Wah-he-joe-tass-e-neen, " The half-white Man," seeing that I was so successful with his head chief's likeness, and probably feeling a little jealous, came and requested me to take his also, which I willingly did, as he had one of the most extraordinary countenances I had met with for some time. He was a man, however, noted as a great hunter, and as an evidence of his tremendous powers of endurance, it was related to me that one morning he had started on snow shoes in pursuit of two moose, and pursued them until they separated. He then followed one track until he killed his prey, cut it up, and put it on scaffolding to secure it from the wolves. He then returned to where the tracts separated, and followed the other; this he also killed, and placed, as he had done the former, returning to his lodge late in the evening. In the morning he sent off three men with dog sledges to bring in the game, and they were three days following his tracks before they got home.

Mah-Min gave one of the missionaries who was up here last summer a very long and serious lecture upon lying. It seems the missionary, who did not smoke himself, had brought with him a carat of tobacco for the purpose of purchasing horses and food from the Indians, should he require them. Immediately on his arrival, the Indians, who had exhausted their stock, eagerly inquired if he had any tobacco, but he was afraid that if he acknowledged he had any they would want it all, and leave him without anything to barter with them, and denied that he had any. Shortly afterwards, when he was about to return, he went to Mah-Min, and told him that he wanted horses and some provisions to return, and that he would pay him for them in tobacco, when Mah-Min said to him, " You preach to the Indians many things, and tell them not to steal or lie; how can they believe or listen to you? You are the father of lies. You said you had no tobacco, and now you say you have plenty."

We had nothing to eat at Rocky Mountain House but rabbits, and even of those we could not get as much as we wanted; this was in consequence of the *cache*, in which the dried meat was placed, having been robbed by the Assiniboines, who, if they could not be honest against the temptations of hunger, at least tried to be as much so as they could, for they placed furs of considerable value in the place of the meat they had stolen. This was the second year they had played the same game; but however satisfactory the arrangement might be to the Hudson's Bay Company, it certainly was anything but pleasant either to their servants or myself; so that after being half starved for ten days, and seeing no signs of the Blackfoot Indians coming in, I persuaded Jemmy Jock to come back with me to Edmonton. This he agreed to do, and he said he had a *cache* of dried meat on the road which would supply us with plenty, so that all we had to do was to ride fast until we came to it.

Early in the morning, we started, taking four extra horses with us as relays. This is done by one man riding in front, then the loose horses, and the other man follows and drives them on; the horses seldom stray or give trouble in this way, and, as they carry no weight, are comparatively fresh when the horse you ride has broken down. We rode the whole day at a tremendous pace, stimulated by hunger, and arrived at the *cache* towards dusk. Having tied our horses, Jemmy went to the *cache*, which was made of logs built together, something like a loghouse, but not very closely fitted together, and began throwing off the heavy logs which covered the top and concealed it. He heard a regular rumpus within, so he called to me to fetch the guns; when I got up, he removed part of the top, and a fine fat wolverine jumped out, which I immediately shot down. The brute must have been starved and desperately thin to have squeezed himself through the openings between the logs, and no doubt impelled by hunger, and the smell of the meat inside, had not thought much of a slight squeeze. However, when he was once in, and had had a good meal, he could not get out again, and the idea of starving himself as long as the meat lasted, did not seem to have occurred to him. This was a great disappointment to us, as there was very little left, and that mangled, torn, and tossed about in the dirt by the animal. We, however, contrived to make a supper, and saved some for the future; but it was so little, that instead of taking our time on the road as we had intended, we had nothing for it but to ride as fast as we could.

The next day was most uncomfortable, as we had a heavy snow storm blowing in our faces the whole day; but we pushed on gallantly, and finished our provisions between supper and breakfast next morning, and on the afternoon of the third day we got into Edmonton, but only with two horses, the others having been fagged out and left behind.

*May 22nd.*—Mr. Low arrived from the east side of the Rocky Mountains, in company with Mr. de Merse, the Roman Catholic Bishop of Vancouver, and Mr. Paul Frazer. The boats and their cargoes had been long prepared, and we only waited for a favourable break in the weather to commence our journey home.

*May 25th.*—The weather having cleared up, we embarked with the before-mentioned gentlemen for Norway House. We had twenty-three boats, and 130 men, with Mr. Harriett as our chief. We saw great numbers of dead buffaloes along the shore of the river, which, from the long continuance of the snow covering the herbage, had become so exhausted, that they were drowned in attempting to swim across the river, in their accustomed migration to the south every spring, and now lay in thousands along the banks.   At night we drifted down with the current, the men tying several boats together, so as to be under the guidance of one man, whilst the rest lay down and slept.

*May 26th.*—We saw several large herds of buffaloes swimming across the river, all going south.

*May 27th.*—What with the strong current, the men pulling all day, and our drifting all night, we again arrived at Fort Pitt, where we got an addition to our party of two more boats.   These boats are all loaded with the furs and pimmi-kon of the Saskatchawan district.   The furs are taken down to York Factory, in the Hudson's Bay, where they are shipped to Europe ; the pimmi-kon is intended for those posts where provisions are difficult to be procured.   We remained at Fort Pitt for two days whilst the other boats were getting ready, and I took advantage of the delay to sketch a Cree chief. He was dressed in full costume, with a pipe-stem in his hand.

*May 29th.*—We left Fort Pitt, quite filling the

river with our fleet of boats, presenting a most imposing and animated appearance, considering that we were navigating inland waters so far from the boundaries of civilisation. We saw great numbers of wolves busily employed in devouring the carcases of the drowned buffaloes, and had some amusing hunts with our boats after them, our men greatly enjoying the sport. We continued our course in great humour and comfort, without meeting with anything which I considered particularly worthy of recording at the time, until

*June 1st,* when we saw a large party of mounted Indians, riding furiously towards us. On their nearer approach they proved to be a large war party, consisting of Blackfoot Indians, Blood Indians, Sur-cees, Gros Ventres, and Pay-gans. We had a Cree Indian in one of our boats, whom we had to stow away under the skins which covered the goods, lest he should be discovered by the party, who were expressly bound on an expedition against his tribe, and whom our disproportionate number could not have opposed had they sought to take him from us. We instantly put ashore to meet them, and Mr. Harriett and myself met them on the banks of the river, leaving strict orders with the men to keep the boats afloat sufficiently near the shore for us to re-embark promptly in case of danger. They received Mr. Harriett, however, in a most friendly manner, he being personally known to numbers of them. They immediately spread a buffalo skin for us to sit down upon, depositing all their arms, consisting of knives, guns, and bows and arrows, on the ground in front of us, in token of amity.

There was, however, one exception to this pacific demonstration, in the case of an Indian I had frequently heard spoken of before, named Omoxe-sisixany, "Big Snake." This chief walked round the party, cracking and flourishing a whip, and singing a war song, evidently desirous of getting up a fight, and refusing to lay down his arms with the rest, although frequently requested to do so. At length, however, he put them down, and sat with the rest, and taking (though with evident reluctance) a few puffs from the pipe which was going the round of the party, in token of peace, he turned to Mr. Harriett and said, that as he had smoked with the white man, he would present him with his horse, at the same time leading up a beautiful brown animal which I had seen him alight from on our arrival, he handed Mr. Harriett the lasso. Mr. Harriett declined his gift, explaining that it was impossible for him to take it with him in the boats.

They told us they were a party of 1500 warriors, from 1200 lodges, who were then " pitching on" towards Fort Edmonton; that is, they were making short journeys, and pitching their tents on towards Edmonton, leaving few behind capable of bearing arms. They were in pursuit of the Crees and Assiniboines, whom they threatened totally to annihilate, boasting that they themselves were as numerous as the grass on the plains. They were the best mounted, the best looking, the most warlike in appearance, and the best accoutred of any tribe I had ever seen on the continent during my route. As Mr. Harriett was very anxious to cultivate the acquaintance and friendship of such questionable characters, he accepted of their invitation to "camp" with them until the following morning, which was exceedingly acceptable to me, as it enabled me to make several sketches, and to hear something about them. After our smoke several of the young Braves engaged in a horse race, to which sport they are very partial, and at which they bet heavily; they generally ride on those occasions stark naked, without a saddle, and with only a lasso fastened to

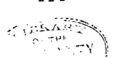

the lower jaw of the horse as represented in Sketch No. 16. I had some difficulty at first in getting the chiefs to let me take their likenesses, but after they comprehended what I wanted, they made no objections.

No. 16. — Horse Race.

Big Snake's brother was the first who sat to me, and while I was sketching, he told me the following anecdote of his brother, of whom he seemed to be very proud. Mr. Harriett understood the language and acted as interpreter.  Some time back, Big Snake had the free admission to one of the American forts near the Rocky Mountains. Coming up one day with two other Indians, to enter the gate, it was shut rudely in his face by the orders of the commander, who had only lately arrived in the country.  This his pride led him to regard as a direct insult; he rode away, and falling in with some cattle that he knew belonged to the fort, he commenced firing on them, and killed thirteen.  As soon as the sentinel, who had ·given the offence, heard the shots, he suspected the reason, and informed the superintendent, who immediately collected his men, and sallied out with them well armed, in the direction of the firing. Big Snake being on the watch, hid himself with his two companions behind a small hill.

The party from the fort apprehending there might be a large number of Indians hid, hesitated to advance within gun-shot; but a negro of the party offered to proceed and reconnoitre. Approaching the hill with great caution, and seeing no one, he began to think they had escaped; but, when within about twenty yards of the top, Big Snake sprang up from his lair and fired, bringing him down, and the next moment bore off

his scalp, and waved it in derision towards the
Americans.

A short time afterwards Big Snake met a large
party of Blackfeet, "pitching" towards the fort
on a trade.    On his arrival amongst them, he
stated what he had done, and dared any one to
censure his conduct on peril of making him his
enemy.    Although the band well knew that what
he had done amounted to an open declaration
of war, and would of course cut off any communication or trade with the establishment, unless
they actually gave up Big Snake as a prisoner,·
yet they suffered their disappointment in silence
rather than incur the anger of one whom they
so much feared.    Another band of the same tribe,
ignorant of the circumstance, arrived at the fort
a few days afterwards.    The Americans, thinking this a good opportunity of chastising the
aggressors, loaded one of their cannons with
musket-balls, and while the unsuspecting Indians
were standing huddled together at the gate, waiting for admittance, applied the fusee.    Fortunately
it did not explode, and the Indians, seeing the
unusual stir and the flash, became alarmed, and
fled.    On a second application of the fusee, it
discharged its murderous projectiles amongst the

fugitives, and killed ten persons, principally women and children.

Some time after, Big Snake heard that one of the most influential Indians of the tribe had blamed him, in a speech, for involving the tribe in much inconvenience and destroying their trade. On hearing these remarks, he directly went in search of the censurer, armed with a scalping-knife, and, on coming up with him, attempted to stab him; his foot, however, slipped in the attempt, which saved the other's life, although he received a severe wound in the side. These two continued for some time after in a state of deadly hostility, until Big Snake was persuaded by many of his friends to make peace, to which he at length consented, and proceeded towards his lodge for that purpose. In the meantime he had told his wife, if she saw any disturbance, to move her lodge instantly to the top of a small hill, a few hundred yards distant, which might be more easily defended. On his arrival at the man's lodge, he found him seated with his wife and children around him, and, taking up one of the children, he began to caress it, and asked it to intercede with its father for the injury he had done him. The man, however, moodily held down his head without any reply, whilst Big Snake again asked the child to take pity on him still. The father remained silent. On which Big Snake, getting enraged at the rejection of the friendly overtures he had condescended to make to one whom he regarded so much as an inferior, and feeling himself humiliated by the refusal, rushed from the tent, seized his gun, which he had taken the precaution of placing within reach in case of emergency, and commenced firing through the skin covering of the tent, killing two of its inmates, and wounding a third; after which he returned to the hill, where his wife was pitching the tent, according to his orders, where he remained and defied the whole camp to molest him.

After I had finished this picture, and the others had examined it with great attention, a general impression seemed to prevail amongst them all that I must be a great medicine-man. And as we encouraged the idea, which afforded us no inconsiderable protection from any treachery on their part, I had no trouble in getting as many sitters as I could possibly manage. Amongst others, I sketched group No. 17, consisting of Big Snake, the centre figure; Mis-ke-me-kin, "The Iron Collar," a Blood Indian chief, with his face painted

Paul Kane del.                                    Vincent Brooks Lith.

GROUP OF SIX INDIAN CHIEFS

Paul Kane del.                                         Vincent Brooks, Lith.

MEDICINE PIPE STEM DANCE.

red; to the extreme left of the picture, is a chief called " Little Horn," with a buffalo robe draped round him, and between him and Big Snake is Wah-nis-stow, " The White Buffalo," principal chief of the Sur-cee tribe. In the background stand two chiefs of inferior quality, one of them has his face painted half black, being in half-mourning for some friend. ) As they were expecting to have a fight with the Crees next day, they got up a medicine dance in the afternoon, and I was solemnly invited to attend, that I might add my magical powers in increasing its efficacy. Amongst all the tribes here assembled, the sacredness of the medicine pipe-stem is held in very high estimation, and it was with much solemnity that I was placed in the best position, to work my incantations; that is to say, to make the sketch No. 18.

Next morning we embarked, after having presented the chiefs with eight or ten pounds of tobacco to be distributed amongst the rest, and had not proceeded many miles, when we had to put ashore again to gratify an old Blood Indian chief, who had arrived at the camp shortly after our departure, and had galloped immediately after us, for the purpose of having a talk with Mr. Harriett, whom he had known many years before, and for whom he entertained the warmest friendship. After the talk, he stripped himself naked, excepting his breech-cloth. Mr. Harriett, not to be behindhand with him, gave him everything but his shirt and pantaloons : it was rather a losing operation for him; although the chief's leather shirt and leggings were quite new and highly ornamented, yet they were not exactly what Mr. Harriett would like to wear, so he gave them to me to add to my stock of Indian costumes. One of the Indians who had accompanied the old chief, noticing I had a new capote on, thought he would try what could be done by an interchange of civilities with me. He accordingly took off a dirty old greasy shirt he had on, and laid it down before me; but as I had no other clothes with me but what I had on, I was forced to decline this most endearing mark of friendship, much to his disappointment, although the scamp could not help grinning as I shook my head in token of refusal.

*June 3rd.* — We were obliged to lie by the whole of this day, on account of the violence of the wind and snow, which rendered any attempt at proceeding very uncomfortable, and almost useless.

*June 4th.* — Early in the forenoon, we arrived at Carlton, and Bishop De Merse immediately took horses to cross by land to Red River Settlement, a distance of sixteen days' journey.

## CHAP. XXV.

THE Crees around this post all took to the woods on hearing of the large party of Blackfeet in their vicinity, and, as we heard, were collecting in large numbers in a camp, about fourteen miles off, for the purpose of opposing the invasion of the hostile tribes.

*June 5th.* — We remained at Carlton during the day, as Mr. Harriett was anxious to hear of the proceedings of the hostile tribes; indeed, he felt rather apprehensive of the treachery of the Blackfeet, and knew that the large numbers of our party would check them from attempting anything which might hereafter call for redress.

*June 6th.* — In the morning a fugitive arrived, bringing news of a battle between the hostile Indians. It appears that the Crees had a medicine dance, and had, according to their custom, erected an ornamental pole, around which they hang their medicine bags, &c., whilst dancing. After the conclusion of their dance, they returned to their camp, a distance of about three miles, which consisted of ninety lodges, leaving the medicine pole standing; shortly after, the invading war party we had met discovered the pole, and on one of their number climbing to the top, to tear off the ornaments, he from the height perceived the Cree camp in the distance, upon which the party prepared themselves for battle.

One of the Cree scouts had also perceived them, but had formed a very erroneous idea of their numbers, and had mentioned them only as a small party. Upon this the Crees immediately proceeded to the attack, thinking to overwhelm them by their superior numbers, and did not discover their error until they were actually engaged. When they perceived that they were so much outnumbered, they retreated to their camp; all but

one chief, Pe-ho-this, who, disdaining to fly, dashed
madly into the midst of his enemies, dealing death
around him with his poke-a-mau-gun or war club.
On every side, bullet and arrow pierced his body;
but he continued the unequal conflict, until his
bridle arm was shattered by a ball, when his
wounded and frightened horse, no longer under
control, dashed with him from the tumult, and
carried him still living to his lodge, but with only
just sufficient strength to enable him to beg his
tribe to take care of his wives and children for his
sake, when he fell dead from his charger.

The whole camp now fled with their women and
children, leaving their lodges standing; except two
old and enfeebled chiefs, who, as is not unusual
amongst Indians under such circumstances, remained in the best lodge, and having dressed themselves in their gayest clothes and ornaments,
painted their faces, lit their pipes, and sat singing
their war songs, until the Blackfeet came up and
soon despatched them.

The Crees had nineteen killed and forty wounded,
besides losing their lodges and a good deal of
property, which they could not carry with them.
The Sur-cees lost Wah-nis-stow, before mentioned,
and having taken six scalps, thought they had

done enough, and returned from the battle to have a dance with the scalps. The Blood Indians, after losing three of their party, also retired after taking a few scalps, leaving the Blackfeet, who had lost six, to bear the brunt of the battle; the Pay-gans and Gros Ventres not having arrived until the fight was over, of course suffered no loss.

Immediately after hearing this, Mr. Harriett ordered us to embark, as he knew that the Blackfeet and their allies would immediately return to their own country after meeting with any success, and having a few scalps to take home, according to the invariable custom of the Indians. We embarked early in the forenoon, and glided quickly down the rapid stream, aided by our oars. We now were out of the buffalo country altogether, and had no fresh meat but some little that we had brought with us for the use of the gentlemen of the party; the men, however, were plentifully supplied with pemmi-kon.

*June* 10*th.* — We arrived at Cumberland House, which we left next morning, having received an addition to our party of three more boats and their crews.

*June* 12*th.* — We arrived at the Paw, where my old friend Mr. Hunter gave me a most hearty welcome. Mrs. Hunter had died during my absence, and he had been waiting for us for the purpose of going down to Norway House. We met here Sir John Richardson and Dr. Rae, *en route* to Mackenzie River, with two canoes in search of Sir John Franklin. From them we first heard of the events that had recently occurred in Europe, the flight of Louis Philippe from Paris, and the revolutionary movements then agitating the Continent.

Whilst walking past the small trading post established here, Mr. Hunter asked me to go in, and we were received very kindly by a little shrivelled up French Canadian, married to a Cree squaw, one of the most extraordinary looking women I had ever seen. She was so fat that she was obliged to sit on a small waggon, in which they drew her about, and her mode of going to bed was by rolling off this on to a buffalo skin. She had not been able to use her legs for many years. I have generally noticed that all Indian women, when brought into the forts, and when relieved from the toils and exposures of their native life, become fat, lazy, and unwieldy.

We left the same evening, bringing Mr. Hunter with us. Few incidents worth noticing occurred on our route. Mr. Harriett's boat, in which I sat, was generally a-head of the party, being lighter and rather better built than the rest. One evening we

got to the place Mr. Harriett selected for encampment considerably before any of the others, and I
got out my drawing materials and took a sketch
of the brigade, as it was coming up with a fair
breeze, crowding on all sail to escape a thunder
storm rolling fast after them.

*June 17th.* — We arrived at the Grand Rapids,
and the whole brigade shot down them, a distance
of three and a half miles; this is the same rapid
where Paulet Paul achieved his herculean feat before mentioned. No rapid in the whole course of
the navigation on the eastern side of the mountains
is at all to be compared to this in point of velocity,
grandeur, or danger to the navigator. The brigade flies down as if impelled by a hurricane, many
shipping a good deal of water in the perpendicular
leaps which they often had to take in the descent.
The whole course is one white sheet of foam, from
one end to the other.

We passed here the brigade of boats bound
upwards for Mackenzie River; they were laboriously
making the portage up, whilst we were shooting
down with lightning speed. The heavily laden
men, as they toiled along the banks, cast many
an envious look at our flying company, who yelled
and shouted with excitement whilst plunging down

F F

the foaming cataract. Having ran the rapids
in safety, we arrived in a few minutes more
at Lake Winnipeg, and encamped on· the shore,
where we cooked and ate our supper. From this
point we had to make a traverse of seventy miles
as the crow flies to Mossy Point, the entrance to
Jack Fish River; but as the wind was against us,
we lay down to sleep.

About 1 o'clock in the morning we were all
aroused, and found the wind blowing fresh and
fair, so that we put off immediately to take advantage of the fortunate occurrence. I was soon asleep
again in the boat, and did not awake till after
sunrise, when I found we were far out of sight of
land and the wind blowing a heavy gale. About 2
o'clock P.M. we rounded Mossy Point, and at 5
o'clock arrived at Norway House, where the brigade
left me, they going on to York Factory, and I remaining to meet Major M^cKenzie, who was expected
soon to pass on his way to Fort Francis.

The annual council of chief factors, which is
usually held at Red River, was this year held at
Norway House, and I had the pleasure of again
meeting with Sir George Simpson, and several gentlemen to whose kindness I had before been deeply
indebted. I was detained here for more than a

Paul Kane, del                                    Vincent Brooks, lith month, ᵃnd though the weather was clear and fine, yet ᵥₑ could not sit in the house in comfort without having the stove lighted. I amused myself in fishing and shooting. I speared a good many sturgeon, which are here very fine and numerous, and also great lots of gold eyes, which are a peculiar species of fish, like the herring, though larger and thicker, but not worth catching. Mr. Rowand said that they eat like mud. I certainly never tasted them but once, and I was not tempted to repeat the experiment.

I was often accompanied in the canoe by Ogemawwah Chack, "The Spirit Chief" (sketch No. 19), an Esquimaux from the Hudson's Bay who had attained to an extreme old age. According to received opinion, he was 110 years old, and the events which he related as having witnessed seemed to warrant the belief. He had an only son, whom I often met, quite elderly in appearance. The mother of this boy had died very shortly after his birth, and there being no woman giving suck near at the time, the father, to soothe the cries of the starving infant, placed the child's mouth to his own breast, and finding that the child derived some benefit from it, he continued the practice for some days, and, strange to say, milk flowed from his nipple, and he brought up the child without the assistance of any woman.

Before leaving Norway House, some Cree Indians arrived, and boasted that one of their war chiefs had vanquished the great Blackfoot chief, Big Snake, in single combat. Big Snake had ridden away from the main body of his tribe, in hopes of stealing some horses, as he thought that the Crees in their precipitate flight were likely to have left them behind; and, hoping to have all he got for himself, he took no comrades with him. The Cree chief discovered him from behind a hill, riding alone on the plain beneath, and, burning with vengeance, rushed at him, without waiting for his other warriors, who were not, however, far off. Big Snake did not see the others, and disdaining to fly from a single foe, he boldly galloped to meet his enemy; but the fight was short, as the Cree succeeded in piercing him with his spear at the first meeting, and he was scalped and dead before the others came up.

*July 24th.* — Major M<sup>c</sup>Kenzie at last arrived with five boats, manned principally with Indians; he only remained a few hours, when I embarked with him; but we only proceeded about six miles when it became dark, and we encamped for the night.

*July 25th.* — We stopped to breakfast at a picturesque little island near the outlet of Lake Winnipeg, after which we passed the Spider Islands, so called from the countless myriads of these insects which infest them. In the evening we encamped at Point de Tremble, on Poplar Point.

*July 26th.* — We left in the morning with a strong breeze, which changed into a perfect gale, making many of our Indians sea-sick. The swells of Lake Winnipeg, from the shallowness of this wide expanse of water when set in motion by a heavy wind, are far more abrupt and dangerous for boats than those of the Atlantic; and I could not but feel very apprehensive for our safety, — a feeling which was evidently shared by Major M'Kenzie, for he kept a signal flying from his mast-head, which the guide well knew meant for him to put ashore, but which he would not obey, as he considered it a most dangerous alternative to change his course; and the shore, from its rocky character, being very difficult of approach in stormy weather. We, however, by dint of constant baling, continued our course in safety until we arrived at

the mouth of Behring's River, which we entered
in safety, much to the relief of the Major's anxiety
for both cargoes and crews.   Here we remained
windbound for the rest of the day and part of
the following.

By way of passing the time, I took my gun and
strolled up the river, accompanied by the guide,
and fell in with a solitary Sotto woman and
child sitting under a tree.   She was quite alone,
as her husband had gone up the river fishing in
the morning.   She did not appear to be at all
alarmed or confused at our approach, and freely
entered into conversation with the guide, to whom
she told her name, Caw-kee-ka-keesh-e-ko, "The
Constant Sky."   Tempted by the beauty of the
scene, and she seeming to be in no wise unwilling,
I sketched her likeness and the surrounding landscape with considerable care.

*July 27th.*—We started rather late, and being
only able to make Rabbit Point, we encamped.
We here found immense flocks of wild pigeons,
and killed a good supply.   Our Indians killed
several skunks, which they prize very much as
delicate eating, preferring them to the pigeons,
although the bare smell of them in our vicinity
almost took away my appetite for the former.

*July 28th.* — About 2 o'clock P.M., we endeavoured to proceed, but only got as far as the Dog's Head, the wind being so strong and unfavourable, that it was thought useless to run any risk for the short distance that we would be able to make against it. In the evening our Indians constructed a jonglerie, or medicine lodge, the main object of which was to procure a fair wind for next day. For this purpose they first drive ten or twelve poles, nine or ten feet long, into the ground, enclosing a circular area of about three feet in diameter, with a boat sail open at the top. The medicine-man, one of whom is generally found in every brigade, gets inside and commences shaking the poles violently, rattling his medicinal rattle, and singing hoarse incantations to the Great Spirit for a fair wind. Being unable to sleep on account of the discordant noises, I wrapped a blanket round me, and went out into the woods, where they were holding their midnight orgies, and lay down amongst those on the outside of the medicine lodge, to witness the proceedings. I had no sooner done so than the incantations at once ceased, and the performer exclaimed that a white man was present. How he ascertained this fact I am at a loss to surmise, as it was pitch dark

r r 4

at the time, and he was enclosed in the narrow tent, without any apparent opening through which he could espy me, even had it been light enough to distinguish one person from another.

The Major, who, with many other intelligent persons, is a firm believer in their medicine, told me that a Canadian once had the temerity to peep under the covering which enclosed the jonglerie, but that he got such a fright that he never fairly recovered from it, nor could he ever be prevailed upon to tell what it was that had so appalled him. After about two hours' shaking and singing, the medicine-man cried out that he saw five boats with the sails set running before the wind, which communication was greeted by the whole party with their usual grunt of satisfaction and assent.

After this, many questions were asked him by the Indians, some inquiring after the health of their families at home, whom they had not seen for many months. Upon putting the question, the inquirer threw a small piece of tobacco over the covering of the tent, upon which the medicine-man agitated the tent, and shook his rattle violently, and then replied that he saw one family enjoying themselves over a fat sturgeon, another engaged in some pleasing employment, &c. &c. I then put a question to him myself, accompanying it with a double portion of tobacco, for which I got a double portion of noise. ) I asked about my curiosities which I had left at Norway House (for want of room in our boats), to be brought on by the canoes which had taken up Sir John Richardson on their return, they not being engaged to carry him further than Prairie River. The medicine-man told me that he saw the party with my baggage encamped on a sandy point, which we had ourselves passed two days before.

However singular the coincidence may appear, it is a fact, that on the next day we had a fair wind, for which the medicine-man of course took all the credit; and it is no less true, that the canoes with my baggage were on the sandy point on the day stated, for I inquired particularly of them when they came up to us.

*July 29th.* — We started very early in the morning, with a fair wind, and stopped to breakfast at the Loon Narrows. We reached Otter Head in the evening, and then encamped.

*July 30th.* — We breakfasted at Point Mille-lac, and arrived at 10 o'clock A.M. at Fort Alexander, where we found a great number of Saulteaux Indians, who come in large numbers about this

season of the year, and disperse themselves among
the small lakes, where they gather great quantities
of wild rice, resembling our own in taste, but much
larger and black. The scarcity of other provisions
in these parts renders the rice very valuable, but
the Indians are so lazy, that they will not collect
much more than they want for themselves without
being bribed to do so, and the clerk in charge of
the establishment is obliged to give them, for that
purpose, a certain quantity of rum to induce them
to go to collect rice for the establishment, and also
to give them some on their return, besides paying
them in goods for the quantity they bring in.
Major M'Kenzie here met his wife and two
daughters, who had been on a visit to Red River.
We remained at Fort Alexander four days, changing our crews, the Indians who had been with us
belonging here.

Before leaving Lake Winnipeg, I would remark
that the whole of its eastern shore, which I had
just coasted, presented a most wild, rocky, rough,
hilly, and almost impassable country, and several of
the Indians who had been through, described it as
being of the same character far back from the
lake, and interspersed with innumerable lakes and
swamps.

Paul Kane, del.

Vincent. Brooks, Lith

WHITE MUD PORTAGE.

*August 3rd.*—We left with four boats, manned with thirty men, twenty-seven of whom were Indians, two French Canadians, and one Orkney man, and commenced the ascent of the Winnipeg River. Mrs. M°Kenzie and her two daughters were to follow us in a light canoe, with a crew of Indians. We had to make several portages during the day, and in the evening got over the portage of the Prancing Horses, a cascade about twenty feet high. We had a whole fleet of light canoes following us, containing the Indian wives and children. Two of them contained brides, who had been married in the morning without any ceremony that I heard of.

*Aug. 4th.*—In the morning, we made the White Mud Portage, which was very picturesque, and of which I took a sketch, No. 20, with the Indians and squaws who were following us, carrying their canoes across; and in the course of the day made another called Little Rock, about seven feet high, and camped at the upper end of it.

*Aug. 5th.*—Left at 4 o'clock A.M., and arrived at the Grand Bonnet, a portage of a mile in length, which it took us the whole day to drag the boats across; the weather was burning hot, and the mosquitoes in legions. The canoes, containing the women and children, kept close at our heels, and always came up to our encampment for provisions; this so reduced our stock, that out of regard to our own safety, we were obliged to put them upon short allowance.

*Aug. 6th.* — We crossed the Second Bonnet, and met some Indians, who sold us a few sturgeon, and crossing Lac de Bonnet, where several of our Indian followers left us for the rice-grounds, we encamped for the night on the banks of the river Malaine. Owing to the low marshy state of the country hereabouts, we were dreadfully tormented with mosquitoes. The poor Orkney man, in particular, seemed to be an especial favourite, and there had been evidently an attempt made to eat him up altogether. In the morning, his face presented the appearance of a person in the small-pox.

*Aug. 7th.* — Passed six portages to-day, one of which is called the Wooden Horse, and encamped at the Grande Gullete. The chief's son, of Rat Portage, who was one of our engaged men, here deserted us, and stole off in a canoe with his two wives.

*Aug. 8th.* — To-day we had to make several portages, and in the evening encamped three miles above the Grand Rapid of this river, having still thirteen canoes of Indians paddling in our wake. This evening we found some smooth flat rocks, which the voyageurs always prefer to grass or earth to make their bed on, and I can say, from experience, that they have formed a judicious estimate of the superior comfort they afford after a hard day's travel; for grass or sand is certainly the worst surface to sleep upon, however soft it may feel at first.

*Aug. 9th.* — We breakfasted at the Barrière Portage, and arrived about noon at the Slave Falls, of which I made a sketch. Three military officers, Captain Moody, Mr. Brown, and Mr. Constable, caught up to us in their light canoes; they were on their way from Red River to Canada, and pushed on after a very short stay. We had hardly bid them good-bye, when Mrs. M‘Kenzie and her two lovely daughters came up, and stayed with us until next morning. Our Indians now refused to proceed further, unless they received an allowance of rum; and the Major was obliged to promise them a supply as soon as he arrived at Rat Portage.

*Aug. 10th.*—Our starting was delayed this morning in consequence of a dense fog, and we only got as far as the Rochers Boules before breakfast; after which, the ladies left us for their residence at Rat Portage. During the day we passed the Aux Chênes, and encamped about four miles below the Point of Woods.

*Aug.* 11*th.*—Our provisions were now getting very low, and we had still further to restrict our distributions to the women and children. On each side of the river for a long distance are innumerable small shallow lakes, bearing usually large quantities of rice; but the water in them had sunk so low this season, that the Indians were apprehensive of a failure in the crop, which would be attended with the most serious consequences, as upon it was placed their whole dependence for food. When we arrived at the Grand Equerre we stopped for the night.

*Aug.* 12*th.* — We passed to-day the deserted Catholic mission called Wabe-samung, "White Dog," from the name of the portage next above it. This was established by Mr. Belcour, a Catholic priest, but he had left it the year before, as he found there was not enough of land near it that would pay for cultivation. The whole country between this and Fort Alexander was rocky and barren, so that no mission could hope to get any Indians to settle permanently near it. In the evening we encamped at the White Dog Portage.

*Aug. 13th.*—We got to the Yellow Mud Portage by breakfast-time, and afterwards crossed the " Grande Décharge," so called from its being the place where the boats are hauled up after the goods are discharged from them, in distinction from a portage, at which latter place, as I have already observed, it is necessary to carry the boats as well as the cargoes. In the evening we encamped at what is called the Fishery, or the place where the people from Rat Portage come to fish. It was with great difficulty we could find a place to sleep on free from ants, whose hillocks we disturbed at every step. I made several attempts to lie down, but they annoyed me so much, that at last I got into one of the boats.

*Aug. 14th.*—Left our encampment at 3 A.M., and arrived at Rat Portage at 10, where we were received by Mrs. M‘Kenzie with the greatest hospitality and kindness. The Indians here subsist on sturgeon and white fish in the summer, and rice and rabbits in the winter. We rested ourselves here two days, and employed ourselves principally in feasting on white fish, to make up for the short allowance of food under which we had lately been suffering.

*Aug. 16th.* — It was with great regret that I parted with the kind Major and his family. The men having made the portage from which this post is named, we left about 2 in the afternoon, and soon entered the Lake of the Woods, where we chose a comfortable little island, and encamped for the night.

*Aug. 17th.*—We threaded our way among innumerable islands, many of them thickly covered with woods, from which circumstance the lake takes its name. We saw on one of them about five acres of cultivated corn, the only instance of the kind I had seen since I left Norway House. There is another island called Garden Island, which lay to the west of our route, about six miles long and about three wide, on which I was told some Indians raised yearly a few bushels of corn and potatoes. At night we again chose an island for our resting place.

*Aug. 18th.*—We were wind-bound until 5 P.M., during which time we were visited by a large party of Saulteaux Indians; we embarked in the evening, but only succeeded in getting on about six miles before we were again obliged to stop, and remained all the next day.

*Aug.* 20*th.*—Made an early start with a fair wind, which carried us into the mouth of the River La Pluie. Here we found some Indians who were gathering snow-berries and sand-berries; the latter are the size of large grapes, of a reddish blue colour. They grow on long vines trailing upon the sand, and are very good eating when washed free of the particles which adhere to them. We encamped about four miles up the river, and were again tortured by our old enemies the mosquitoes, aided by detachments of black flies.

*Aug.* 21*st.*—Roused by the flies, we started early. Our route up the river was much enlivened by the antics of the Indians when tracking, that is, hauling the boats up the current, which they do for days together whenever the banks, or indeed the bed of the river, will admit of it; for they seemed to be perfectly amphibious, wading about in the water, and swimming from side to side as a matter of course, without thinking of getting into the boat, and making great fun of one of our Canadians who had got into a canoe with two squaws, to cross.

*Aug.* 22*nd.* — The men woke me up at 2 o'clock in the morning from my warm blankets, for the purpose of getting under way; but when just ready to start, we were prevented by a violent storm of

G G

rain, which continued until about 6 o'clock, when we immediately set off. The country about here is very swampy, but, from its height, I think much of it might be drained, and adapted for cultivation. I noticed all along the banks of this river, that wherever pine trees had been burned down, poplars invariably sprung up in their places, although no other poplars could be seen in the vicinity.

*Aug. 23rd.* — We left our encampment at 1 A.M., so as to make sure of arriving at Fort Frances before night. The Indians tracked with the line the whole day, frequently up to their middles in the water, and often swimming; this wearisome toil they kept up for sixteen hours, with the exception of one hour, during which we stopped for breakfast, never for one moment losing their cheerfulness and good humour. I scarcely think that any other race of people could go through such fatigue with the same alacrity and energy.

At 5 o'clock P.M. we reached Fort Frances, so named after the sister of Lady Simpson. Here the annual three months' voyage terminates, that being the time which it takes to convey the furs to York Factory, in Hudson's Bay, and bring back the outfit of goods. The fort is situated near where

Rainy Lake disembogues into a river of the same name, forming a beautiful cascade. The Indians catch great quantities of sturgeon at the foot of these falls in the month of June. The sturgeon here are very small — seldom weighing more than 40 or 50 lbs. — at least in comparison with those taken at the mouth of Frazer's River on the west side of the mountains, which often weigh from 5 to 7 cwt.

Fort Frances has usually about 250 Indians in its neighbourhood, who have a half-breed missionary of the Methodist church resident amongst them; but I understood he was about to leave them, disheartened by the small success attendant upon his exertions. The Indians live here as at Rat Portage, on rice, fish, and rabbits. The last are so numerous in the winter, that one man caught eighty-six in one night, being only unsuccessful with fourteen snares out of the 100 he had set in the evening.

The skins, like the Canadian, are far inferior to the European rabbits': the only use to which I have seen them applied has been in the manufacture of rabbit-skin robes, which are made by cutting the skin with the hair on into strips, which are twisted and netted together in such a manner as to keep the hair outwards on both sides of the robe.  The people of the fort grow some wheat and potatoes, but though there is some very good land about, they find it impossible to induce the Indians to cultivate it.  The crop of wheat which they got in while I was there, was almost entirely spoiled by smut, and they were obliged to wash it before they could turn it to any account.  I remained here eighteen days waiting for the passing of the express canoe which annually carries the letters from the interior posts to Lachine.

*Sept.* 10*th.* — The express canoe arrived in the evening with Mr. M'Tavish.  He was come direct from York Factory, where he had been stationed for fourteen years, and gave a most dismal account of the climate and country; he was now going to the Sault St. Marie, to the charge of which post he had been recently appointed by way of giving him a little taste of civilisation, of which he rather stood in need.

*Sept.* 11*th.* — We started at 6 o'clock in the morning, and got through Lac la Pluie by 5 in the afternoon; after this we had to make two portages, and encamped just before dark at the second.

*Sept.* 12*th.* — Started at 3 o'clock A. M., the morning was very cold and foggy; and we had a severe frost during the night. We breakfasted at the Grand Chute, and had a very severe day's work afterwards, as we had to make four bad portages, and did not encamp until 9 o'clock at night; the men having worked eighteen hours steadily. We were lucky enough to meet some Indians after dark, from whom we obtained a good supply of delicious white fish. We now exerted all our energies to hasten our journey as the danger of ice setting in was becoming imminent, and with great labour we arrived at the Mountain Portage on the evening of the 18th.

*Sept. 19th.* — I got up at the first appearance of day, that I might have the opportunity whilst the men were making the portage, of again visiting the Kakabakka falls. As the day dawned the magnificent spectacle gradually cleared to my view in all its mighty grandeur and magnificence, and I felt more impressed than ever with the opinion that these falls far surpass the Niagara in beauty and picturesque effect, and would have much liked to have taken another sketch of them; but my admiring contemplations were hastily cut short by a peremptory summons from the canoes, which were waiting for me. I hastily rejoined them, and we dashed down the uninterrupted current forty miles

to Fort William, where we arrived early in the
afternoon.   On leaving Fort William, we suffered
a great deal the next five days from the high cold
wind, which frequently stopped our progress.

*Sept. 24th.*—We were wind-bound at the mouth
of a small river, and as there seemed no prospect
of a change, I followed the stream up about ten
miles until I came to a cascade.   The interior of
the country as far as I went seemed to be of the
same character as the coast, high mountain rocks,
interspersed with a few trees of stunted growth
and scanty herbage.   I was lucky enough to shoot
four ducks, which proved a most acceptable addition to the pemmi-kon and fish which we had
brought with us.   We got off next day, although
the weather was still bad, but we were anxious to
get to Michipicoton, as there is a post there, and
we might obtain some little comfort at least, if we
were detained.

*Sept. 27th.*—We arrived at the post about
9 o'clock in the evening, and remained there the
whole of next day.   The post is situated in a deep
bay at the mouth of the river, and is surrounded
by some of the best land to be found on the British
shores of Lake Superior.   The head chief of the
Ojibbeways, who resides near the post, sat for me

in his red coat trimmed with gold lace. These coats are given by the Company to such Indian chiefs as have been friendly and serviceable to them, and are very highly prized by their possessors. His name was Maydoc-game-kinungee, "I hear the Noise of the Deer."

*Sept. 29th.*—We started very early in the morning, and encamped that evening opposite to Montreal Island.

*Sept. 30th.*—We got to Montreal River, where we stopped for two hours for breakfast, passed Micah Bay at 1 o'clock, and encamped at night at the Isle aux Sables.

*Oct. 1st.*—We stopped to breakfast at 4 o'clock near Gros-Cap, a porphyry rock rising 1500 feet above the level of the lake, and got to the post at Sault St. Marie by 2 o'clock P.M. Here I consider that my Indian travels finish, as the rest of my journey home to Toronto was performed on board steam-boats; and the greatest hardship I had to endure, was the difficulty I found in trying to sleep in a civilised bed.

## Census of Indian Tribes inhabiting the North-west Coast of America, for the Year 1846.

| Traders' Name of Tribe. | Indian Name of Tribe. | General Residence. | Men. | Women. | Children. Boys. | Children. Girls. | Slaves. Male. | Slaves. Female. | Canoes. | Guns. | Houses. | Language. | Remarks. |
|---|---|---|---|---|---|---|---|---|---|---|---|---|---|
| Nass Indians | Kit-ha-teen | Nass River, from entrance upwards in the order they are put down | 182 | 109 | 126 | 103 | ... | ... | 121 | ... | ... | Chymsyan. | Generally trade at Fort Simpson. |
| | Kit-a-hon | | 117 | 111 | 97 | 104 | ... | ... | 111 | ... | ... | | |
| | Ke-toon-ok-shelk | | 146 | 118 | 48 | 69 | ... | ... | 40 | ... | ... | | |
| | Kin-a-roa-lax | | 98 | 100 | 43 | 82 | 4 | 8 | 52 | 21 | 32 | | |
| | | | 543 | 488 | 314 | 308 | 4 | 8 | 324 | 21 | 32 | | |
| Chymseyans | Kis-pa-cha-laidy | Chatham's Sound, from Portland Canal to Port Essington, into which Skeena River falls, both mainland and neighbouring islands | 116 | 150 | 99 | 71 | 4 | 7 | 104 | 40 | 104 | Chymsyan. | Trade at Fort Simpson, and generally reside at no great distance from the Fort. |
| | Ket-lane | | 129 | 184 | 75 | 76 | 6 | 4 | 167 | 29 | 29 | | |
| | Kee-chis | | 71 | 75 | 43 | 80 | 1 | - | 71 | 20 | 28 | | |
| | Keen-ath-toix | | 68 | 74 | 48 | 89 | 2 | 2 | 62 | 20 | 12 | | |
| | Kit-will-coits | | 64 | 78 | 41 | 86 | 10 | 8. | 78 | 28 | 15 | | |
| | Kitch-a-claith | | 81 | 86 | 20 | 28 | 1 | - | 34 | 14 | 8 | | |
| | Ket-at-sah | | 104 | 85 | 50 | 58 | 4 | 1 | 125 | 28 | 32 | | |
| | Ken-chen-kieg | | 87 | 68 | 48 | 62 | 4 | 4 | 74 | 48 | 19 | | |
| | Ket-an-dou | | 54 | 70 | 85 | 43 | 8 | 2 | 49 | 8 | 11 | | |
| | Ket-wilk-ci-pa | | 18 | 18 | 11 | 8 | - | - | 18 | 4 | 4 | | |
| | | | 787 | 778 | 465 | 446 | 40 | 28 | 702 | 284 | 257 | | |

| Group | Village | Locality | | | | | | | | | | Nation | Remarks |
|---|---|---|---|---|---|---|---|---|---|---|---|---|---|
| Skeena Indians | Kee-chum-s-kai-lo | } Lower part of Skeena River | 59 | 28 | 35 | 28 | 1 | 1 | · | · | 10 | Chymseyan | } Trade at Fort Simpson, and with the Chymseyans: they may be reckoned as a part of the Chymseyan tribe. |
| | Kit-se-lai-so | | 72 | 49 | 29 | 81 | 8 | 2 | · | · | 20 | | |
| | | | 181 | 72 | 64 | 59 | 4 | 8 | · | · | 30 | | |
| Sabassas Indians | Keet-heat-la | Canal de Principe | 289 | 179 | 160 | 120 | 15 | 20 | | | | Chymseyan | } Frequent Fort M'Loughlin and Fort Simpson. |
| | Kil-cah-ta | { Entrance Gardener's Canal } | 68 | 66 | 20 | 22 | 14 | 9 | | | | | |
| | Kit-ta-muat | North Arm | 80 | 75 | 24 | 18 | 14 | 11 | | | | | |
| | Kit-lope | South Arm | 66 | 60 | 26 | 20 | 7 | 8 | | | | | |
| | Nees-lous | Canal de la Beddo | 26 | 27 | 13 | 14 | 8 | 5 | | | | | |
| | | | 474 | 407 | 243 | 194 | 58 | 58 | | | | | |
| Milbank Sound | Onie-le-toch | } Milbank Sound | 467 | 454 | 119 | 166 | 22 | 22 | 488 | 174 | 46 | Ha-eelb-zuk or Bellabola | } Trade at Fort M'Loughlin. |
| | Weetle-toch | | 112 | 81 | 89 | 46 | 1 | 2 | 105 | 80 | 8 | | |
| | Kok-wai-y-toch | | 66 | 59 | 44 | 51 | · | · | · | · | 11 | | |
| | Kee-tay-toch | Cascade Canal | 94 | 89 | 57 | 49 | · | · | · | · | 18 | | } Visit Fort M'Loughlin, but not frequently. |
| | Kui-much-qui-toch | Deane's Canal | 86 | 41 | 19 | 21 | · | · | · | · | 6 | | |
| | Bella-hoo-la | { Entrance Salmon River | 161 | 168 | 87 | 98 | · | · | · | · | 30 | | |
| | Gua-shil-la | Rivers' Canal | 71 | 69 | 29 | 86 | · | · | · | · | 8 | | |
| | Natal-se-moch | Smith's Inlet | | | | | | | | | | | |
| | Wee-ke-moch | Calvert's Island | | | | | | | | | | | |
| | | | 1007 | 961 | 894 | 462 | 28 | 24 | 588 | 204 | 122 | | |

| Traders' Name of Tribe. | Indian Name of Tribe. | General Residence. | Men. | Women. | Children. | | Slaves. | | Canoes. | Guns. | Houses. | Language. | Remarks. |
|---|---|---|---|---|---|---|---|---|---|---|---|---|---|
| | | | | | Boys. | Girls. | Male. | Female. | | | | | |
| Chilcat, several tribes | Chilcat - | Lyn's Canal - | 267 | 116 | 71 | 66 | 42 | 86 | | | | | |
| Cross Sound Indians | Ueena-caw - | Cross Sound - | 258 | 284 | 108 | 88 | 40 | 54 | | | | | |
| Auke - | Auke - | { N. entrance of Tako River } | 72 | 61 | 85 | 81 | 2 | 2 | | | | Klem-e-kate. | Trade at Sitka, Tako, and Stekini |
| Tako Samdan and Sitka | Tako Samdan and Sitka | { Tako and Sitka Rivers, south of them on mainland } | 127 | 116 | 71 | 66 | 59 | 60 | | | | | |
| Hootsinoo - | Hootsinoo - | | 274 | 248 | 85 | 76 | 48 | 41 | | | | | |
| Hanaga - | Hanaga - | { Hood's Bay } | 89 | 80 | 29 | 27 | 27 | 24 | | | | | |
| Kake - | Kake - | | 169 | 106 | 70 | 64 | 24 | 20 | | | | | |
| | | | 1249 | 961 | 469 | 418 | 242 | 287 | | | | | |
| Stekini Indians - | Sick-naa-huly - | | 81 | 24 | 30 | 27 | 2 | 4 | 38 | 17 | 8 | | Trade generally at Stekini, but frequently visit Fort Simpson, Tako, and Sitka. I have not been able to ascertain their numbers, but they are said not to be so numerous as the Chymeeyans. |
| | Ta-ee-tee-tan - | | 88 | 29 | 16 | 9 | 8 | 4 | 43 | 86 | 4 | | |
| | Kaas-ka-qua-tee - | | 59 | 41 | 10 | 6 | 6 | 18 | . | 19 | 4 | | |
| | Kook-a-tee - | Stekini River | 187 | 67 | 86 | 82 | 2 | . | 63 | 49 | 9 | Klen-e-kate. | |
| | Naa-nu-aa-ghu - | | 83 | 117 | 60 | 46 | 82 | 52 | 85 | 76 | 15 | | |
| | Tal-qua-tee - | | 52 | 51 | 27 | 83 | 2 | 4 | 52 | 85 | 6 | | |
| | Kick-sa-tee - | | 51 | 21 | 21 | 18 | 4 | 4 | 84 | 19 | 5 | | |
| | Kaady-ett-ee - | | 61 | 60 | 40 | 19 | 4 | 8 | 42 | 88 | 8 | | |
| | | | 562 | 410 | 240 | 190 | 55 | 80 | 862 | 280 | 59 | | |

| Tribe | Subdivision | Locality | | | | | | | | | Total | Family | Remarks |
|---|---|---|---|---|---|---|---|---|---|---|---|---|---|
| Port Stuart Indians | A-he-alt | Port Stuart | 50 | 45 | 42 | 49 | | | | | 10 | | |
| Tongass Indians | Kee-tah-hon-neet | South entrance Clarence Straits | 85 | 90 | 60 | 65 | | | | | 18 | Klan-e-e-kate | Generally trade at Fort Simpson, but occasionally visit Stekini. |
| Cape Fox Indians | Lugh-ee-le | Cape Fox | 45 | 50 | 89 | 48 | | 6 | 9 | | 9 | | |
|  |  |  | 180 | 185 | 141 | 157 | | 6 | 9 | | 87 | | |
| Kygarney Indians | You-ah-noe | South side of Prince of Wales' Archipelago | 68 | 70 | 44 | 52 | | | | | 18 | | |
|  | Clict-ars |  | 98 | 105 | 102 | 112 | | | | | 26 | | |
|  | Qui-a-han-less |  | 80 | 85 | 42 | 41 | | | | | 8 | Hai-dai | Frequent Fort Simpeon, Stekini, Tako, and Sitka. |
|  | Uon-s-gan |  | 117 | 121 | 118 | 107 | | | | | 27 | | |
|  | Show-a-gen |  | 58 | 61 | 54 | 61 | | | | | 14 | | |
|  | Chal-chu-nie |  | 65 | 62 | 69 | 68 | | | | | 18 | | |
|  |  |  | 481 | 454 | 414 | 486 | | | | | 111 | | |
| Queen Charlotte's Island Indians | Sa-lan-na | Queen Charlotte's Islands, beginning at North Island, north end, and passing round by the eastward | 80 | 76 | 69 | 71 | | | | | 20 | | |
|  | Nigh-tan |  | 70 | 69 | 72 | 69 | | | | | 15 | | |
|  | Mosette |  | 630 | 650 | 589 | 604 | | | | | 160 | | |
|  | Ne-coon |  | 24 | 27 | 29 | 42 | | | | | 5 | | |
|  | A-se-quang |  | 84 | 81 | 27 | 28 | | | | | 9 | | |
|  | Skit-e-gates |  | 191 | 182 | 176 | 189 | | | | | 48 | Hai-dai | Most of these people frequent Fort Simpeon; but several of them never see any establishment. |
|  | Cum-sha-was |  | 80 | 74 | 68 | 69 | | | | | 20 | | |
|  | Skee-dans |  | 116 | 121 | 98 | 105 | | | | | 80 | | |
|  | Qnee-ah |  | 87 | 79 | 68 | 74 | | | | | 20 | | |
|  | Cloo |  | 169 | 164 | 105 | 107 | | | | | 40 | | |
|  | Kish-a-win |  | 80 | 74 | 85 | 90 | | | | | 18 | | |
|  | Kaw-welth |  | 181 | 146 | 145 | 189 | | | | | 85 | | |
|  | Too |  | 45 | 49 | 50 | 52 | | | | | 10 | | |
|  |  |  | 1786 | 1742 | 1576 | 1689 | | | | | 430 | | |

| Traders' Name of Tribe. | Indian Name of Tribe. | General Residence. | Men. | Women. | Boys. | Girls. | Slaves. Male. | Slaves. Female. | Canoes. | Guns. | Houses. | Language. | Remarks. |
|---|---|---|---|---|---|---|---|---|---|---|---|---|---|
| | Na-wee-tee - | | 90 | 100 | 99 | 91 | 18 | 12 | 100 | 90 | 15 | | |
| | Qua-coith - | | 800 | 350 | 320 | 400 | 28 | 22 | 260 | 50 | 80 | | |
| | Quee-ha-qua-coll - | | 400 | 500 | 500 | 590 | 24 | 36 | 460 | 70 | 40 | | |
| | Mar-ma-li-la-cal-la | | 400 | 500 | 500 | 590 | 18 | 22 | 500 | 120 | 40 | | |
| | Claw-et-sus - | | 500 | 600 | 650 | 700 | 17 | 28 | 600 | 180 | 50 | | |
| | Mar-til-par - | | 500 | 600 | 650 | 700 | 19 | 21 | 600 | 120 | 50 | | |
| | Nim-kish - | | 400 | 500 | 500 | 590 | 16 | 24 | 460 | 70 | 40 | Qua-coith. All these tribes are said to speak the same language, or only a provincial difference. | A few of these tribes used occasionally to visit Fort M'Lough-lin; but generally they trade with the steamers or other vessels that visit Queen Charlotte's Sound, and do not see any establishment. |
| | We-wark-ka - | About Queen Charlotte's Sound | 330 | 400 | 500 | 680 | 48 | 62 | 260 | 50 | 80 | | |
| | We-wark-kum - | | 380 | 400 | 500 | 680 | 45 | 65 | 260 | 501 | 80 | | |
| | Clal-lu-is-is - | | 450 | 500 | 650 | 700 | 12 | 18 | 500 | 100 | 40 | | |
| | Cam-que-kis - | | 50 | 70 | 100 | 100 | 8 | 12 | 40 | 80 | 10 | | |
| | Leek-que-libla - | | 50 | 70 | 100 | 100 | 9 | 11 | 40 | 80 | 10 | | |
| | Cle-Hure - | | 500 | 600 | 650 | 700 | 23 | 17 | 600 | 100 | 50 | | |
| | Sol-il-enu - | | 200 | 280 | 250 | 270 | 24 | 26 | 140 | 100 | 20 | | |
| | Quick-sul-i-nut - | | 200 | 280 | 250 | 270 | 22 | 28 | 140 | 80 | 20 | | |
| | A-qua-miah - | | 200 | 280 | 250 | 270 | 20 | 80 | 140 | 70 | 20 | | |
| | Cle-li-kit-te - | | 200 | 280 | 250 | 270 | 24 | 26 | 140 | 80 | 20 | | |
| | Nar-kock-tau - | | 400 | 500 | 500 | 590 | 16 | 24 | 500 | 100 | 40 | | |
| | Que-i-nu - | | 200 | 250 | 270 | 280 | 19 | 28 | 200 | 70 | 20 | | |
| | Cex-e-ni-nuth - | | 300 | 400 | 500 | 680 | 46 | 54 | 260 | 50 | 80 | | |
| | Te-nuckt-tau - | | 200 | 280 | 250 | 270 | 22 | 18 | 400 | 100 | 20 | | |
| | Ol-cle-la - | | 180 | 200 | 210 | 230 | 12 | 18 | 200 | 80 | 20 | | |

Queen Charlotte's Sound and Neighbourhood

| | | | | | | | | | | | Remarks |
|---|---|---|---|---|---|---|---|---|---|---|---|
| Ne-cul-ta | Johnson's Stra. | 380 | 400 | 500 | 680 | 45 | 55 | 260 | 50 | 80 | Qua-colth. All these tribes are said to speak the same language, or only a provincial difference. |
| Quee-ha-ni-cul-ta | Johnson's Stra. | 380 | 400 | 500 | 630 | 48 | 52 | 260 | 50 | 80 | |
| Comoux | Johnson's Stra., south entrance | 380 | 400 | 500 | 630 | 44 | 56 | 260 | 50 | 80 | |
| | | 7870 | 8890 | 9949 | 11491 | 627 | 745 | 7580 | 2841 | 785 | |
| Quane | Cape Scott | 50 | 60 | 70 | 70 | 4 | 6 | 50 | 60 | 10 | A few of these tribes used occasionally to visit Fort M'Lough-lin; but generally they trade with the steamers or other vessels that visit Queen Char-lotte's Sound, and do not see any establishment. |
| Ucle nu | Scott's Island | 20 | 15 | 20 | 20 | - | | 80 | 6 | 4 | |
| Kus-ke-ma | Outside Van-couver's Island | 380 | 400 | 600 | 600 | 44 | 56 | 260 | 50 | 80 | |
| Quat-si-nu | South of Cape Scott | 380 | 400 | 600 | 600 | 47 | 68 | 260 | 50 | 80 | |
| | | 780 | 875 | 1290 | 1290 | 95 | 115 | 600 | 166 | 74 | |

Queen Charlotte's Sound and Neighbourhood.

LONDON:
PRINTED BY SPOTTISWOODE AND CO.
NEW-STREET SQUARE.

LaVergne, TN USA
04 October 2010
199521LV00003B/19/P